MAJOR REASONS FOR INVESTING IN PRIVATE COMPANIES

1. A belief (or hope) that extraordinary financial gains will result.

2. A desire for personal involvement in an interesting and rewarding experience.

3. An interest in helping an entrepreneur or the community.

4. A need for tax benefits, which may offset some of the potential loss.

5. A desire for power and influence within the community.

STAGES OF SUCCESSFUL CORPORATE DEVELOPMENT

1. Idea — inspiration — concept.

2. Presentation of idea to others for approval, collaboration, and initial (seed) financing.

3. Creation of product or service.

4. Testing and test marketing of product or service.

5. Acquisition of capital for start-up.

6. Further product development.

7. Commercial introduction of product or service.

8. Development and expansion of business.

9. Reinvestment of retained earnings in product improvements or new projects.

THE MAGAZINE FOR ENTREPRENEURS

Venture's

GUIDE TO

INVESTING IN PRIVATE COMPANIES

THE MAGAZINE FOR ENTREPRENEURS

Venture's

GUIDE TO

INVESTING IN PRIVATE COMPANIES

**A FINANCING
MANUAL FOR THE
ENTREPRENEURIAL
INVESTOR**

ARTHUR LIPPER III
WITH GEORGE RYAN

DOW JONES-IRWIN Homewood, Illinois 60430

ISBN 0-87094-480-0
Library of Congress Catalog Card No. 83–73366

Printed in the United States of America

1 2 3 4 5 6 7 8 9 0 K 1 0 9 8 7 6 5 4

To Nancy L. Stuart—
thanks for the
last 25 years

PREFACE

The unsung heroes of our American form of capitalism are the private individuals who provide financing for the more than 11,000 companies formed every week in the United States. These informal investors, aptly known in the business world as angels, venture where bankers fear to tread.

The entrepreneur starting up a new business, without sufficient capital and credit of his own to get it under way, normally has three sources of possible funding: venture capitalists, the stock market, and individual investors. However, venture capitalists and other professional investors are involved in a maximum of only 1500 of the more than 600,000 companies started each year. The entrepreneur's chances of funding are not good, to put it mildly. Very few entrepreneurs can expect to be the beneficiary of a public offering. This leaves the huge majority of new companies to be funded by other than professional, or even experienced, investors.

Profit is not the sole motivation of many of these individual investors—they are often just "helping out" someone. Yet, the fact that most new companies fail for one reason or another is a reality that most of these angels will have to face sooner or later. All too often, these business failures result in recrimination, broken friendships, and sometimes even financial disaster.

This book is for the individual investor who has $50,000 to $250,000 of "disposable" assets to invest in private companies. Its purpose is to show the individual how to maximize profits and minimize losses. Its recommendations are based on more than 20 years of experience on my part in startups and seed-capital financings. My aim is to enable the entrepreneurial investor to do a better job of investing.

Some business observers detect a trend away from the highly managerial organizations of the 1960s and 1970s toward entrepreneurial enterprises. They see this change as part of a resurgence of America's tradition of self-reliance and personal independence. The social benefit which I hope will result from this book is that its readers, who make more money when right and lose less money when wrong, will be in a position to participate in the financing of an ever increasing number of new ventures. Only through new company formation will our country be able to solve the problems of underutilization of its people and resources. It is also only through new company formation that many individuals will ever be able to utilize their talents to achieve true economic freedom through the accrual of wealth.

This book is *not* for those wealthy individuals who are naturally risk-averse and intent upon maintaining economic and social status quo. Nor is this a book for those who wish to gamble and see entrepreneurial investing as a means to fast and vast riches. The former should probably invest only in real estate, and the latter should learn the intricacies of futures and options.

Investing in entrepreneurs, for that is the real investment which is being made when one invests in new private companies, can be enormously rewarding, as well as highly frustrating and very expensive. The rewards can be much greater than financial gains, and the losses can result in much more pain and subsequent sacrifice than the investor expected.

Parenting a successful private company to the point of its going public or sale is an exhilarating experience. Of course, money accompanies this success. One can make, as I have made, 40, 50, or more times the amount originally invested. The great fortunes created in this country since World War II have been for the most part a result of either real estate speculation or entrepreneurial activity; the early investors, particularly those who invested at the outset with the founding entrepreneurs, have benefitted extraordinarily. Everyone has heard of the financial rewards of early and successful investment. All anyone needs in their lifetime is one such "hit."

The frustration, embarrassment, and pain of failure can be of such magnitude that marital and familial relationships become strained beyond repair. The loss of self-esteem in situations of significant financial loss can be serious for an investor. Whereas the entrepreneur in failure can feel he had no choice but to make the attempt, win or lose, the investor is not provided with a similar ego-protective device. He did not *have* to make the investment and, therefore, must accept the responsibility, in his own eyes, of being stupid or greedy, or both. The failure of a private company is usually a great deal more traumatic than watching the price of a stock plummet on the stock exchange.

Women readers may have noticed by now that both the investor and the entrepreneur are referred to as "he." This usage has been adopted solely to spare the reader—female and male—of the repetitious use of "he or she" and circumlocutions involving the word "person." Of *Venture* magazine's subscribers, 95 percent are men; 98 percent of the Association of Venture Founders are men. However, most social trends would seem to favor an increased number of successful women entrepreneurs and investors in the future. Currently, there seems to be a much greater interest and participation on the part of women in entrepreneurial activity than ever before.

According to John Maynard Keynes, mere thrift is not enough by itself to build cities or improve mankind's possessions. He wrote in *Treatise on Money:* "If enterprise is afoot, wealth accumulates whatever may be happening to thrift; and if enterprise is asleep, wealth decays whatever thrift may be doing." Entrepreneurs represent America's spirit of enterprise, and they in turn must depend on individual investors to get their projects off the ground. Very often such investors make more than financial contributions to the new company, putting to the entrepreneur's use their experience, skills, and contacts.

I do not claim that I can be of assistance in finding the right entrepreneur for a particular investor. But I do believe that as a result of reading this book, the prospective investor will be in a better position to recognize the right entrepreneur for him (or, as is more likely, the *almost* right entrepreneur). Most importantly, this book should point out to both investor and entrepreneur what in all likelihood will occur in their business relationship, and how they can avoid, by prior agreement, common points of friction caused by the entrepreneur's nonachievement of projections. I do not claim to have all the answers to private company investing. I do not even claim to have as many investment answers as I have investment scars. I do understand the essence of the transaction which occurs between investor and entrepreneur, and I have been a player in the game a sufficient number of times to understand the rhythms and evolutions of both personal relationships and new company development. While deals are not all alike, entrepreneurs tend to have many characteristics in common.

This book could easily have been entitled *Do as I Say and Not as I Have Done.* It could also have been entitled *I Wish I Had Always Done as I Now Know Enough to Say to Do.* As I guess is true with most books offering advice based upon experience, I am attempting to do the almost impossible—to pass on the benefit of experience. I must also admit that, even with the experience, I do not always follow the advice offered herein. However, when I do let myself get so over-enthusiastic with an entrepreneur or project as to disregard the lessons learned previously, I do so with a knowing smile and some feeling that I am about to experience déjà vu and relearn the same lessons. As Royal Little writes in his wonderfully instructive and entertaining book, *How to Lose $100,000,000 and Other Valuable Advice,* "almost anyone can afford to make a single mistake, but when you make the same identical mistake twice, it is time to visit the headshrinker!" I've lived long and actively enough to have run out of possible new mistakes, so many times I just keep making the same ones over and over again. Hopefully, this book will spare readers the same masochistic exercise. All who are considering becoming angels would do well to read Royal Little's book. There is a lot of wisdom dispensed with humor and humility. Private company angels should also realize that increased humility is one of the probable results of private company investing, unless the investor is very lucky, in which case arrogance will usually result.

Arthur Lipper III

ACKNOWLEDGMENTS

Many people helped me write this book. Many of them dislike me. Some of them I now dislike. The particular people to whom I now refer are those with whom, or through whom, I have lost money. The mistakes made were all mine. They were, for the most part, mistakes of judgment regarding people and not situations. Sure, some products did not work and some markets were not there as hoped or projected, but the real problem was one of people-judgment error. A good manager can find or create a new product if the original one does not work as hoped. A good entrepreneur can find another way of marketing or maneuvering if the planned approach turns out to be wrong. Being an investor in private companies is not a popularity contest. The private company investor just does not have the luxury of selling his stock, as does a stock market investor, if he becomes disenchanted with management. He has to either await his destiny or try to do something about it. The latter seldom creates friends. I won't list those from whom I have learned the hard and disagreeable lessons, the essence of which has resulted in some of my approaches to investing and certain advice offered in this book. As they read the book, however, I hope that they will recognize themselves and, perhaps, with the passage of time, understand better the lessons which were there for both of us to benefit from in the future.

Other people helped with this book in a more direct manner. Those people gave generously of their time and counsel. They put up with my interviews and questions. They offered me the use of materials they had prepared for their own use. They are all very busy people and were most gracious in the gift of time and attention, and I thank them greatly. A list of these "angels" of informational input follows.

I would also be remiss if I failed to mention the constructive ease of working with George Ryan. George is a true professional writer and editor. When I first met George he said "What kind of a book do you want me to do? A western, romance, adventure?" He, at the time, knew almost nothing about the subject and now, after much study, is almost an expert. Of course, if he tries to use his book-only knowledge, he is likely to end up paying some tuition in the form of a few losses—but then, that's how one learns.

Of course, my wonderful wife, Anni, had to put up with almost total social withdrawal as it was necessary for me (us) to go "cold turkey" in terms of time spent with friends during the months of intensive effort it took to complete the book. As all who know her, and me, will agree, she is next in line for canonization anyway. Neither entrepreneurs nor entrepreneurial investors are easy to live with, and combining the two can be deadly for a relationship. Ours, due to her good judgment and firm guiding hand, has endured for more than 22 years, and we have both enjoyed a great return on our investment.

One cannot create a book such as this without the dedicated assistance of those with whom one works on a daily basis. Eileen Broderick has kept everything organized and flowing. It is not an easy job when there are also the daily demands of working with someone such as myself who has more than a few activities going most of the time.

The following knew they were helping me create *Venture's Guide to Investing in Private Companies* and I thank each of them.

Burt Alimansky—*Alimansky Planning Group*
Howard Arvey—*Arvey, Hodes, Costello & Burman*
Marshall L. Burman—*Arvey, Hodes, Costello & Burman*
Scott Hodes—*Arvey, Hodes, Costello & Burman*
Fred Shapiro—*Author*
Herbert S. Meeker—*Baer, Marks & Upham*
William R. Chandler—*Bay Venture Group*
W. R. Berkley—*W. R. Berkley Corporation*
Harold E. Bigler, Jr.—*Bigler Investment Company, Inc.*
David L. Epstein—*J. H. Chapman Group*
Frank J. A. Cilluffo—*Cilluffo Associates, L.P.*
John L. Hines—*President, Continental Illinois Equity Corporation*
James Bergman—*DSV Partners*
John A. Canning, Jr.—*President, The First Chicago Equity Group*
Martin L. Solomon—*First City Holdings*

Joel Leff—*Forstmann-Leff Associates*
Stanley C. Golder—*Golder, Thoma & Company*
Evelyn Berezin—*The Greenhouse Investment Fund*
E. F. Heizer, Jr.—*Chairman, Heizer Corporation*
Howard Stevenson—*Harvard University*
Norman Mesirow—*Mesirow & Company*
Arthur D. Little—*Chief Executive Officer, Narragansett Capital Corporation*
Royal Little—*Narragansett Capital Corporation, Textron*
Steven D. Oppenheim—*Oppenheim, Appel, Dixon & Company*
Seth H. Dubin—*Satterlee & Stephens*
Raymond J. Armstrong—*Starwood Corporation*
Richard Testa—*Testa, Hurwitz & Thibeault*
Gerald Tsai, Jr.—*Vice Chairman, American Can Company*
William Wetzel, Jr.—*University of New Hampshire*
Karl H. Vesper—*University of Washington*
Dan W. Lufkin—*Venture Capitalist*
Jonathon B. Levine—*Business Week*
Carl Burgen—*Editor-in-Chief, Venture Magazine*
J. Patrick Welsh—*Welsh, Carson, Anderson & Stowe*
E. C. Whitehead—*Whitehead Associates*

I also wish to express my appreciation to Stanley E. Pratt and Norman Fast of Capital Publishing Corporation for so graciously allowing the use of certain articles appearing in various annual editions of the *Guide to Venture Capital Sources*. This valuable reference source and directory has become an industry standard. Readers of this book will note in the appendices several interesting and relevant articles which have appeared in *Guide to Venture Capital Sources* and are advised they will find many more in the original source.

A. L. III

CONTENTS

Enforcement of Agreement between Investor and Entrepreneur. Letters of Intent. Shareholders' Agreement as Management Tool.

THE INVESTOR 1

When asked whether individual investors should invest in private companies (as opposed to those that are publicly traded), almost without exception the advice of the experts interviewed in the preparation of this book was that they should not.

However, this advice misses the question behind the question. The real issue is this: Are the potential benefits of investing in private companies sufficient to justify the increased risks of failure and, most importantly, the sacrifice of liquidity? Each year, several million Americans vote yes to this question by writing checks, signing subscription agreements, executing partnership forms, and making bank loan guarantees.

This book is intended to assist you, the individual investor, in making better decisions as to whether you should or should not invest in private companies, and if you do invest, how to do so more effectively.

The primary reason the vast majority of the professional investors interviewed advised against individuals investing in private companies was the inherent illiquidity of almost all private company investments. In reaching their conclusion, the professional investors were contrasting private against publicly traded investments. They were contemplating direct investment rather than indirect ones using the medium of guarantees, and they were primarily thinking of those which related to companies that had the potential for either becoming public or being purchased by larger companies within the span of a few years.

Clearly we would all like to find, and have the necessary courage to invest in, future Apples, MCIs, Federal Expresses, and the hundreds of other companies which have gone public and, thereby, made instant millionaires of the original investors as well as the founding entrepreneurs. However, for each of these winners there have been many more losers in which the investors have lost all of their original investment and, frequently, substantially more.

How you can lose more than the amount that you invested is the subject of a later section and is perhaps one of the more important risks of private company investment to be understood.

The point under consideration in this chapter is whether you, the investor, can afford to be in the game at all.

It must be recognized that once a private company has received monies from investors, there are basically only two ways in which these investors can either make a profit or at least break even. One way is for the company to be profitable and, therefore, either repay obligations or declare dividends. The other way is for something to be sold. That something can be either assets of the company or the securities owned by the investor. In either case, the company will probably have to enjoy some measure of success if the investor is to have a satisfactory experience. Yet, it is not always so. The company can be sold, or the investor can sell something to someone before the company achieves its projected results. For example, most (in number, not aggregate value) initial public offerings are of companies not yet profitable, and the existing shareholders most frequently already have large "paper" profits based upon the capital valuation indicated by the offering price.

The question of who should invest in a private company really cannot be addressed until the motivation for investing has been determined. Lots of people should make private company investments—if they can afford to do so, if they wish to gain a sense of participation in the growth and development of a company not generally available through investing in publicly traded stocks, and if they wish to assist in the creation of new jobs and economic opportunity in America.

No one should invest in a private company more than he can afford to lose. This trite-sounding statement is more profound than it may at first appear. In a private company investment, the investor is likely to have a total result—either his monies are likely to be totally lost or the result will be totally satisfactory. A satisfactory result will probably come at a time beyond the control of the investor and not close to the time of original investment. When progress is not satisfactory, there is usually no easy way for the investor to exit, take a loss, save the balance of his investment, and redeploy his assets.

The investor would do well to prepare a personal-business plan or personal-financial projection in order to determine the exact amount of money he can afford to lose. It is all well and good to say "I have $50,000 with which to speculate," but does that assume a similar level of disposable assets in future years? Can he foresee possible demands for investable funds for other projects? These and similar questions will assist the investor in estimating how much of his capital he can truly put at high-risk. It is not as simple a determination as is generally thought.

As publicly traded securities have a liquidity that is absent in private company investments, it is reasonable for the investor to expect a higher rate of return from the latter when similar risk levels are involved. In other words, if a net 15 percent annual average compound pretax return is anticipated by the investor from the investor's publicly traded securities, then something higher must be projected from his nonliquid investments. He must be compensated for the sacrifice of liquidity. Most of the professionals interviewed suggested that, for companies of similar quality, the private company's projected investment return would have to be three to five times that of the publicly traded company before they would consider it worthwhile. Of course, these calculations presume a sale of the purchased securities and are not usually reflective of either a dividend or interest income assumption. Therefore, since a 15 percent annual return compounded over five years doubles the amount of the principal, thereby producing a 100 percent gain, a cumulative gain of 300 to 500 percent is indicated as an appropriate five-year minimum objective for an illiquid investment.

One consideration of whether or not to invest in *anything* must be the level of the investor's own financial sophistication. In the case of private company investing, the investor's level of sophistication should be higher than that needed for publicly traded stocks because of two reasons. First, very few other people will review the company's investment offering proposal, so the investor must rely more than usual on his own judgment. The standard investment services do not follow private companies, investment banking firms and securities analysts do not cover them, and the financial press does not typically comment on them or their prospects. Second, much less financial information is generated by the private company in the normal course of events than by its publicly traded counterpart. Also, the quality of the financial information provided by the private company will probably not be at as high a level as that of a similar publicly traded company, which has disclosure requirements and public-shareholder liabilities. The investor does not need a graduate degree in finance, but he does need, for private company investing, to truly understand cash flow analysis and that which goes into the making of projections of financial results.

Of course, if the investor is lucky—very lucky—or is making the investment for purposes other than straightforward financial gain, he need not have a high degree of financial sophistication. Yet, he will need the solace of having a sense of humor (or at least a sense of human inability to predict future events), since private company investment is an area in which Murphy's law—anything that can go wrong, will go wrong—can be seen in its most spectacular applications. The private company investor must maintain a sense of detachment and objectivity. This detachment can result from the size of the investment being relatively modest or from the investor's overall approach to high-risk investments.

In determining the appropriateness of a private company investment, the availability of the investor's time is a significant consideration. A good deal of time is required to adequately monitor the progress of a private company, for the reason, as mentioned previously, that in all likelihood there will be no one to do it for the investor but himself. The investor must also expect to have to put questions to the private company, and expect the company to live up to its description as "private" in its reluctance to disclose information. Entrepreneurs are frequently "too busy" to be terribly communicative with investors once they are in control of the investors' money.

Howard Stevenson, the Harvard Business School professor most concerned with entrepreneurship, recommends the following to the investor: "Every time you have a dumb question, ask it. Very often, these turn out to be the most probing questions an investor can put to an entrepreneur."

Stevenson says also,

> The investor must not forget his skills and regard himself solely as a supplier of money. Money is not the most difficult thing in the world to come by. Usually, skills or other resources are more scarce than money. But, before investing his skills, the investor has to estimate how much time he can take off from his regular business. Thus, a dentist has special skills to be an investor in a dental supply company if he can also spare the time.

The appropriate size of a private company investment relative to the investor's own assets or future income levels is a matter which must take into consideration the age, health, financial resources, and socioeconomic and ethnic backgrounds of the individual investor. Whether the investor can *take* a loss is more than just a question of the money involved. Will it embarrass you? Have you been brought up to believe that it is wrong to lose and only acceptable to be a "winner"? Are your friends all winners or very security conscious and, therefore, risk-adverse to the point of being frightened by, or contemptuous of, those who sometimes lose or put themselves in a position of risk? If so, your position in private companies should be very minor, and probably not of a size which can help or hurt you very much. All things considered, 20 percent of an investor's common-stock portfolio or a similar percentage of an individual's ordinary income seems like a reasonable figure to use once the investor has passed the point of needing money to support present life style necessities.

The issue of concentration or diversification of private company investment simply compounds the questions posed earlier which relate to the time and money availability of the investor. Diversification is one of the guiding principles of all portfolio management, especially when speculation in unknown future events is a large factor. However, if the private company investor is going to be active and participating, as opposed to passive, concentration is probably a more advantageous program.

Active or passive investment is a basic decision the investor must make. This decision is very bottom line in that many of the other conclusions flow from it. If the investor wishes to be passive, he is probably much better off with a portfolio of publicly traded issues, since purely economic justifications for private company investment by most individuals are difficult to find. For the individual motivated by a desire to be actively involved in "growing" a business, some private company investments are worthy of consideration.

Understanding the true intent and motivation of the investor is essential in weighing the merits of any investment. Many private company investments are made on a quasi-obligatory basis because of a special relationship between the investor and entrepreneur/manager seeking the funds, such as an investment requested by a family member, good friend, customer, business associate, or political personage or an investment made simply to assist someone. In other words, the investor's exclusive concern is not profit. Recapture of capital may not even be a major concern when compared to the real reason for making the investment.

These quasi-obligatory investments are probably the most common type of private investment made and involve two primary concerns. One is the perception of fairness from the perspective of the recipient of the funds. The other is that the investment be structured in such a manner as to free the investor from the obligation to make any follow-on investments, unless he wishes to make them solely on the basis of profit expectation.

If current return or future income, as opposed to capital gains, is the investor's primary objective, many private company investments can be structured to be attractive. Security of his principal will probably be this type of investor's greatest concern.

Large capital gains are most investors' aim, ultimately through selling the interests purchased to someone else, and such transactions must be structured very differently from either income-oriented or quasi-obligatory investor transactions.

In many instances, the development of an eventual adversarial relationship is almost inevitable between the investor and the entrepreneur/manager. This unpleasant fact of life can be a result of two factors or a combination of both: (1) the entrepreneur feels he has given the investor too good a deal on the project that he created; and (2) the investor blames the entrepreneur for his inability to achieve the results predicted in the time frame which the investor feels was used to induce him to invest. Both parties feel, and frequently so, that they have been taken. Often, the honeymoon period is short. On the other hand, as with some marriages, the relationship between investor and entrepreneur can evolve and mature from what was probably a set of unrealistic expectations in the first place. However, recognizing the fact that most new businesses cease to exist within five years of incorporation, investor unhappiness with entrepreneurs can be said to be natural, predictable, and widespread.

The investor taking stock of risk and reward relationships should consider the personal aggravation involved in dealing with personalities who may have a naturally antipathetic posture to those having excess money with which to invest. Many investors in private companies are unprepared for the personal involvements which result. These involvements can be the very best part of private company investing, but they can also be the most painful and disagreeable.

How much easier it is to sell a stock or a bond on the open market than it is to have to tell an entrepreneur, with whom you have been in constant contact for several years, that you have decided not to do something which would have permitted the company to continue along lines wished by the entrepreneur. How do you tell the entrepreneur/manager of a business, who has become a friend, that your condition for providing additional funds is his leaving the company? What about when the entrepreneur/manager is a relative or the son of a friend or a customer? How do you tell the founder that his business, in its success, has outgrown his abilities and that for the company to further prosper, he will have to change (reduce) his position within it? On the other hand, there can be no more satisfying development than seeing a group of hardworking and capable young people "making it big" and feeling that you, as the investor, were at least partly responsible.

The sacrifice of liquidity required by private company investment is a manner for serious consideration. Alternative uses for the capital and its possible future needs must be reviewed. However, the most important aspect is understanding the motivation of the investor and structuring transactions accordingly.

The investor should be aware that he often has more to offer a private company than hard cash. He may have technical know-how or marketing knowledge to contribute, or his very involvement with the company may permit it to achieve better banking or customer relationships than would otherwise have been the case.

For another general overview of the informal investor, see Appendix A.

It has been suggested to me that a simple how-to approach to private company investment would be more "positive" than my investor-beware approach. I think that the private company investor can benefit from a how-to book. However, my concern is with a more fundamental problem most investors have—unrealistic expectations of wealth enhancement. These are the expectations that allow them to be persuaded by entrepreneurs into ventures of such impracticality and high risk that they are almost certain to incur losses. The last thing such investors need is a how-to book. I, therefore, feel there is a more urgent need to *warn* investors of the pitfalls they will assuredly meet, and how these pitfalls may be circumvented or at least lessened.

A book advising entrepreneurs not to be entrepreneurs would be a total folly—they have little control over their destiny in this regard. This book is certainly not written to advise private company investors not to invest but solely to help them make better decisions in their investments, thereby making more money and/or losing less. It is extremely important for the investor to lose less, since he can go on to another enterprise with the money he salvages from a failed one. Conversely, once he loses all his money, he is out of the game.

THE ENTREPRENEUR 2

What real knowledge have I, an investor, about entrepreneurs? Being an entrepreneur, having financed, studied, and liked entrepreneurs, having fought and litigated with them—in all humility, I claim a certain authority in describing and dealing with them. My observations are based also on my roles as chairman and founder of the Association of Venture Founders and chairman and CEO of *Venture: The Magazine for Entrepreneurs.* Incidentally, my observations and views are very similar to those of academics who have made formal studies of the character traits and common experiences of entrepreneurs.

The entrepreneur as such is not the subject of this book, nor is the entrepreneur in general a social phenomenon about which I have particular insight or information. The person I refer to as an entrepreneur throughout this book is that rare breed, and sometimes endangered species, the *successful* entrepreneur. The distinction I am making here is similar to the one between people with artistic tendencies and successful artists. People with artistic tendencies outnumber by far successful artists. In the same way, there are lots more people with entrepreneurial tendencies than there are successful entrepreneurs. The reason for this is that tendencies have to be developed, through experience or education and training, into abilities and skills. Raw talent and desire alone are not enough.

One of the areas of great loss in natural wealth this country suffers is that of failing to identify young talent and develop it fully for the benefit of the individual, as well as the community at large. In general, I believe that gifted children are the world's largest wasted asset, since they hold the power, if developed fully, to solve the problems of mankind. Gifted children are the most highly leveraged of investments. Unfortunately, an early aptitude for athletics is the only classification of giftedness that gets special treatment in most countries.

Luck plays a big role in the life of the successful entrepreneur and those in his orbit. However, most entrepreneurs are people who feel the need to be in control of their lives and dislike the very idea of luck. Typically, they are not gamblers and do not think of themselves as risk-takers. I suspect that a customer profile of an Atlantic City or Las Vegas casino's partons would show relatively few entrepreneurs as opposed to wage earners who feel the need for some unrestrictive randomness and the something-for-nothing excitement of gambling much more than the successful entrepreneur.

The luck which plays a role in the entrepreneur's life is that of location, of childhood years, of timing, of inspiration, and of associations. Location is important, since it determines the likely area of exposure and focus—there aren't too many high-tech startups in Montana. Timing is, perhaps, the most important consideration, because the entrepreneur is more likely to be too early in an area of development than too late. Only major companies can afford the expense of being too early. Many of my own investments and entrepreneurial activities which failed to achieve success were years later successfully developed by others with less vision but better judgment and more money. On the other hand, the entrepreneur who has an "idea" feels almost a compulsion to go into business, as soon as he can marshal the forces of development and production, since his need is for achievement and recognition more than profit.

Chance associations are part of entrepreneurial luck; for example, the military service buddy, the college roommate, or childhood friend who in later years can provide special assistance. Successful entrepreneurs tend to be able to identify a single person who made a real difference in their lives. This extremely important mentor relationship seems to have been a random occurrence in most cases.

Among other traits, the entrepreneur is an achiever. The goal orientation of entrepreneurs may have something to do with the fact that most of the successful ones have had a particularly strong relationship with their fathers, either good or bad. I suppose I can expect now to hear from all those successful entrepreneurs who were orphans and those who see themselves as having been maternally motivated.

Another striking statistic is that the majority of successful entrepreneurs were either first-born or only children. Of course, the first born is always the only child for a period of time and, therefore, for a while at least, can be the focus of his parents' attention. A conviction that society suffers from a lack of willingness to identify and fully develop gifted children as a national natural resource, and that many achieving gifted children received special early nurturing, led to my founding the *Gifted Children Newsletter*,[1] of which I am chairman. The newsletter serves as a communication and networking medium for parents.

The entrepreneur is an early riser. In a survey of the first group of members of the Association of Venture Founders, it was found that only 3 percent rose after 8 A.M. and that the vast majority rose before 7 A.M. This is not surprising since most entrepreneurs are people of high-energy level, are achievement-oriented, and love what they are doing. They can't wait for the day to begin. They seem to require less sleep than others and tend to be in good health, perhaps as a result of their high energy.

Despite the fact that entrepreneurs have no special physical characteristics, many successful ones recollect that as children they felt that they were different—taller or shorter, thinner or fatter, and so on. The most commonly shared characteristic of entrepreneurs is that they had a job or jobs during childhood. The kinds of jobs are not significant, only that they worked for a tangible reward at an early age, and that the work was performed for others and not as a family duty. Obviously, there is a bias in this toward city and suburban children and away from rural children. But then most successful entrepreneurs are not farm-bred.

Successful entrepreneurs are usually married. Those I know tend to stay with one wife over the years I have been acquainted with them. This is not to say that divorce statistics are different for entrepreneurs than for others at similar socioeconomic levels but rather that the entrepreneur is truly married to his business and is not likely to be interested in creating change in his home life. Problems arise when his spouse cannot sufficiently identify with his business to accept the sacrifice of his attention. There are just so many waking hours in the day and product development seems to take precedence over child development and *nothing* is as important as generating cash flow.

Entrepreneurs are often described by others as "compulsive" or "driven," yet do not see themselves in such a light, feeling that all they are doing is "getting the job done." Others may find the entrepreneur abrasive, since his need to please has been replaced by the sometimes conflicting needs to achieve and prove something.

This "composite portrait" of the successful entrepreneur has been put together for the purpose of aiding the investor in identifying him. Not everyone who has these characteristics will make a successful entrepreneur, but they will certainly not be held back by them. If it were solely the business that the investor had to consider, the personality of the entrepreneur would have little interest for him. But the entrepreneurial investor invests in entrepreneurs. It is the entrepreneur who is subject of the investor's investment rather than his product. Products can be created, altered, or replaced, but entrepreneurs have to be found and attracted to the right deal.

---

[1] *Gifted Children Newsletter*, P.O. Box 115, Sewell, NJ 08080.

For another general view of the entrepreneur, see Appendix B.

The following is an editorial which appeared in the September 1983 issue of *Venture* magazine.

CHAIRMAN'S COMMENT

Entrepreneur is a word used with ever greater frequency. That's because there's more entrepreneurial activity going on and because the entrepreneur has a better image these days. The word is now less likely to evoke an image of a Walter Mitty or of a fast-talking broker than previously. Nevertheless, the word is not satisfactorily defined. The Webster definition of one who "organizes and manages a business undertaking, *assuming the risk* for the sake of profit" is clearly restricted to those entrepreneurs who are entirely self-financed. As most successful entrepreneurs require outside funding, there must be a better and broader definition.

In a speech describing entrepreneurs to an audience responsible for pension fund investing for major companies, I suggested the following definition of an entrepreneur who should be attractive to the venture capital investor. Readers having good ideas for definitions of an entrepreneur are asked to send them along to me.

The entrepreneur is someone who: makes something commercial happen.

The successful entrepreneur is someone who: makes something commercial happen which benefits others.

The commercially successful entrepreneur is someone who: makes something happen which benefits others and produces a profit.

The commercially successful business entrepreneur who is attractive to investors is someone who: makes something happen which benefits others, and which produces a profit of sufficient magnitude to justify the risks inherent in providing the funding for the entrepreneur.

Profit is the key word. The entrepreneur should not lose sight in seeking funding that the enterprise must produce a profit of sufficient magnitude to be an attractive alternative to competitive investment opportunities. To the investor, the art of investing is one of comparing ever-present alternatives. The professional investor must always be invested, but not in any one deal or type of security. The entrepreneur is different. He is typically single-project focused and therefore may benefit in motivation but suffers in objectivity and realism.

Venture as a magazine is really all about profit. We are focused only on that which is intended to ultimately produce a profit, or about those who have achieved profit. We also believe that loss avoidance or minimization is an integral part of profit making for both the investor and the entrepreneur, and for that reason, frequently publish articles on how entrepreneurs manage their companies to best effect.

I am always interested in learning from readers ways in which the magazine can be of more service. If you have thoughts, please share them with me. Profit is the name of our game and we know that profits are earned by benefiting others.

Arthur Lipper III
Chairman

FINDING PRIVATE COMPANY INVESTMENT OPPORTUNITIES 3

OBJECTIVES OF INVESTOR

We have all heard the golden rule of business: He who has the gold makes the rules. There should also be an intelligent private company investor's golden rule: He who has the gold should first understand his own true objectives and then make the rules.

Understanding what is in the investor's own self-interest is very different from negotiating the hardest deal possible with an entrepreneur. If the investor is going to have to depend on that entrepreneur to manage the enterprise, the hardest deal will most often not be the best deal for the investor.

What return do you really expect on your investment? Why exactly are you investing in the enterprise? To show how smart or adventuresome you are? To be the Ted Turner of your country club? To seek the highest possible current rate of return on your money? Ideally, you are accepting the challenge of private company investment with a balanced view of its risk and reward parameters, but you must also understand on a very personal level why you are investing. These personal reasons are the ones that cause the investor to ignore the advice of others, for better or worse. There are many valid reasons for an individual to invest. The only ones you really need to understand are your own.

The investor cannot use the entrepreneur as his sounding board, because, in most cases, the entrepreneur will agree to almost anything proposed by the funding source if he has been rejected often enough by others. The funding source has the responsibility to do the right and fair thing, and what turns out to be fair for the entrepreneur most often turns out right for the investor.

HOW MANY OPPORTUNITIES SHOULD BE SOUGHT?

It is less a matter of the investor actively pursuing a certain number of opportunities than of his being exposed to a sufficient number of deals to be in a position to judge the good from the bad. The average professional in the venture-capital field probably reviews 400–500 investment proposals and business plans in the course of a year, and his success in part will depend upon his having accurate and up-to-date information on what is available. The individual investor should not even try to cope with large numbers of proposals, but he certainly should see a number before feeling confident to tell whether he is being offered a fair deal in terms of the risk being assumed and the current marketplace value for similar deals.

The chances are that if this is the investor's first private company investment, he will put the bulk of his money in the first proposal which comes along that he finds attractive, regardless of what it is. Obviously, such a decision increases his chances of losing the bulk of his money. Holding back a part of one's investment capital for the purpose of refinancing the chosen enterprise will be discussed elsewhere. But should the investor concentrate on a single venture, or should he deliberately try to diversify his holdings? The investor with $50,000 to $250,000 to invest hardly expects to build a highly diversified portfolio, but he can put, say, $20,000 each into five new companies instead of $100,000 into one. Five companies will demand more of his time and energy than one; yet, on the other hand, since so many new companies fail, he may feel he has a better statistical chance of success with five rather than one. Such reasonable diversification makes sense, so long as the investor keeps in mind that the limiting factor is more likely to be his own time more than money. Time spent working with entrepreneurs and reviewing financials can seem endless, and it is terribly important for the individual investor to understand the magnitude of the commitment he is making, in terms of time as well as money.

Building upon the strength of one's experience and skills is one aspect of being a successful investor. Such knowledge gives the investor strength, and that strength permits a concentration of effort and financial investment. When an investor finds a good opportunity in an area in which he is knowledgeable, he should concentrate on it, since it would be foolish for him under these circumstances to diversify simply for the sake of diversification. However, just because an investor knows something about the textile business does not mean he should invest in textiles, unless that particular segment of the textile industry is attractive in terms of future investment. By embracing only the familiar, one can turn a strength into a weakness.

Daniel Lufkin—one of the founding entrepreneurs of Donaldson, Lufkin and Jenrette, a director of many successful companies, and legend in the venture capital business—told me,

> All sorts of Wall Street research reports describe the latest technology, the newest microprocessor, and so on. The advice I give is don't listen to other people when they tell you what you should invest your money in. Listen to yourself. By this I mean, pay attention to the products that you buy and use regularly. These products solve a need that you have. Obtain information from the companies that make them. In other words, think along familiar lines rather than looking for exotic things in which to invest.

James Bergman—a general partner in DSV Partners, the very successful Princeton-based venture capital organization—took this approach:

> The private company investor who has not the knowledge or contacts to get in on the leading edge of new high tech companies might very well concentrate on suppliers of such companies. For example, he might avoid becoming involved in a genetic engineering company but invest in a company that produces instruments for genetic engineers.

Diversification of investment can be more rewarding in prestartup companies, or seed-capital investments, than in those in the startup or development stages, because so many prestartup companies never get off the ground. But, diversification (particularly if it involves high-return, high-risk enterprises) can never be a substitute for knowledge gained through the commitment of time, energy, resources, contact, and study. The private company investor looking for significant risk reduction through diversification is recommended to get into a fund or play the stock market.

WHEN YOU ARE THE ONE THE OPPORTUNITY FINDS

When offered that chance-of-a-lifetime opportunity, the investor has to ask himself, with some degree of harshness, why he is the lucky one to be selected. If you do not know the person making the offer, and if he does not come to you with the endorsement of someone you know and respect, you should be wary. It is reasonable for the investor to ask such an entrepreneur to provide a list of the investors he has already approached. If such a list is forthcoming, the investor can then contact the people named in it to ask them why they did not invest in the venture. They may have made an excuse to the entrepreneur, wishing to spare his feelings or to avoid argument, saying they had no funds available or so forth. These investors are frequently more likely to tell a fellow investor the real reasons for their refusal to become involved. In many cases, the investor can be sure that such a list of investors exists or could be made, and the reason the entrepreneur approached him was that his name was next on that list after all those who preceded him had turned down the deal.

The entrepreneur is probably aware that many professional investment managers and venture capitalists are reluctant to invest the time to study a business plan unless it arrives with some sort of referral, which is frequently taken as an endorsement. The entrepreneur should not be surprised, therefore, when the investor asks him for references, such as a letter of reference from a bank, an attorney, or an accountant. One professional often asks an entrepreneur for five references, telling him to make one of them someone who dislikes him, without saying which one that is.

WHO IS MAKING THE OFFER AND WHY?

Not only must the investor be wary of strangers offering him deals, he must also closely examine the credentials and motivation of *any* man offering or promoting a deal. My experience is that a financial intermediary, or "middleman," is more likely to misrepresent a deal than is an entrepreneur. The entrepreneur knows that he is going to have to justify, in an ongoing relationship with the investor, all his initial representations and projections, whereas the financial intermediary may be interested only in making the sale, collecting his fee, and moving on to other deals. Having said that, it must be pointed out that the presence of a reputable financial intermediary or investment banker can add enormously to the credibility of a proposal. Such an investment banker's reputation is on the line, and he is probably assuming some legal liability in making the offer, notwithstanding claims to the contrary.

William R. Berkley, a successful entrepreneur and founder of W. R. Berkley Corporation, is a firm believer in checking out references. He often goes one step further, sometimes with rewarding results, by checking on the validity of the reference. For example, when an entrepreneur tells Berkley, "Talk to John Smith at Citywide Bank, he'll vouch for me," Berkley does no such thing. Instead, he or his own banker calls someone else at Citywide and asks them about John Smith and the entrepreneur. Sometimes, the endorsement is warm and is all the more reassuring coming from a third party; sometimes, the warning is straightforward, acknowledging there are troubles with the account; and, at other times, the answer is evasive, which must be taken as a tipoff that all may not be well.

Some sophisticated investors expect that an entrepreneur or promoter will offer an investigatory background report on himself, such as prepared by Bishop, Pinkerton, or Proudfoot. These reports note negative happenings in the career of the subject, such as litigation, poor credit ratings, divorce, prior directorships, and associations with a bankrupt company. The reports are not expensive, generally running from $150 to $700, depending on the amount of information required and the availability of data.

The investor should look for an experienced entrepreneur whose record casts no doubt as to his integrity. He should not accept previous wrongdoing on the part of the entrepreneur as an "early mistake." But, neither should the investor always expect to find someone without a business mistake or failure in his career. The entrepreneur's integrity is the issue, not his perfection of business judgment. The investor should look for openness and candidness about prior business disappointments and, perhaps, failures on the part of the entrepreneur. There will frequently be an invention he was unable to finance or a situation he was unable to control. You won't have to ask him to tell you about his successes; he will do so without prompting.

When a financial intermediary is involved, the following are fair questions for the entrepreneurial investor to ask. How exactly is the middleman involved in the deal? Does he have an ongoing interest in the company as part of his fee? Is he in fact investing in the company himself? And if not, why not? If the investment is good enough for you, why isn't it good enough for him?

DEAL EVALUATION

It is vital for the investor to understand that deal evaluation is a two-part decision-making process. The first part occurs to everybody—will the company be successful? Success or failure is 90 percent of the average investor's decision-making focus, whereas it should really be no more than 60 percent. The second part, all too often played down, concerns the *worth* of the deal the investor gets for his money. What will he have to pay for the projected success? What is his cost of admission? What is his sacrifice of liquidity? How much of his time will it take, how much travel and worry will he be burdened with, and to what risk will he be exposed? Will he have to put in additional monies? What is the valuation? How much is this business *worth* today in terms of currently available alternatives?

Take a startup business with a typical business plan, one which predicts losses in the first through third years, a small profit in the fourth year, and a big profit in the fifth. Suppose that the entrepreneur's projections are correct and that a profit of $500,000 after taxes is made in the fifth year. Using as a guideline a publicly traded stock of a comparable company being worth 10 times its annual earnings after taxes, a public company with earnings of $500,000 would be worth $5 million. However, private companies are often valued at a fraction of the value of public companies. Suppose, therefore, that the private company is worth $2,500,000 or 50 percent of the public company's market valuation. Now the investor is not being offered 100 percent of the company in exchange for his investment; if he is being offered 50 percent, the projected value of his share of the company in five years will be $1,250,000. He must then ask himself if $1,-250,000 in 1989 dollars is worth the investment he is being asked to make in 1984 dollars, considering also the risk, time, and effort that will be required on his part. Of course, if it is realistic to assume that the private company will go public within the five years, a higher valuation is warranted.

The well-informed investor will be aware of stocks doubling or tripling their value in a single year in the stock market. He will consider his ability to sell downtrending public stock in order to cut his losses, and how there is no convenient way of admitting a mistake and bailing out of a private company investment. Perhaps, he will think of putting his money into second mortgages, where he can get a high current return on his investment. Having considered these alternative investment opportunities, the investor will be justified in expecting a much higher rate of return from a private company investment, with its inherent risk and illiquidity, than from a publicly traded transaction.

The success of an investor, therefore, often has more to do with the structure of the investment and pricing of the deal than it has to do with the company's ultimate commercial success.

WHERE THE GRASS LOOKS GREENER

With the rise of industries overseas and with the incentives offered investors by some of these countries, American investors are often tempted by foreign opportunities. Also, there is a certain glamour to having investments in faraway places. The American investor's one worry may be whether the party will be over by the time he gets in.

In the oil business, they say one should be wary of the drilling opportunity that has to come east of Houston for financing. Similarly, the American investor should wonder why the persuasive Australian entrepreneur sitting across the desk from him could not raise sufficient funds for his enterprise locally in Sydney or wherever. Why has this American investor been so lucky?

As a general rule, the greater the distance between the owners of the money and the management of the enterprise, the less likely the success of the investment. This can be put in a more positive way: the greater the distance between the investor and the company, the greater the need for a strong and directly involved local partner in the investment.

Distance can be intellectual instead of geographical, with similar results. It is my belief that individuals from, or operating within, smaller, socially constricted communities, such as islands, tend to be relatively more stable and conscious of their reputation than those from geographical frontiers who tend frequently to be contemptuous of the status quo embracing the establishment and its financial institutions. So, too, on intellectual frontiers. The investor, being seen as a part of the establishment, is frequently viewed as fair game and may be divested of his investment without a great deal of entrepreneurial concern. This attitude, which amounts almost to a contempt for people with money, is prevalent in elements of the scientific community and is only increased by the large amounts of money the investment community, including venture capitalists, so readily make available to academics unburdened by prior profit-making responsibilities or history. With investors (and their shepherds), there is all too often an inverse correlation between an understanding of technology and willingness to speculate on future commercial success. Those doubting the validity of this observation are invited to review initial public offering prospectuses of prior bull market periods and of the current one in a few years time, with the appropriate inquiry, "where are they now?"

RESPONDING TO ADS SEEKING MONEY OR "PARTNERS"

The advertisement saying "Partner Wanted" is essentially a way of avoiding security act violations, since securities may not be sold directly through newspaper ads. Nearly all ads for such partnerships are simply solicitations for money in exchange for an equity interest; the prospective "partner" is rarely requested to contribute anything more than his money.

Generally, I would not recommend answering such ads. Yet, if you decide to do so, do not send your name and address. If you do, chances are you will end up on a suckers list—to be pestered continually in the future. Informing strangers that you are in a position to invest $50,000 or more can have serious consequences. You may respond through a post-office-box number or have your lawyer respond stating that he has a client who is interested and that all correspondence should be addressed to the law firm. In all cases, the offering must be made in writing. Do not ever respond to anything over the telephone. Ask for a business plan, get them to send references, and keep your distance early in the relationship.

The chances of coming across a scam or confidence game through such ads are clearly high, regardless of the publication's respectability. However, an ad in a restaurant trade publication stating "Partner Wanted for New Restaurant in Aurora, Ill." may prove to be attractive and easily verifiable, while a blind ad in another publication with vague wording about a "business opportunity" is obviously in a different category.

PLACING ADS

Placing ads is an entrepreneurial act in that the investor takes the initiative. He can also more easily set up his own standards and conditions. If you wish to invest in a business in a particular geographic area, say a small town in New Hampshire, placing a "money available" ad in the local paper may be one of the more effective ways of going about it. (Contacting a business broker in the area is another effective way.) If you have a knowledge of some field of technology, lasers, for instance, placing an ad in the appropriate trade journals indicating the availability of funding will doubtless elicit some interesting replies.

You have to be careful in the wording of the ad not to mislead the reader as to your capabilities or resources. You also must give enough information about what it is you seek in order for the reader to respond efficiently. If you want a business plan first time around, say so. If you want references, state that all responses must include references. The more specific you are, the more restricted will be the number of responses you receive, but you will probably have better quality responses.

The same precautions hold for placing ads as for responding to them: do not give your name and address, and deal through a post-office-box number or your lawyer. Respondents to such ads may also elect to retain their anonymity at first, and this indicates a desirable level of sophistication. Clearly state that all submissions will be treated in confidence. Also state that, unless accompanied by a stamped and addressed envelope, submissions will not be returned. Without such notice, the investor is likely to find himself with either a large postage bill or a flock of unhappy entrepreneurs.

CONTACTING INVESTMENT BANKERS

Investment bankers are an excellent source of investment opportunities. However, they are not, as a rule, experienced in investments in the range of $50,000 to $250,000, except when such an amount represents part of a much larger investment. Indeed, the relative smallness of the amount involved may be the primary reason why the investment banker is not interested himself and is willing to pass the opportunity on, or it may be that the deal does not fit his particular interests at the moment. Investment bankers also have available to them a wide range of opportunities for secondary financing of companies beyond the startup stage and, at times, of companies in trouble, which may be of great interest to the investor. The investor's own commercial banker, attorney, or accountant can often recommend a reputable investment banker.

Investment bankers having interest in smaller companies tend to flourish with an active new issue market. When the stock market declines and interest in new issues contracts, the number of smaller investment bankers tends to diminish. The size and quality of investment bankers range from very small and unscrupulous to large and prestigious. Size, however, is not indicative of quality. The roles of the investment banker and venture capitalist are not to be confused. Typically, the venture capitalist is not involved in the act of transferring ownership of securities to others. The investment banker, in marrying other people's money to management, takes some form of commission, as opposed to the investor or venture capitalist, who puts in his own funds or those for which he is responsible.

Independent financial planners or individual financiers also may have investment opportunities available. The general role of a financier is to provide funding for projects, without it being significant whether the funds are his own or those of others.

The investment banker who has an office in the community in which the investor lives has a greater motivation to deliver a good deal than has another investment banker, finder, or intermediary with a base of operations elsewhere. This issue of reputation within a community is vitally important. When a local investment banker, who sees a range of investment opportunities, offers a deal to a local investor, it normally means that the banker thinks highly enough of the proposal to risk his reputation locally by recommending it. The banker may or may not know the entrepreneur well but presumably has checked him out; the investor should certainly enquire about this.

In the crudest sense, an investment banker can serve as a protective device for the investor in that the investor can sue him if the banker made any misrepresentations that induced the investor into a bad investment. The most important aspect of the presence of an investment banker in a private company is in terms of future exit. Whether the company is successful or unsuccessful, the investment banker is going to be helpful to the investor who wants out of the deal. Because of the banker's contacts with other investors, he can be of great assistance when a company needs additional funds.

Investment bankers can act both as general and limited partners in venture partnerships. As well as participating in the high anticipated returns some private company investments offer, they may regard the young companies as future underwriting clients for initial public offerings. The banking firm involved may also have a general interest in the field in which the new company will operate. Because of fees and/or free stock, or other forms of carried interests, the investment banker's involvement can be quite costly to a private company.

The most advantageous situation for the investor is where the investment banker tells him, "The company needs $100,000. I am going to invest $10,000 of my own money, will you invest the other $90,000?" Although the banker will probably be collecting a 10 percent fee and, therefore, will not be at the same risk level as the investor, the fact that the banker is investing his own money in the enterprise indicates his level of confidence to the investor.

COMMERCIAL BANKS, INSURANCE COMPANIES, AND OTHER INSTITUTIONAL REFERRALS

Although regulations prevent many commercial banks from directly investing in private companies, they often become involved when young companies cannot pay back bank loans. The bank's loan officers are usually glad to hear from an investor willing to assist in their salvage operations, and when a bank wants badly to extricate itself from a situation, the investor can often pick up a real bargain. However, it may be an expensive bargain in that the investor himself may not be able to turn the company around. The commercial lending officer at the bank will no doubt have turned down some loans for lack of collateral, and he is often willing to put the investor in touch with these deals. He can certainly provide introductions to local businessmen and provide other valuable contacts.

Insurance companies have long been involved in venture capital investing to various degrees, and are normally attracted only by very large deals. As with commercial bank officers, their staff members can provide the investor with important personal introductions in the local business community.

Anywhere businessmen tend to congregate will prove fertile ground for those seeking private company investments. Business clubs and organizations, such as the Rotary Club, the Association of Venture Founders, and the Chamber of Commerce, are recommended; so too are state and municipal development authorities. High-potential opportunities are not typical of businessmen's clubs, and high-tech deals are even rarer. The professors at the nearest business school will have a greater exposure to such deals. They often sit on private company boards of directors and frequently possess an interestingly different perspective on investment opportunities. Trade shows and conventions, particularly those in which exposition booths can be visited, provide opportunities for investor research regarding the business of the exhibitors. Such trade shows are in themselves highly educational for private company investors.

The individuals must make an attempt to become a part of what William E. Wetzel, Jr., calls the network of informal investors. Bill is the professor of Business Administration at the Whittemore School of Business and Economics. He has studied informal investors and has written extensively on the subject. His "Angels and Informal Risk Capital" article appearing originally in the 1983 Summer edition of the Sloan Management Review is "must" reading (Appendix Q).

Though my own observations differ slightly from those of Wetzel regarding some aspects of the angel's motivation and expectations, I accept his views, particularly relating to investors in "small technology-based firms" or STBFs. The reason for the differences of expectation and motivation is that in Bill's survey, it would appear, most of the angels flocked together in a group and most of my advice is intended for the solo angel.

This difference prompts some thoughts on the flocking of angels. My principal concern would be "who's the boss angel?" There has to be a "leader of the money," as in most cases there is going to be some post investment interaction with the entrepreneur and the cohesiveness of the investor group will permit a better investor result than if the group is fractionated. The entrepreneur is going to probably fall short of his projections and, therefore, require greater financial assistance than had originally been expected. There is always a feeling, in part true in most cases, that the entrepreneur has worked very hard, and it is not his fault that "things did not work out as planned." That is, of course, the first time. The reaction of the investor(s) is likely to harden with repeat performances which are experienced. But what about the first time when there is a group of equals (or is it co-equal with angels?). Are all of the angels on the board of directors? Do they all agree as to their best course of action? Are they investing as a group either legally or in practice? What should be done with the one dissenter who favors holding the entrepreneur to his original projections? Does not the situation of flocked angels create a "we the money and they the management" situation which, by the very description, must become adversarial? Is the result the operation of two boards of directors, money, and management?

Of course, it depends on the size of the flock and the relationship between the angels but, in most cases, I would have the angels invest through an entity rather than directly in bits and pieces in the company directly.

The reason for this view—and remember in this book I serve, or at least attempt to, the interests of investors over those of entrepreneurs—is control of the enterprise. Structured properly from the investor's perspective, early stage financings should permit the investor to assume a position of protecting his interests as they become increasingly threatened. The manner of accomplishing this is, in one word, *control.* This is not to say that investors have to exercise the control they have as soon as they acquire it—or ever, for that matter.

The investing group can always merge itself into the investee company. Also, the investing entity might develop a separate life of its own if the angels all interact well together. After all, investors in private companies usually expect to invest their talents, and if a group of talented people got together to band their common interests for one project, why not consider additional projects?

Investors in private companies should always meet and get to know their partner angels before the deal jells. Meeting for the first time at a creditors' meeting would be silly. Do not let the entrepreneur simply put together a "private placement" of investor slices of the same pie. There is strength for the investor in getting the circle together.

Bill's article makes a point which must be understood by both investors and entrepreneurs. That point is that the winning investments must result in large enough gains for the investor to provide an acceptable overall result *after* deducting the losses. If the investor is going to lose half his investment in four out of five deals (a great result), how much does he have to make in the fifth to give him a net 30 percent annual average compound result? Don't bother doing the calculation for a five year period . . . it's a lot. The point is simple and it's the essence of this book. The less you lose in private company investing, the less dramatic need be the winning (and, therefore, likelier) investment result to yield an overall satisfactory investment experience.

The number of informal investors is staggering, and their investment resources exceed the funds available to professional investors. Assume that there are many as 600 venture capital-providing entities in the United States and that each of these is responsible for totally funding two startups a year (probably a high estimate). Thus, of the more than 600,000 businesses started each year in the United States, only 1,200, at the most, are financed by professional venture capitalists. Subscribers to *Venture* magazine alone were involved in 156,000 business startups in 1982 according to a subscriber study. Unfortunately, the degree of involvement is unknown and there may be some duplication of responses as to individual businesses in the astounding 156,000 figure. From these figures, the informal investor can readily see his potential value to entrepreneurs relative to that of professionals. Entrepreneurs have good reason to refer to the informal investor as an angel. The perception of the investor as angel is likely, however, to change 180 degrees when the sophisticated investor finds he must protect his interests versus those of the entrepreneur.

For an article on professional investors organizing their own companies, see Appendix C.

FRANCHISES

Whereas a very high percentage of all new businesses fail in the early years, the reverse is true of franchised operations. The reason that only a very small percentage of franchisees fail is that the franchisor, in most cases, has had to have had sufficient success to prove the fundamentals of the business and that he also imposes discipline and provides systems which otherwise might not have been available to the individual entrepreneur. The franchisor tells the entrepreneur how to purchase, how to hire, what hours to run his establishment and so forth, thereby saving him a great many mistakes. The investor recognizing this knows that, with the benefit of the franchisor's supervision, the entrepreneur is less likely to fail than would be the case were he to be on his own.

One hears the somewhat vague, and probably overstated, estimates that 90 percent of all new businesses fail within the first five years. Interestingly, only 5 percent of franchisees fail. One proviso that must be mentioned in regards to the low failure rate of franchisees is that it is possible for the franchise to "succeed"—from the franchisor's point of view—when the original failing franchise-investor team is replaced without delay by another such team or indeed a series of them. Franchise resales, even at losses to the original franchisee, are not counted as failures.

Franchises need not necessarily be thought of in terms of roadside pizza stands. A seat on the New York Stock Exchange is a form of franchise, entitling its holder to solicit and transact business on the Exchange but also binding him to its rules and requiring him to pay fees. The local dry cleaner may be a franchisee, with the equipment manufacturer or process owner the franchisor. Holiday Inn and Coca-Cola bottling franchises have had highly publicized success stories. An investor with 10 McDonalds franchises would today be a very rich man. Franchises are rare in manufacturing businesses, and the investor will not find one in computer chips. Service businesses where the product is an intangible constitute the most successful area for franchises, and this area is not nearly as well understood by private company investors as it might be though there are an increasing number of service companies making initial public offerings. Of course, these are more likely to be franchisors than franchisees.

When investing in a well-known franchise with a good bottom-line income, the investor can borrow more money and leverage himself more highly because of the franchisor's name recognition factor. Any investor who has confidence in a young entrepreneur/manager could do a lot worse than to set him up as a franchisee in a well chosen franchise.

Entrepreneurial investors sometimes have a general contempt for franchises. They have heard horror stories of how the franchisee is always taken advantage of by the franchisor, of how they can be squeezed out of their franchises, if successful, by the franchisor raising the prices of supplies they must purchase from him, and of the huge merchandise turnover needed to produce even low profits. As in any area of business, in franchises there are bad deals, good deals, and very good deals. Before going into an invest-ment, the investor should enquire from other holders of the same franchise how it has worked out for them. He should try to spot the success factor or factors common to all their franchises and judge whether his prospective franchise also has this factor. For example, in a business that sells low-priced items to a population with low mobility, the site of the franchise will probably be its overwhelming factor of success.

Some private company investors say that while a franchise can make an attractive investment with lowered risk, it does not deliver the high potential they seek from investments. Obviously, "high potential" in the fast food business must be defined differently, or at least viewed differently, from what it is in the semiconductor business. Holders of Mexican fast-food franchises have been pleasantly surprised by the high potential of their businesses. The holder of a McDonalds franchise a block away from a new junior college is in a high-potential situation.

The following article on investing in franchises was prepared by Deloitte Haskins & Sells and appeared in the DH&S *The Week in Review,* July 1, 1983.

INVESTING IN A FRANCHISE

Franchising continues to be a growing form of business because it offers a means through which individuals with limited capital and experience can own or operate their own business. During recent years, franchising as a type of business operation has been expanding rapidly and entering into new areas of application. Retail franchising amounted to $334 billion or 32 percent of the total U.S. retail sales in 1981.

Franchising is a form of licensing by which the owner (the franchisor) of a product, service or method obtains distribution through affiliated dealers (the franchisees). The franchisee is often given exclusive access to a defined geographical area. In addition, the franchisor usually provides certain other benefits including: (1) location analysis and counsel, (2) store development aid, including lease negotiation, (3) store design and equipment purchasing, (4) initial employee and management training, (5) advertising and merchandising assistance, (6) centralized purchasing, and (7) standardized procedures and operations.

To build and protect its goodwill, the franchisor usually exercises some degree of continuing control over the operations of franchisees, and requires them to meet stipulated standards of quality. The extent of such control varies. In some cases, franchisees are required to conduct their operations in strict conformity with a manual furnished by the franchisor. In return, the individual franchisee can share in the goodwill built up by other outlets which bear the same name.

Evaluating a Franchise

An investor would be well advised to obtain independent professional assistance in reviewing and evaluating any franchise under consideration. Such assistance is particu-larly important in reviewing the financial statements of the franchise and the franchise agreement to be signed.

Before signing a franchise contract, you should carefully consider the following:

Exactly what can the franchisor do for you that you cannot do for yourself?

Is the franchising firm adequately financed so that it can carry out its stated plan of financial assistance and expansion?

How many years has the firm offering the franchise been in operation (and what kind of reputation does it have)?

Are there any lawsuits or other controversies outstanding between the franchisor and any of its franchisees?

Has the franchisor furnished audited financial statements indicating net profits for one or more going firms?

Under what circumstances can you terminate the franchise contract and at what cost to you?

If you sell the franchise, will you be compensated for the goodwill you have built in the business?

In addition, you should also make a thorough review and evaluation of the following matters before making a final decision:

The amount of equity capital needed to purchase the franchise and operate it until you reach the breakeven point or start making a profit.

The payments you make that will be considered deductible for tax purposes and those that will be considered a capital cost.

Where you can obtain financing, if necessary.

Your aptitude and attitude toward the type of activity involved.

Competition already existing in your territory for the product or service you contemplate selling.

Further information about franchises including a listing of franchisors with a brief summary of their franchise arrangements, the Code of Ethics adopted by the International Franchise Association, and other considerations of a potential franchisee, is included in a handbook entitled *Franchise Opportunities Handbook*. This book is available at $10 per copy from the Superintendent of Documents, U.S. Government Printing Office, Washington, D.C. 20402.

These are just some thoughts to consider. Your tax advisor and financial consultant can provide more detailed information and should be consulted before any action is taken.

Those considering investing in franchisors or franchisees may also find interesting the following "Chairman's Comment" appearing in the January 1984 issue of *Venture*.

CHAIRMAN'S COMMENT

I recently attended a seminar on Franchisee/Franchisor Relationships (known in the franchising industry as "zees" and "zors"), created and conducted by Robert E. Kushell, founder of Dunhill Personnel Systems and sponsored by the International Franchise Assn., Washington. The IFA is a 381-member organization, the members of which have more than 100,000 zees. This particular meeting was attended by representatives of 35 zors. The average annual growth in zee units predicted by the attending zors for the next three years was more than 180 percent. Predictions of ten-fold growth were not unusual. Of course, it is easy to be misled by the use of percentages when the base is small. Accepting such projections is not easy. But it's a big country, and many of the newer zors have enormous energy, motivation, and momentum going for them. Some of the zors had familiar names; many were new to me. For those interested, we can provide a list of IFS members.

There are some interesting trends emerging. The franchising industry is broadening, and food operations, though still a large part of the zor population, are being challenged for zee fees by a diverse range of retail and service businesses. The zors' claim is much the same: A zee, with average intelligence, hard work, the necessary amount of capital, and most importantly, a willingness to follow the zor's formula, will succeed. Strangely enough, it does seem to work out that way. Whereas the average life expectancy of a newly formed business is tenuous at best, only about 10 percent of zees fail in the first five years. The zor's requirement that the zee unswervingly follow instructions raises questions regarding entrepreneurial tendencies of the zee.

Predictably, rapid growth and zee success have given rise to communication problems, and the Garden of Zor is on the verge of becoming more of a Zoo of Zees and Zors. The zees, with success, are becoming restless. The zors must continually stroke and assist existing zees while, at the same time, pursuing the primary business of most zors, the creation of new zees. The care and feeding of zees is becoming increasingly important as now, on the horizon, are two unions of zees. The Washington-based National Alliance of Franchisees has an estimated 10,000 member constituency. More recently the American Franchisee Association, Santa Monica, has announced its formation. Many zees of a particular zor have already formed, frequently with the cooperation and sponsorship of the zor, an advisory board or council to better communicate with their zor and to define and assert their demands. The zor is naturally concerned by the prospect of zee defections, and the zee, as he becomes more sophisticated, demands more assistance for the royalty flow he is providing the zor. There comes a time in the development cycle of most zees when they feel they know as much or more than the zor. Zees then may question whether they need to use the zor's name on new units. The zor may be in a situation of a zee's very sucess breeding discontent. Of course, not all zees are successful.

With annual zee sales of $400 billion, representing one third of all retail sales, franchising is an important, rapidly growing aspect of America's economy. *Venture* intends to continue, and expand, our editorial coverage of the interesting world of zees and zors.

Arthur Lipper III
Chairman

ACQUISITION OF DISTRESSED ASSETS

Some private company investors have been extremely successful in buying assets from creditors or through various bankruptcy proceedings. It is not my style to do so, because I think of myself as a creator of assets rather than an acquirer. Yet, I am fully aware that such transactions may be the single most profitable area of private company investment. Even at the creative end of things, I am forced to be involved with enough pain and anguish on the part of entrepreneurs and investors so as not to want involvement in situations which have their roots in the financial loss and possible disaster of others. Those reading this may be surprised at this idealistic, unrealistic, or, perhaps, quixotic sentiment expressed by one who no doubt they have come to think of as hardbitten, tough, callous, money-grubbing, and so forth. I am tough. One has to be to survive in commerce, which is an environment that is often hostile. But, it is one thing to be a tough survivor in competitive situations, as I am, and quite another to deliberately search for benefits from the misfortune of others.

NEWSLETTERS, MAGAZINES, AND OTHER PUBLICATIONS

Every industry has at least one newsletter or periodical. One or more of these publications are often essential reading for anyone who wishes to stay abreast of developments in the particular industry. Most of these publications are not angled toward the investor. However, their editors and writers are normally responsive to queries on the part of investors. Needless to say, they may not be willing or in a position to actually recommend specific investments, but more often than not, they will steer the investors to individuals who can provide them with the information they seek.

Bill Berkley told me how he felt about the importance of reading in the following way.

Imagine a man who goes into a pet shop and buys a tank and a hundred dollars' worth of ornamental fish, but won't bother to buy a booklet on how to take care of them. This is how most individual investors invest in private companies. They don't know what they are doing. Unfortunately, it is not the same as investing on the stock market. Essentially all that is needed (in stock market investing) apart from funds are common sense and a certain amount of knowledge that can be gained from reading. The private company investor needs a broad overview of what is happening, what is going on in the business, what deals are being done, what they look like. This is an investment in itself, of knowledge and time, and may take place over years. I do not mean 10 hours a day, but reading on a regular basis over a period of time to learn what is going on. Most investors like the excitement of private deals, but do not understand the commitment of time and learning required in order to participate in a success-oriented way.

GETTING TO KNOW ENTREPRENEURS

Entrepreneurs are not hard to meet. Almost by definition, entrepreneurs are open people. Both entrepreneurs and investors in entrepreneurs generally have no reluctance whatsoever to share experiences with others. The experienced investor in private companies knows the dangers of the game and welcomes the association of others with money and intelligence. As with successful entrepreneurs, successful private company investors have no choice but to keep themselves open to experience and listen carefully to what newcomers have to say.

Essentially, private company investing is a people business. Go to people who can introduce you to people. Invest in people you can rely on in a personal sense. When the investor has selected an industry he feels comfortable in and decides has extraordinary growth potential, he can ask the suppliers to that industry to recommend entrepreneurs and investments to him. After all, few people know an industry better than those who sell to it. Thus, wholesale meat or vegetable suppliers can be an investor's best guide to a promising new restaurant opportunity.

THE IMPORTANCE OF CONTACTS

Almost without exception, professional venture capitalists and others who invest, rather than lend, will confirm that very few deals are done, let alone seriously looked at, without an introduction or endorsement being involved. Members of the "venture clan" provide entrepreneurs with these introductions and endorsements in order to assist each other by lightening a little of the burden of individual decision-making. Professional venture capitalists tend to have herd instincts similar to those of other professional investment managers. Reliance on his own decision-making and judgment is essential to the investor, since only future events will demonstrate the wisdom of his investments. Unlike the investor, the lender normally has collateral to provide security and justify the risk assumed relative to the anticipated return. The lender seeks only the difference between his cost of money and the interest or rent received for it. This limited-return possibility is the reason that lenders are so reluctant to provide capital to entrepreneurs, other than to those dealing in asset-related transactions. The approach of entrepreneurs who deal in real property and the redeployment of assets is very different from that of entrepreneurs who develop concepts and build companies. Almost by necessity, those dealing in current assets are more financially sophisticated than those dealing in the future creation of assets. Entrepreneurs who deal in assets, like lawyers, tend to look backward to precedent rather than forward to future events.

Dealing in hard assets is frequently a matter of deriving benefits from the mistakes of others. The seller either is making a mistake in selling (he does not have the buyer's sophistication, or economic power to cause change, or vision), or he is selling the property for less than he paid for it.

The entrepreneur building a company from scratch must depend on financing from those who have been convinced that the entrepreneur's view of the future will evolve. A large part of this conviction comes from "knowing" that the entrepreneur is not going to do something that will embarrass or harm the provider of funds. Thus, the investor relies on the integrity of the entrepreneur, and this integrity is the matter implicit in all introductions and endorsements. An introduction or endorsement is in part a warranty. Entrepreneurs are well advised, therefore, to obtain as many introductions and endorsements as possible, particularly from people themselves in positions of trust, such as bankers and attorneys. Providers of capital, however, need to inform themselves on the depth of knowledge of the person who provided the introduction. Of course, an investor should never lightly give an entrepreneur an introduction to fellow investors. He will certainly not be thanked by them if they subsequently lose money on this entrepreneur's project.

Contacts are vital to the investor. The great advantage the professional investor has over the informal investor is that he can check out deals and people more quickly and effectively. After all, knowing people is the professional's stock in trade. Investors find it easier to make contacts than do entrepreneurs, since the investor has something to give those from whom he is seeking information, whereas the entrepreneur is frequently viewed as someone who wants something from everyone with whom he comes in contact.

EVALUATING THE INVESTMENT OPPORTUNITY $\quad$ 4

"BIG" AND "SMALL" CONCEPTS

Venture capitalists frequently take the position that they wish to invest only in companies that have the potential of $100 million in sales. This position is taken because they are usually considering investing solely in companies they hope will go public, possibly even becoming major companies. Professional venture capitalists must achieve a significant return on the money they invest and, like any investor, must keep the number of their investments within a manageable number. The average venture capital pool certainly exceeds $10 million dollars, and investments are often limited to a $250,000 minimum to keep their number within bounds. Venture capital pool managers also recognize that they will have to invest significant time in companies they have funded.

The investor with $50,000 to $250,000 to invest should relate the "bigness" of the concept to the capital he has available. Clearly, there is no sense in investing a large amount of money in an enterprise that will generate for the investor, assuming everything goes well, $20,000 a year in profit. There is nothing wrong with $20,000 a year worth of extra income, but there is no reason to invest more than a few thousand dollars in something which has the potential of generating only $20,000. The company concept has to be big enough to make the investment worthwhile. A correlation must exist between the size of the investment and the size potential of the prospective business.

As a general criterion, I would require a company to have the potential for a 10-fold return on investment to the investor in a five-year period. Yet, there is nothing sacrosanct about this rule. Exceptions are made for companies where the potential is less but so is the risk. At the other end of the spectrum, nonleveraged equity deals with an expectation of a 5-year 100-fold return on the investors' money are most often silly. The greater the expectation, the greater the probability of disappointment.

Small ideas are worthy of investment if they require small amounts of money, time, or risk.

For a discussion of prestartup seed capital, see Appendix D.

THE NOT-FOR-PROFIT-ONLY INVESTOR

The investor whose investment decision is premised on something other than achieving a maximum return on his investment is the major source of funding for new companies. Of the more than 600,000 new companies started in the United States annually (probably only half of these are able to hire even a single employee), less than 2 percent have any professional investor input or participation. In other words, the professional investment and venture capital community is involved in only a presumed maximum of 1,200 new companies each year. Actually, the major venture capital organizations were involved in only 330 startups in 1982. It is worth remembering also that of the 20,000-plus public companies, there are regularly quoted markets for less than 10,000. We are a country of small businesses. It's all part of the American dream and tradition.

Who finances all these new companies other than professionals? Relatives, friends, business associates, and informal investors (or angels) are the primary source of funds. However, relatives and friends form by far the largest category. Apart from cases in which an entrepreneur uses his own or personally borrowed funds, my guess would be that relatives and friends finance over 80 percent of new businesses. If a knowledgeable source suggested a 95 percent figure, I would not be surprised. I also would not be surprised if family funds greatly surpassed the amount of friend-generated funds.

The relative or friend is really a not-for-profit-only or perhaps even obliged investor. The investment is not one which he would normally seek out or choose to participate in were it not for the relationship.

Since the majority of new business ventures fail, relatives and friends must assume that the opportunity they are being asked to consider will also probably fail and almost certainly will fail to achieve the projected and desired results within anything like the business-plan-projected time frame. This assumes, which I doubt, the existence of a business plan. In addition, since most failures are due to insufficient planning and, as a consequence, inadequate funding, the relatives and friends must expect that the goals of the new company will not be accomplished with the amount of money originally estimated or provided.

It does not take much imagination for the relative or friend to see how such an ongoing demand for more money for a failing enterprise could put a strain on the personal relationship as well as, if acceded to, place the provider in financial jeopardy. In order to preserve friendships and familial relationships as well as one's capital, it is better to *donate* the funds requested with the specific statement and understanding that no subsequent investment will be made to protect the money already "invested." Although this may amount to effectively giving the money as a gift, it is better to psychologically write off the amount as a loss and go on to other deals than to become embroiled in a continuing financial and emotional disaster. Of course, if the enterprise is successful, the recipient of the funds always has the option of repaying the money and/or sharing appropriately the rewards of the investment.

The not-for-profit-only investor should first, however, insist that the entrepreneur prepare a business plan—by which incidentally, he will be doing the entrepreneur a great favor—and then base the amount of money he provides upon the apparent viability and requirements of this plan. In such a case, the investor would not want to negotiate with the entrepreneur for his own maximum advantage or, as normally would be the case, shift the reward balance in his favor. He would not wish to penalize the entrepreneur for risk, charge high money rent, or put in place the same sort of penalty clauses for nonachievement that he would with an entrepreneur to whom he was not related. Here, the investor genuinely wants to help and is not seeking a maximum or even normal return on his investment. I suggest a contract which simply states that the entrepreneur will, at some point in the future, either return the funds or provide the investor with an appropriate interest in the business, leaving the amount of interest and equity up to the entrepreneur. If the deal works out, the parties can easily be satisfied; and if it does not, the loss has already been emotionally recognized by the investor.

Some treat such a request for funds not as an investment but as they would a personal loan. They provide the money but do not tally it as an asset on their balance sheets. To look upon the transaction as a loan to a friend without high expectations of getting any of the money back is generally a much more realistic approach than to expect to recoup the investment through further cash infusions.

To whatever extent possible, tax considerations should determine the deal structure, since losses will probably develop and may be more useful to the investor than the entrepreneur recipient of the funds.

Almost inevitably more money will be required. Further investment based upon that often used rationale of hostage ransom for the initial investment is the worst basis for investing in anything. The investor who finds himself compelled, for whatever reason, to make the initial investment must ensure that he will not feel equally compelled when the 2nd, 3rd, 5th, or 10th calls for money are made. It is vital that the recipient of the funds know that the provider of the funds is making his full commitment at that point in time—once only, even at the risk that the money he has "invested" will be lost or jeopardized should he fail to reinvest. Should the new business prove to be a success, the investor, of course, can always change his mind.

ENTREPRENEUR ENTHUSIASM IS CATCHING . . . INVESTORS BEWARE

To be even a fledgling entrepreneur, an individual must possess powers of persuasion. Typically, the entrepreneur can also persuade himself of almost anything. The investor catches the enthusiasm and is swept along in the project, frequently forgetting the risks and the probability that projected results will not be achieved. The enthusiasm of the entrepreneur is to be guarded against. I used to keep a sign in my Singapore office: ALL LOANS APPEAR SOUND AT THE TIME OF GRANT. I only wish my manager there had fully understood its meaning.

Good advice for investors, even those who like to get things done immediately, is to wait one week after negotiating the final terms of a deal before executing any document. During that week, the investor should compile two lists. The first should enumerate the good things that can occur to the company being financed and the effect of those good things on the earnings, *along with the need for additional funds.* The second should be a list of the bad things which may possibly thwart the efforts of all concerned. Inevitably, the list of bad possibilities will be longer than the list of good ones, but that in itself should not dissuade the investor, since it is the probability of occurrence that counts more than the raw possibility.

Lists made jointly by the investor and entrepreneur are a good idea, both prior to the investment decision and afterward, perhaps even on a monthly basis, in order to anticipate problems and to update the business plan.

The business plan should be viewed as a working document, not simply a means of raising capital. The plan should be updated monthly, and, from this, the investor can learn the entrepreneur/manager's areas of strength and weakness in projecting various aspects of the different elements of the business. Values indicating the probability of achievement should be assigned to projections. Clearly, those projections of events occurring further in the future will be assigned lesser probability weightings than those occurring sooner. However, certain business areas can be projected more easily than others. Among the more difficult are those under the control of others, such as sales to customers and the development of anything new or different.

Investors should beware the entrepreneur who can foretell the future with perfect clarity. Professional venture capital providers are amused by business-plan projections carried out to the last dollar and cent. Reid Dennis, the managing partner of Institutional Venture Partners, tells of being put off by an entrepreneur who gave the clear impression of never having made a mistake. A man who sees himself to be free of failures may just have chosen not to recognize them—and if he cannot recognize failures, he cannot deal with them or learn from them. One cannot stress the need for entrepreneur integrity too much, and part of integrity is being honest with oneself.

INVESTOR EXPECTATIONS VERSUS ENTREPRENEUR EXPECTATIONS

A man can have an excellent business idea, the quality of which may soon outgrow the individual with the idea. This is the classic case of the inventor who has the concept but not the ability to create the business. The investor must never forget that he is investing in the business and not in the product of the business—that is, the investor must never fall in love with the product concept. He is really investing in the entrepreneur as a person, betting that the entrepreneur can transform the concept into a profitable ongoing business. If you are not a good judge of people, you will probably not make a good investor in private companies.

One hears that excuses must be made for geniuses. Geniuses probably cost investors much more money than they make for them. An investor has to recognize what he is investing in. He hopes to find an individual who has the ability to manufacture a product or create a service and sell that product or service at a profit. The world does not beat a path to the door of the manufacturer of a superior mousetrap. Geniuses are terrific, but businessmen are relieved that most of them are in academic life, because they clutter up the commercial landscape. Typically, a lot of debris follows the genius-turned-businessman.

A neat and thoroughly prepared business plan is a favorable sign that the entrepreneur is competent at least as a planner and possibly as a marketer. I like to meet the entrepreneur in his home and have some sort of feel for his family life and relationships before making an investment. If he cannot maintain some sort of order and discipline in his personal life, he is unlikely to be able to do so in his professional life.

The investor should be able to like the entrepreneur/manager as a person, although it is a mistake for them to become social friends, certainly in the early stages of the relationship. The adversarial relationship between money and management is inherent in business. Some of the hard decisions the investor is going to have to make can very quickly become clouded by a friendship he has developed with the entrepreneur/manager. It is very hard to reach a decision under the best of conditions that a manager must be replaced or that his role must change as a condition for putting new money in, and it is that much harder when the investor has become a friend and confidant of the manager and manager's family. Good decisions are hard enough to make on an impersonal basis, and they are almost impossible to make when there is a heavy level of personal relationship.

The argument that the relationship between investor and entrepreneur is similar to that of a marriage is answered by the fact that nearly two thirds of all marriages fail and that the investor can reasonably expect strain in his relationship with the entrepreneur. The investor wants to like the entrepreneur, wants him to succeed, and wants their relationship to be amicable. However, their relationship is complicated not only by failure but often also by success. The entrepreneur may grow to feel he has given the investor too good a deal and become resentful of the profits earned by him, conveniently forgetting, or possibly never having understood or recognized, the risks the investor originally assumed. Joining a country club is a wiser way to make friends than investing in private companies.

The investor must look for a certain toughness in the entrepreneur, he must be realistic and have backbone. For example, if a manager or prospective manager has a present business position, he might be asked how many people he has fired in the past year. If he has not fired anybody, is it because he is not sufficiently demanding? People are a commodity in the business world, and excellence within an organization is dependent upon continually improving through training, motivating and upgrading the staff. Such decisions are never pleasant to make, but if a man is not willing to assume responsibility for continually upgrading the human resources of a company, he should not be ready to assume responsibility for running a company.

While the relationship between investor and entrepreneur may be naturally adversarial, it need not necessarily be unpleasant. The investor should make it clear from the outset that he is a businessman. He should be direct, precise, and never vague. The investor must listen carefully and remember everything he is told, and, for this purpose, it is a very good idea for him to keep a notebook for each of his private company investments. After a while, an interesting library can evolve.

A looseleaf or flimsy notebook is much less effective than a well-bound substantial notebook suggestive of permanence. By visibly taking notes during meetings and conversations, the investor is proclaiming his expectation that there will be a large amount of accountability required. Obviously, a certain amount of intimidation is involved. Everything of importance that the entrepreneur/manager tells the investor should be logged in, both before and after the investment is made. If these points are not logged in, the investor has no really effective means of knowing what he had reason to believe prior to making the investment and during the early stages of the business. The investor will in all likelihood be called upon to make an additional investment, and, at that point, he needs to be able to judge both the predictive and operational ability of the entrepreneur. If the entrepreneur has proven himself to be consistently overly optimistic, according to the entries in the notebook, the investor probably should discount any projections that he is now making and, perhaps, walk away from the deal. Records kept of a successful business startup can be a useful future reference source for both investor and entrepreneur. Conversely, the log of a failed business venture can provide equally valuable information and may even represent evidence of what the investor was told when induced to make the investment.

A notebook is a way for the investor to let the entrepreneur know that he is taking seriously what he is being told and that he will hold the entrepreneur accountable for that which he undertakes to accomplish. The investor is not trying to entrap the entrepreneur, to get him to say something he did not intend to say, or to make bigger projections than he wishes to make. He is simply forcing him to be precise, and thereby establishing the good communications that are an absolute necessity between the owner and user of the investor's money.

The first conflict between investor and entrepreneur is likely to occur in negotiation for interest in the company. After startup, conflict may be expected if the first level of projections are not achieved. These may not necessarily be earnings projections—they may be projections of when equipment will be installed, when a secretary will be hired, when certain studies will be delivered, when auditors will deliver their report, or when lawyers will finish a contract. Since the entrepreneur most often has made in good faith the projection that has failed to materialize, the investor, before reacting himself, must make sure he understands what exactly the original projection was and who or what was responsible for its nonachievement. Just as important, the investor must understand the significance of the failure. He should certainly not permit himself to become the heavy over a minor item. Yet, it is perfectly appropriate for the investor to say to the entrepreneur, "John, in our meeting of six weeks ago, I indicated in my notes the fact that the lawyers would finish the contract by this time, and now you tell me they say they need another two weeks. Don't you think we should try another law firm for future contracts?"

The investor can come up with constructive suggestions in cases where delay is costing the company money. He is a captive partner in the business. Although the instrument the investor holds may be a debt instrument, an unsecured creditor in a private company is normally, or should be, treated as a partner in the business. Even while the investor is contributing constructive suggestions, he must remain aware that his most important role by far is holding the entrepreneur accountable for his projections. When the call comes for more money, the investor has to be able to develop a judgment on the entrepreneur's ability based upon his track record.

Some of the unachieved projections may be beyond the control of everybody involved. However, such explanations merit close examination. For example, if equipment was not delivered on time through no apparent fault of the entrepreneur, had he checked with the shipper two weeks before scheduled delivery to make sure the equipment would arrive on time? It is one thing for equipment to be late and for all concerned to know well in advance that it will be late and quite another to discover a few days beforehand that the equipment will not arrive on time and find it is now too late to make alternative plans. One of the chief roles of any manager is to ensure freedom from surprise.

A common area of contention is the involvement of the entrepreneur's family in the business. One aspect of this is putting members of the family on the payroll. I see nothing wrong with this, so long as they are paid a fair wage, not an exorbitant one, and so long as they pull their own weight.

Some investors take the view that family members on the payroll are detrimental to the company because of the attitude of other people within the company toward nepotism. Because of the dedication and effort required from a manager to make a new company successful, I think it is beneficial for his wife to be involved and to have a sense of participation.

As long as the business is going well, an investor can only benefit from an entrepreneur's identification with the company, and that identification is obviously heightened when it is a family affair. The problem arises when the business starts going badly and the investor, by virtue of his having to invest additional money, finds himself in a position of increased influence and control in the company and decides that part of the problem is the entrepreneur himself. The greater the sense of personal identification, the more difficult it is to dislodge the entrepreneur/manager.

Members of the entrepreneur's family are frequently at odds with the investors, because they see the effort, anxiety, and involvement of the entrepreneur and do not see the fear, concern, and risk assumption of the investors.

A situation that frequently evolves is where the entrepreneur's wife poisons him against the investor. She and the entrepreneur often feel, and sometimes express, that they should not have given so much of the company to a man who simply wants to make a profit—to him it's "just an investment," to them it's "their lives." The entrepreneur often feels that the investor is undeservedly getting a higher rate of interest on his money than a bank or others would charge. All too frequently, the entrepreneur, now that the business is successful or its prospects more attractive, would like to replace the investor(s) with new ones on terms more favorable to the entrepreneur.

Differences often arise when the investor requires the entrepreneur to issue personal guarantees, which in some cases is neither an unreasonable request nor an unusual one. From the investor's standpoint, it remains an open question whether the entrepreneur should be financially at risk in the venture. Some professional investors think that too much pressure on an entrepreneur is a bad thing, whereas others will invest only in situations where the entrepreneur has something to lose as well as gain. I have found that entrepreneurs are primarily ego-driven and that they work neither more nor less hard when they are at financial risk.

One disadvantage of putting the entrepreneur at financial risk is that this can give him the status of being a creditor of the company. Such an entrepreneur-creditor with the right to attend and participate in creditors' meetings could use his minor holdings to become a major nuisance in winding up a company's affairs or in selling it.

One straightforward way for the investor to seek guarantees is to require the entrepreneur to become a personal guarantor of company obligations if a particular ratio falls below a stipulated amount (for example, if sales of a certain amount are not achieved by a certain date). In other words, the entrepreneur, who is in a position to do so, undertakes an obligation which is contingent upon the passing of a certain event which he claims is within his control and which then becomes a factor in the investor's decision to invest.

There should be a contract or shareholders' agreement which provides the investor with the right to change management and the functions of management at such time as his investment is placed in jeopardy. The investor should have increasing control or influence in a business in inverse proportion to the achievement of projections.

WHAT IS THE INVESTOR BETTING ON?

Howard Stevenson of Harvard summed up this concept in his interview with me.

My personal opinion about investing, whether it be the stock market or startups or real estate, is that you need to know what you are betting on. You should be able to write down the five things you are betting on. These factors might involve the adoption of a new technology or the emergence of a new market; for example, in a real-estate deal you may be betting on your ability to rewrite the leases or a decline in interest rates or the passing of a new zoning law.

The investor might even imagine himself being asked to write a short account of his investment for *Fortune* or *Forbes* [or of course *Venture*]. What exactly is he betting on? What does he consider to be within the control of his management? Can volume of sales or projected profits be undermined by lack of cost control and inventory control? How sound is the basic business concept?

ADVICE OF EXPERTS

Before investing in a business, every investor has to question his own level of expertise in the area. For example, if an entrepreneur claims to be an expert engineer, does the investor have enough personal knowledge to tell whether this is a valid and sensible claim? If he cannot decide himself, does he know where to find the answer? Most investors sooner or later will find their own managerial capacities brought to the test in judging the performances of entrepreneur/managers. To be a good investor in other people's businesses, you have to understand your own strengths and limitations. You should not permit yourself to make an investment in a person without having the ability to make a valid judgment about him.

Lots of experts are willing to sell their time on some basis to investors. The more technical the subject area, the easier it is to identify an expert. These are recognized authorities who contribute to journals on the subject, who teach the subject at universities, or who work in the field or a closely related field for other companies.

I always like to hear what someone who knows a particular business has to say about the person I am thinking of investing in. However, Bill Berkley, founder of W. R. Berkley & Co. and an active investor in private companies, thinks that experts and consultants are of little use to a venture capitalist. He believes that it is sufficient for the investor to understand the numbers and that every business ultimately converts into what those numbers are. Thus, before recently buying a major dairy business, he found out how it worked for only the price of a lunch with a retired milk company executive.

An expert may be found or retained for an investor by his law firm, an investment banker, or a management consultant firm. Many of the larger management consultant firms profess an ability to provide expert advice in almost any area. A well known and respected academic's daily consulting fee ranges from a couple of hundred to as much as $2,000. His total fee will probably be very small in comparison to the amount being invested in the enterprise, while his advice can go a long way in improving the decision-making process regarding the investment. The cost of such advice is of course tax-deductible, as are most expenses incurred in investigating a possible investment, so long as the investment qualifies as being a business and not a hobby.

Academics are usually more available to investors than executives in the same business area. The latter of course, are the real experts but are often wary with those they think likely to be competitive with them. A retired executive who was well placed in a company with a business similar to the one of interest can contribute valuable advice, both on a one-shot and on-going basis, and frequently on very favorable terms.

LEGAL REPRESENTATION

I recommend that arbitration provisions be included in contracts rather than leaving disputes to be settled by litigation. Arbitration is frequently a more cost-effective procedure, although at times, court litigation can yield a more favorable result. However, you may need advice on whether you should go to a regulatory agency, a state body, or a courthouse, especially if you feel that a fraud has been perpetrated. The friend you went to college with and who is now such a crackerjack tax lawyer will probably not be the man you really need. The investor should avoid the general practitioner of law and go to a corporate lawyer with corporate finance expertise. Since it is a critical decision as to who represents the investor, it is perfectly reasonable to ask the attorney whether he has previously represented investors in the size of transaction in which the investor is involved. As well as avoiding lawyers with too little experience, the investor must avoid those accustomed to representing venture capitalists in deals worth millions of dollars, since such deals may have little relevance to the smaller scale problems of the investor. Ideally, a lawyer should be familiar with his client's investment from his initial decision to put money in the business and should have advised in preparing the contract. It is also reasonable to require that the entrepreneur accept the investor's attorney as attorney for the company after the deal if the investor is providing the bulk of the funding.

However, I think it is a mistake to ask most lawyers for business advice. Lawyers are trained to search in the past for precedents and, therefore, tend not to be very forward-looking. A typical lawyer will find a reason to advise his client against going into almost any transaction, because he sees the worst case side of the deal and is also aware of the history of most transactions. Lawyers must be regarded as useful servants by the investor, but as nothing more. An experienced lawyer's advice is invaluable to an investor in how to go about becoming involved in deals upon which the investor has already made his business decision. The extent to which a lawyer should be actually involved in negotiating the transaction is open to discussion.

For a discussion of legal documents of venture financing, see Appendix E.

SONY'S CHAIRMAN ON LAWYERS

Akio Morita, chairman of Sony Corporation, is one of the world's most successful business entrepreneurs, and as such, his views are always worthy of study. The January–March 1983 issue of *Japan Quarterly*, published by Asahi Shimbun, Tokyo, printed a revised version of a speech given by Mr. Morita at the Kennedy School of Government, Harvard University, in 1982. New York & Foreign Securities Corporation, of which I am chairman, obtained permission to reprint this article, since I believed many of the points made are so interesting and valid. Mr. Morita does not waste words—in any language.

DO COMPANIES NEED LAWYERS?*
Sony's Experiences in the United States

Akio Morita

Ladies and gentlemen, I am very pleased and honored to be a speaker here this evening. I met Dean Allison for the first time just over a year ago in Japan at the Shimoda Conference, at which time I mentioned to him the many legal problems a Japanese company encounters when it does business in the United States. He immediately invited me here to speak on the subject, and I agreed. Later, when he informed me that I was to speak on the theme "The Role of Lawyers in Handicapping Entrepreneurial Efforts in the United States," I half regretted accepting his invitation. To deal with such a theme adequately is almost as difficult as it is to cope with lawyers in this country.

Before I begin, I want to make it very clear that what I have to say is my personal opinion and carries no legal meaning. I don't want to find myself later ensnared in a lawsuit.

Our company established an American subsidiary—our first overseas venture—in 1960 with three American and three Japanese employees. The reason we decided to handle our American operation ourselves, rather than use the services of a general trading company, was that our company then, as now, was in the business of creating new products; since only we really understood how to use our new products, we could not expect those outside the company to market them effectively.

---

* Copyright © 1983 *Japan Quarterly*. This article is a revised version of an extemporaneous speech given at Kennedy School of Government.

When we started operations here, I knew nothing about American management practices, but I quickly learned that they differ substantially from those of Japanese. In Japan employment is generally for life; once we hire a person we almost never let him go. In this country, however, I found that management can fire an employee at any time. At first it seemed as if America was a paradise for management, but then I learned that even management can be fired. That came as a real shock.

American employees know that if they make a serious mistake they are likely to be fired. As a result, they seek to justify everything they do. That is why your consultant business thrives. If you follow the advice of a consultant and do poorly you can blame it on the consultant. By contrast, in Japan, since we do not fear losing our jobs should we make a mistake, we feel more free to try ideas we think good for the company.

In 1962 we decided to issue shares of stock on the New York Stock Exchange, and I discovered a basic difference in our thinking vis-à-vis contracts. Before we could issue stock we had to register our company with the Securities and Exchange Commission. To do so we had to have an army of American lawyers come to Japan to examine our records. We had many contracts with other companies, all of which, it seemed, had to be translated into English. When we translated them and showed them to an American lawyer he shook is head. What, he asked, do these contracts mean? What confused him was the final chapter of each contract, which said that in the event of disagreement, both parties to the contract agreed to sit down together in good faith and work out their differences. In fact all Japanese contracts contain such a provision. This concept baffles Americans, who take an adversary approach to contract disputes: one side, they believe, is right, the other wrong, and a judge is needed to arbitrate. Having studied science, I can understand the logic of their thinking. Logical as it may be, I do not feel that it works in the best interests of American society.

What accounts for our differing perceptions of the contract? Perhaps most import is the fact that Japan is a homogeneous society, while the United States is not. Japanese society is built on a base of Asian ethics and custom. Japanese think of themselves as members of one large family. When there is a disagreement in the family, the only reasonable thing to do is for the people involved to sit down together and work it out.

Invariably disagreements will arise between parties to an agreement and on occasion one will breach the contract. In Japan he will be asked to reconsider his action and compromise. In America, however, breach of contract results in legal action. For this reason a businessman here needs a lawyer at all times.

A lawyer's job is to anticipate legal problems. When a contract is drawn up, lawyers recommend provision after provision until the contract is as thick as a book and difficult to understand. Even so, legal problems arise since it is impossible to anticipate everything. The net effect of this concern with being protected against all conceivable eventualities is to make companies overly cautious. Our company employs many lawyers and engages the services of a number of law firms. They give us all sorts of advice, much of it conflicting. If we paid too much attention to their advice we would be unable to do any business at all.

Some leading American businessmen have become aware of this country's over-reliance on lawyers. A close friend of mine, John Opel of IBM, discusses the problem in an article titled "Our Litigious Society." Ten years ago, he says, some 87,000 cases were filed in U.S. federal courts. Today the number has nearly doubled, and he predicts that by the year 2010 one million cases will be filed each year. Just think of the legions of lawyers that will be needed to handle so many cases!

Already, I have been told, you have a half million lawyers in this country, and their number grows by 39,000 every year. By contrast, we have about 17,000 lawyers in all of Japan, and their number grows by only 300 a year. Per capita, then, you have about 15 times more lawyers than we do. In Japan many bright students who in America would become lawyers instead study engineering; Japan, with a population half that of the United States, produces twice as many engineers a year. Thus, industry in our country has access to far more engineering talent.

Even more disturbing than what seems to me is a tremendous waste of human resources in America is the fact that lawyers at times create business, encouraging their clients to sue over the most trifling matter. One is always in danger of being sued in America. In Japan, one who sues and loses must pay the defendant's litigation costs, which works to deter capricious lawsuits. Nor do we have anything like your contingency-based lawsuits, where lawyers and companies start lawsuits as joint ventures.

Science and technology have developed to the point where it is no longer easy to achieve a major breakthrough. While it used to be that one person working alone could come up with an important invention or innovation, today it requires a team of scientists and engineers. Moreover, vast sums of money are needed. To be a leader today, a company must have determination, a frontier spirit.

Sony first began development of the videotape recorder 25 years ago. At that time Ampex was the only company making a video recorder—a large monochrome unit filled with vacuum tubes that was used in television stations. Our company was making tape recorders and was just starting to transistorize televisions. My colleague, Ibuka Masaru, hit upon the idea of combining the two technologies, and we started the project. After many years of determined effort and the expenditure of huge sums of money, we finally succeeded in developing the Betamax.

In our case it was possible to pursue a long-range project like the video recorder because we were willing to take the risk. In this country, however, since management may be fired if it fails in a project, it is often unwilling to take big risks. In America business colleagues are suspicious of one another; after all, since people move around freely between companies, your colleague today may be your competitor tomorrow. Management does not trust employees, and employees do not trust management. Government and business regard each other as adversaries. Even married couples, it seems to me, are overly suspicious of each other. Ultimately, your lawyer is the only person you can trust, because the privacy of conversation and correspondence between lawyer and client is protected by law. How can business be expected to prosper in a climate of fear? What happened to your daring frontier spirit?

In Japan we customarily trust one another, and that goes for government and business as well. More than 50 percent of a company's profits go to the government in the form of taxes; it is as if they were engaged in a joint venture. Thus it only seems reasonable that they cooperate. Within a company, employees work together for the company's sake. Decisions are made with long-term objectives in mind. Employees are not afraid to make mistakes because they know they will not be sued or lose their jobs. We advance as a team.

To operate in this country, however, we must be good corporate citizens and follow your laws and regulations. Although we are a Japan-based company, our American subsidiary, Sony America, is an American company. I speak from experience when I say that it is no easy thing to do business in America.

In 1968 an industry association committee filed a complaint with the Treasury Department, claiming that Japanese TV makers were dumping their products in this country, thereby harming domestic manufacturers. Sony was included in the complaint despite the absence of any evidence of wrongdoing on our part; it was a good example of the legal harassment so common in the United States. In the fall of 1969, after an investigation of the complaint, we were advised by the U.S. Customs Service that we had been cleared of the charge. But in 1971 the Treasury Department concluded that all Japanese television manufacturers were guilty of dumping; despite the lack of evidence implicating Sony, we were included in the ruling because we are a Japan-based company. While we were protesting the ruling, we were named in an antitrust suit by an American television maker on the basis of the Treasury Department's ruling. Finally, after four long years of petitioning and delays caused by turnover in government personnel, misplaced documents, and numerous errors in dumping calculations, the Treasury Department agreed to exclude Sony from its ruling.

At this point we thought that our troubles were over, but we were wrong. The Treasury Department insisted on examining our records of television imports for the preceding three-year period. We had to provide it with mountains of documentation. Then in 1978, without any notice, the Treasury Department changed its method of calculating dumping. Still more documentation was needed. Later in the year, however, it decided that the former method of calculation should be used after all! The investigation dragged on and on and still the Treasury Department could reach no conclusion. Then in 1980 authority for administering an anti-dumping law was shifted to the Commerce Department, which reached a settlement with the nine Japanese television manufacturers involved. Immediately an American industrial committee and one company obtained an injunction preventing implementation of the settlement, so our problems continued. Finally in March 1980, the Federal District Court in Philadelphia dismissed the 10-year-old antitrust case against Sony. We were ultimately vindicated in court but only after years of expensive litigation.

Lawyers perform a necessary function in any society, but when their activities begin to handicap entrepreneurship you have a serious problem. I hope that you will reflect upon what I have said here today. I do not think it is too late for American business to recover its frontier spirit.

CONCLUSION

The important aspect of evaluating an investment opportunity is how the economic potential of the opportunity relates to the amount of money to be invested and the risk associated with the investment. The investor must never lose sight of the fact that he must evaluate the opportunity relative to the *total* amount he will be called upon to invest, recognizing that he will in all probability have to choose whether to reinvest or suffer significant dilution. The amount of money invested in the startup stage will probably have to be increased 5 to 10 times to bring the company to a semimature stage. The investor will have to invest his time and energy, as well as his money. Will all this be better than earning a trouble-free return by investing in an aggressive mutual fund?

The investor must be clear in his own mind about what his interest in a company means to him and how much he wishes to be involved in the affairs of that company. He must not confuse his objectives, as the investor, with those of the entrepreneur, and he must maintain his vision of where the company can go.

The risk factor must be carefully examined by the investor. Having accepted the risk levels involved in a private company investment, the investor should then compare the expected returns from that venture with those from another investment of equal risk but with a far lesser degree of involvement and greater liquidity.

EVALUATION OF THE ENTREPRENEUR AND MANAGEMENT TEAM

5

PURCHASE AGREEMENT REPRESENTATIONS AND WARRANTIES BY THE COMPANY

The investor has a right to believe that which the entrepreneur seeking funding tells him. As an extension of this, the investor has a right to recover his investment, to the extent lost, if it can be shown that the entrepreneur misstated or failed to bring to the investor's attention information which might have changed the investor's mind about the project.

Although it is the company which must provide the representations and warranties, I believe it is reasonable to require the entrepreneur to do so as well. After all, he is going to be the primary beneficiary of the funds the investor is providing. It is also a good idea to get the entrepreneur's attorney to provide, to whatever extent possible, his "opinion" as to the factuality and completeness of the statements made by the company.

The headings for the following checklist were kindly provided by Jim Bergman, general partner of DSV Partners. They may be overly comprehensive but provide an idea of the points to be covered.

Organization, Standing, and so forth. The investor has to know that the company is empowered to be in business and do the things which are necessary to earn a profit. Articles of incorporation and bylaws will have to be provided and reviewed. The investor has to be careful that all of the company's subsidiaries are accounted for, since an unmentioned subsidiary may have liabilities for which the company is responsible.

Qualification. A company should be licensed to do business where it does business, or a statement should be provided to the effect that its lack of a license will have no material adverse impact on the company's business, and so on.

Financial Statements. All the financial statements (and footnotes thereto) which have been provided should be in a form acceptable to the investor or, more probably, to the investor's counsel and accountant. Where the investor is investing in a going business, that company's accountants (actually their insurance company) has a good deal of liability in the event the investor loses money and can show that audited statements presented him were inaccurate due to the auditor's failure to investigate and confirm. This is of course the virtue, for the investor, of an audited statement. The investor should not, in my opinion, be a "nice guy" or "good loser" when losses occur. If it can be shown that any of the professionals providing service to the company, or to the investor, failed in their duty, they should make good to the investor. They received payment for professional service after having presented themselves as being professional. As a practical matter, if they believe they have any liability at all, most professionals will be pressured into offering a settlement by their insurance carrier and by the prospect of spending a lot of time in litigation. I believe that investors generally do not protect their interests to the extent they would if those interests belonged to others and they were responsible as fiduciaries. For this reason, I recommend that investors think of themselves as fiduciaries of their own money.

Tax Returns and Audits. The investor does not want to invest in a company only to find out subsequently that the company has undisclosed tax obligations.

Changes, Dividends, and so on. This is simply a statement of fact that since the date of the last financial statement provided to the investor, no dividends have been declared or paid, nothing of significance has occurred without having been brought to the attention of the investor *in writing,* and no agreements have been made which might change the investor's decision to invest, including wage changes and labor problems.

Title to Properties. The properties owned by the company are in good repair, and no other party has an interest in them. The investor should also know if the company is complying with local zoning laws.

Litigation. The investor has a right to know if there are any legal actions pending or even threatened against the company. This is a very important disclosure area. All too frequently, the investor finds a suit against his new company about which the entrepreneur either had knowledge or should have had knowledge.

Compliance with Other Instruments.   The company and its officers have to state that they are running the business in a manner which is consistent with the law and regulations to which they are subject and with agreements with other parties. It is not possible for an outsider to make these statements, since only those responsible, and the company lawyers, can or should know the details.

Debentures and Conversion Stock.   All instruments issued by the company are authorized, valid, and enforceable.

Securities Laws.   No violation of securities laws is caused by this transaction, and the transaction is not conditional to its compliance with these laws.

Patents and Other Intangible Rights.   The investor must know if the company has the unencumbered rights to the patents and processes which are necessary to conduct the business. He must also know, and fully understand the implications of, the full details of any royalty arrangements.

Capital Stock.   This is the amount of authorized and of outstanding shares, including shares reserved for the conversion of warrants and options. It is in this clause that the statement must be made regarding the existence, if any, of preemptive or similar rights.

Outstanding Debt.   A full description must be provided.

Schedule of Assets and Contracts.   The descriptions in this inventory of assets and contracts must be full enough to permit the investor to comprehend their significance.

Corporate Acts and Proceedings.   The company's board of directors and shareholders must have done whatever is required to accomplish the transaction.

Accounts Receivables.   The accounts receivable on the balance sheet must be real, and the customers must have no valid reason for not paying within a reasonable period. An adequate bad-debt reserve should have been established, and there should be no offsets that would preclude payment of the receivables.

Inventories.   Inventories should be fairly reflected in the financial statements and should be priced in a manner known to and agreed upon by the investor. In this clause, there should be a statement concerning the continued availability of raw materials, and so forth.

Backlog.   The statement concerning the backlog situation should be of a date immediately prior to the execution of the contract.

Purchase Commitments and Outstanding Bids.   The investor should be aware of commitments already in place which will, or may, require the company to spend money or incur liability.

Insurance Coverage. An inventory and description of policies should be provided, including a disclosure of the company's previous relationships with the insurance companies with which policies are carried. As Royal Little advises, "Be sure that sufficient product liability insurance is being carried."

Brokers or Finders. Unless otherwise noted, no financial intermediary fees will be paid by the company relating to this transaction. The company will have to indemnify the investor against any claim by a party known to the company or the entrepreneurs involved for compensation as a finder or broker.

Conflict of Interest. The investor should know if any of the officers or directors of the company have any conflicts of interest due to owning interests or having a fee relationship with any organization or entity with which the company does business.

Disclosure Memorandum. This is a statement to the effect that the memorandum provided to the investor describing the business contained only true and complete statements. It is up to the investor whether he wants "projections" to be warranted and to what degree.

Relationship with Employees. Labor difficulties and the potential for unionization of the staff are disclosure points which should be covered.

Disclosure. This is a catchall which reaffirms that all statements made to the investor are true and complete and that all relevant information known to the entrepreneur has been made known to the investor.

INVESTIGATING THE ENTREPRENEUR

The investor should be forthright with the entrepreneur and not wait until the last minute to put questions to him. The investor must be clear in his own mind as to what answers he expects to his questions. For example, before asking an entrepreneur whether he smokes marijuana or snorts cocaine, the investor should have considered his own attitude to the significance of this. In most cases, the investor will find himself teaming up with a first-time entrepreneur who has no track record of failure and successes. Investigation of such an entrepreneur has to center, out of necessity, more on his personal qualities than business achievements.

The investor should make a list of the questions he intends to put to the entrepreneur. The following areas are worth considering.

The entrepreneur should be requested to provide a short biography. This biography need not extend more than four or five typed pages and should include personal, as well as business, data.

An investigative agency report of the entrepreneur should be secured. In a leaflet entitled *Investigative Services for Management,* Pinkerton describes its procedure as follows:

Increasingly management is turning to Pinkerton's for help in investigating the background of job applicants as it becomes more difficult to judge or confirm data appearing on application forms—and even harder to detect the deliberate inaccuracies or omissions that often occur.

Pinkerton's offers two basic types of applicant investigations: *background investigation* for the more sensitive, responsible positions and *personnel investigations* for less demanding, high-turnover situations.

The *background investigation* encompasses the following:

1. A thorough check of personal references to determine reputation, family status and other personal characteristics pertinent to the position desired.

2. Verification of claimed education, school activities and grades.

3. A financial check to determine credit history, indebtedness and possible civil suits.

4. A check on litigation records and criminal records where permitted by law.

5. Investigation of past employment record including the determination of job stability, attitude, reputation among associates and superiors, and reason for leaving. Periods of unemployment are also checked.

6. Neighborhood background, based on interviews with neighbors to ascertain reputation and conduct.

7. Check on community activities, including affiliation with clubs, charity organizations and business groups. Establish social habits and reputations.

The *personnel investigation* would cover only three or four of the above areas as considered appropriate and is offered at a pre-agreed flat rate per item.

Because of our network of offices, it costs no more to check an applicants background anywhere from coast-to-coast than it would on a local basis. Regardless of the city of origin, the investigation is considered "local" to the office responsible for the investigation.

The entrepreneur must expect to find himself in stressful situations. Has he performed well under stress previously?

The entrepreneur should be asked to provide personal, as well as business, references. The friend given as a reference should be queried about the quality of his relationship with the entrepreneur—that is, whether he considers himself to be a friend or merely an acquaintance. The investor must make it clear to the friend why he is asking these questions—he and the entrepreneur are starting a new company. The investor should also ask if the friend would like to invest. And if not, why not? Does this friend know other people who know the entrepreneur? Anyone with whom he has had a disagreement? Anyone with whom he has been in business? Any lawyer or accountant who has done work for him?

Does the entrepreneur like to go to Atlantic City or Las Vegas? Does he play the commodity markets? Most good entrepreneurs abhor speculation on random events, insofar as the game of chance or commodity market is random; they like to feel in control of the future. While it is possible for a gambler to make an excellent entrepreneur, a fond-

ness on his part for high-risk speculation should tell the investor
something.

Is the entrepreneur willing to take a psychological test? If he objects,
would he be willing to do so under the conditions that he took the
test independently and showed the results to the investor only at
his own volition?

CHECKING REFERENCES

The private company investor is a buyer of people. He wants to back
an entrepreneurial manager who has flexibility of mind coupled with dedication of purpose. He needs a man who can start a company (for instance,
an appliance store), see it not working out as planned, and, in response,
switch the facility to one which rents appliances and start a mail order
business from the same location.

The entrepreneur who the investor wishes to find has a number of
qualities, including a sense of ethics and an integrity fully consistent with
those of the investor. There will be an enormous difference in feeling on
the investor's part about a deal which failed for any number of reasons
and one which failed through malfeasance of its entrepreneur/manager. In
one case, the investor will feel foolish for having made a mistake, while
in the other he will feel anger at having been cheated. Yet, he will know
that he could have done something to prevent himself from being cheated,
and, therefore, he has a much greater level of personal responsibility for
the loss. He could have checked out the entrepreneur better.

I am not suggesting that fraud is prevalent among entrepreneurs. On
the contrary, I know of very few instances of fraud being perpetrated by
entrepreneurs who start businesses. They are too optimistic, too future-
looking, and too secure in the belief in their own ability to cause future
events to occur. The less motivated, more cynical businessman or corporate
executive is more prone to take advantage of opportunities to profit at the
expense of others and may be less concerned with the consequences. The
entrepreneur may well deceive, but it is usually himself whom he deceives
first.

Integrity is not the only quality required on the part of the entrepreneur,
but it is the one always required. As far as I am concerned, when there is
evidence of a background "problem," I do not accept an explanation such
as "I was young and made a mistake."

The investor should require of the entrepreneur a list of references
which the investor can use as a starting point in looking into the entrepreneur's background. One of two things can emerge from a background check.
One is the desire to be in business with the individual being investigated,
almost regardless of the nature of the business. The entrepreneur just checks
out wonderfully well. My advice is to go with him if you can find any
justification for his project. A good man will make it work—even if not
in the manner originally contemplated. The second thing that can emerge

from a background check is a feeling of doubt. If the investor develops some doubt about the entrepreneur as a person, he should drop the deal. He should simply walk away from it. First and foremost, the investor is a buyer of people.

Clearly, the entrepreneur expects strong recommendations from those he has listed as references. Through those listed as references, the investor can find the names of others who know the entrepreneur, and these may be the people who can provide the investor with the most dependable information on the entrepreneur.

Burt Alimansky of the Alimansky Group asks the entrepreneur for five references, including one who dislikes him, without saying which. We can all think of someone who dislikes us and sometimes with cause. It may be someone we have fired, beaten in competition, or mutually disliked instinctively. From such an individual, a different picture of the entrepreneur may well emerge.

However, the key information to be gained from references is the names of others who know the entrepreneur. One of the outstanding advantages of the professional venture capital investment manager is his ability to immediately check out people. It is an invaluable resource. Background checking is very important, and the investor should probably check out the entrepreneur with a minimum of 5 and, preferably, 10 individuals.

James Bergman, a venture capitalist and general partner of DSV Partners in Princeton, New Jersey, told me, "In a reference check, most people do not want to say anything bad about a person. However, if you give them the opportunity, they are often willing to name someone who might have something unfavorable to say."

It does no good, or only very little, to ask for references and either not check them at all or not check them effectively. As Burt Alimansky suggested, it may be a good idea also to ask the entrepreneur for the name of one person who dislikes him. The value of the detractor is that he may lead the investor to others and, thus, cause a more balanced picture of the entrepreneur to emerge. However, the fact that there are people who dislike the entrepreneur should not dissuade the investor. Running a business is not a popularity contest. I think there is too much concern among executives for being liked; many seem to believe that leadership and popularity are in some way linked.

Integrity, in the fullest sense of the term, is the most critical element with which the reference checker must be concerned. Integrity includes being honest, and realistically so, with oneself. It also includes a whole spectrum of dealings with others, not being restricted to whether the subject of the review ever "stole" anything. The further back one goes into the life of the person being checked, the more reliable the results. The reference and background checker is seeking character flaws as indicated by acts, and should not be concerned with snooping into the acts themselves.

I once had the background researched of a prospective employee, whom I unfortunately hired. It was found that he, while in the military, had stolen (used without authorization) gasoline for personal purposes. Now that is not a big thing, especially since it had occurred 20 years earlier. However, I later came to wish I had then recognized the significance of this minor infraction. This individual ended up by costing me millions of dollars, because he was basically contemptuous of authority and not terribly concerned with the use, let alone sanctity, of other people's property. He was also not very intelligent, and this I should have noticed, if nothing else, from the record of his mediocre school grades. Yes, school grades can be important in contributing to the whole picture of the individual.

I mentioned this individual's contempt for authority. Authority is an important concept for the investor and entrepreneur to understand. They would in a perfect world have mutual respect for each other; the world being lacking in perfection, the investor should insist, by his bearing and deportment, on having authority. Authority in this case results from having something—money—that someone wants, whereas respect must be earned. This kind of authority is reflected in power. The investor's power is his ability to say no.

All too frequently, the entrepreneur is contemptuous of money—or at least the present owners of the money. This is an understandable attitude in as much as the entrepreneur has a strong personal image of what he needs to accomplish, of the value and merit of his idea, and of the need for the product or service he wishes to provide. After many instances of rejection by those with money to invest, he naturally comes to see himself as intelligent and those with the money he needs as being either too stupid or too greedy to agree to whatever he is proposing. To survive and persevere, the entrepreneur must have many of the same self-protective qualities of the salesman who suffers daily rejections. One can, of course, wade into deep psychological waters here by questioning whether they may have some need to be punished and speculate about that previously noted very strong relationship with their fathers.

REFERENCE CHECK QUESTIONS

You should always first tell the person being queried the exact reason for your interest. For example, you are considering investing in a project in which the person about whom you are enquiring is likely to play a major role. Therefore, you, the investor, have to learn something about his background not only to find out whether you should, or should not, invest in the project but also to determine the person's relative strengths and weaknesses so you can try to create a situation and environment most productive for all concerned.

1. When did you first meet _____ and under what circumstances?
2. What was the nature and quality of the relationship?
3. Are you still in contact with _____ and with what frequency?
4. What bad things can you tell me about _____'s performance under pressure?
5. Does he seem to seek stressful or comfortable situations?

6. How does he handle failure or situations when they do not develop as he planned or would have liked?

7. In instances of failure or problems, does he tend to blame himself, others, or circumstances beyond his control?

8. When he fails to succeed, how long does it take him to bounce back with an alternative means to accomplish the same goal or with another new idea? Does he get "frozen" into one approach?

9. What can you tell me about the family relationships of _____?

10. Can you think of anyone who might question his integrity?

11. Do you know any people who dislike or have had disagreements with _____?

12. Other than the names of such individuals, can you tell me anything about the problem or disagreement?

13. What are the best things or strongest points you can tell me about _____ from the perspective of a future partner or investor?

14. Have you been able to observe how _____ works with other people? Does he work better with peers or those he is supervising? How does he relate to superiors?

15. Does he complete projects undertaken or does he become distracted?

16. Who do you know who is closest to _____ or in a very good position to provide insights into him?

17. Did you expect this contact and have you had others of a similar nature? If so, from whom? Did you tell them the same as you are telling me?

18. What do you think _____ will be doing 10 years from now? What do you think he really wants to be doing 10 years from now?

19. If you had the opportunity to invest, alone or with others, in a business to be managed and possibly controlled by _____, would you invest?

20. If you did not have the money to invest, would you borrow it if there were no interest payments and if you only had to repay, in the case of loss, 50 percent of the amount borrowed? If not, why not?

Although there are other good questions to ask—and still more will evolve from this list—the above are key questions that will provide meaningful insights into the character and personality of the entrepreneur and his relationship to the person whose name he has provided. Remember, it is important to get to talk to people who know the entrepreneur and whose names he has not given as references.

It is a good idea to make notes during the interview, because it is easy to forget who said what and in which context. You will want to weight the responses as to the nature and quality of the relationships. You may also in the future wish to go back to the listees.

Reference and background checking are the areas of greatest amateur investor weakness. The inherent and intentionally developed advantage of the professional venture capital investor is that he is probably a working part of a well developed network of other investors and industrial, academic, banking, and professional contacts which can provide a very quick, detailed, and frequently accurate picture of the subject of the investigation. The informal investor, and particularly the investor who has some sort of not-for-profit-only relationship with the entrepreneur, is in a disadvantaged position to check out the entrepreneur seeking funding. However, it is vital that the investor do so, since one never really knows another person until there is a shared common experience of stress or danger.

CONFIDENTIALITY AND NONDISCLOSURE

It is only fair to both parties that the entrepreneur be accorded the right to buy from the investor, at the investor's cost, all investigative reports and so forth within a 60-day period from the time at which the investor and entrepreneur agree that no deal is imminent. During the period, the investor would agree to treat as confidential all such reports and other intelligence developed by him. Of course, material given the investor by the entrepreneur can be provided on the condition that it remain the property of the entrepreneur and that the investor has no right to divulge it without the entrepreneur's permission.

Many entrepreneurs are convinced that they have top secret information and have made major discoveries. This, combined with the fact that rubber stamps marked **CONFIDENTIAL** are readily obtainable in stationery stores, can result sometimes in a somewhat paranoiac presentation by the entrepreneur to the investor. All too frequently, the entrepreneur requests, or even tries to demand, that the investor execute a confidentiality and nondisclosure agreement with him prior to his divulging certain aspects, or perhaps the major element, of the proposed business. The investor should not sign anything without adequate legal advice, nor should he, in my opinion, accept anything marked *confidential* without an understanding of what, if any, liability is being incurred. It is not unknown for an entrepreneur to allege that an investor or prospective investor damaged him by an unauthorized disclosure of confidential material.

Many major manufacturers require entrepreneurs and inventors submitting inventions to them to sign a "disclosure release." In essence, this release says that the only rights the inventor has are those which are covered by his patent application and which are ultimately allowed.

On balance, I would be opposed to the average investor signing a nondisclosure or confidentiality agreement without there being a very good reason to do so. The investor can always discuss with his attorney any liability he might assume by discussing with others the results of an investigation he has undertaken, particularly one with negative results about an individual entrepreneur who has not given the investor authority to make disclosures.

It may be constructive for all concerned if the investor informs the entrepreneur at their first meeting of the minimum investment objectives acceptable to the investor, as well as the form of investment he usually finds attractive. If there is too wide a chasm on broad points, it is unlikely there will be eventual agreement on the details. See Appendix F for the "Statement of Policy and Procedure for Those Seeking Funding used, at times, by Arthur Lipper Corporation. See also Appendix G for the request for prospectus used by Continental Illinois Venture Corporation and Continental Illinois Equity Corporation.

EVALUATING THE ENTREPRENEUR AS MANAGER

The terms *entrepreneur* and *manager* are often used interchangeably in this book, because, in a startup situation or development-stage company, these titles are frequently borne by a single individual. Usually, the investor negotiates with the entrepreneur on the understanding that the entrepreneur will be the company's first manager. In almost all cases, the entrepreneur is initially the manager and then, as the company grows, the managerial function is taken over by others. It is worth noting that one of the major problems of small companies, particularly those which are growing rapidly, is that the entrepreneur fails to recognize that others can do a better managing job than he can.

Many of the entrepreneurs an investor meets have neither the background nor particular talent for managing a company. They will only rarely have experience as a chief executive officer and commonly will have never had the responsibility of personnel management. Being a good scientist, engineer, or marketing man is not the same as being a good chief executive officer of an entrepreneurial and developing company. It is critical for the investor early on to determine the breath of the entrepreneur's skills, and individuals having the experience and skills which the entrepreneur lacks should be put on the payroll. The investor can either suggest these individuals or propose to the entrepreneur that the entrepreneur find and attract them to his management team.

ESTABLISHING GOALS FOR MANAGEMENT

One of the requirements of any successful relationship in commercial terms is that the manager, as well as members of the staff, knows what is expected of him in the way of performance. Thus, appropriate goals and objectives should be established for management. The best approach is for each immediately senior person to discuss goals and objectives with each immediately junior person, giving the latter a chance to make his own input. When the person whose performance is being measured plays a role in establishing his own objectives, he will generally establish them higher than those which would have been imposed upon him by the senior person.

The objectives to be achieved by management are not only those of sales and earnings, but include such things as retaining the services of a certain number of engineers by a certain date, concluding the negotiations for a specific contract by a certain date, having a production line up and running by a certain date, and having a sales/marketing presentation package put together by a certain date. To insist on the completion of assignments on schedule is important, because the greatest losses or expenses in any new company are those which are caused by a failure to coordinate properly the use of resources, which include people.

The thought here is that there should be a staging, or scheduling, of expense items associated with specific company activities. To acquire space, people, and other items of expense prior to the time that one is fully able to utilize them is wasteful. A large wall chart showing clearly what is expected week by week is an extremely useful management tool.

The investor should be aware of the activities to be completed by agreed upon dates. If he is not, he will not be in a favorable position to judge the efficiency of management and whether he should provide additional funding when and if it is needed. Further, only by understanding the scheduling of expenses will the investor be able to judge the probability that the business-plan projected results will be achieved.

MEASURING MANAGERIAL PERFORMANCE

As in establishing goals for the management, the investor should have more than simply net earnings as his gauge in measuring managerial performance. Lower than projected results in the face of negative factors not anticipated, or even anticipated, in the business plan may demonstrate superior management skills, because, without these superior skills, management would have achieved even lower returns. Conversely, higher than projected results are not in themselves necessarily indicative of superior management, because the projected results could have been deliberately underestimated in order to assure management's ability to achieve them or might have been boosted by a general price rise in the industry which was not anticipated. Measuring managerial performance is one of the big areas in which management consultant firms offer services, and many books have been published on the subject.

In relating to new companies, the investor must demonstrate a realistic understanding of the problems, and it is up to management to make the investor aware of the problems and not to blandly suggest that everything is just fine. Entrepreneurs are well advised to treat investors as true partners, letting the investor know problems as the entrepreneur and management sense them, rather than waiting for the problems to become fact.

MANAGERIAL COMPENSATION

In my opinion, the need to provide monetary incentive for the entrepreneurial manager is frequently exaggerated in the mind of the investor. Of course, the entrepreneur will always present such a need in order to extract the best deal from his standpoint from the investor. The entrepreneur is primarily motivated by ego, need for recognition, and need to accomplish objectives. His overall money interest in the enterprise is set out in the terms of the deal with the investor, whether it be stock, a share of profits, or whatever. His actual monthly paycheck (executives should be paid monthly and staff every two weeks) should reflect the amount which he *needs* to have to live on a scale roughly equivalent to that on which he lived prior to funding of the company by the investor. Incremental amounts may possibly be offered based on the achievement of objectives and, of course, also possibly as a percentage of profits earned. However, if this approach is used, the profits-earned factor should include only those profits over and above those which were projected in the business plan and which have already, therefore, been paid for by the investor, since these were the profits used as an inducement to get him to invest. The entrepreneur should not be paid more than once for the same performance.

I believe that incentive compensation should be on a pool basis, shared among a number of members of the management team and not just exclusively for the entrepreneur. All too frequently, members of the management team other than the entrepreneur are not adequately or fairly taken care of in terms of stock distribution or whatever form the deal takes in the contract between entrepreneur and the money interests. It is important to develop a team spirit and also not to become too personality-dependent. Therefore, I subscribe to the procedure of allocating perhaps 20 percent of the profits of a company over and above an agreed upon amount to an employed executive incentive pool.

Martin Solomon, a very experienced investment manager who has had lots of private company investment experience, had this to say:

> Normally an entrepreneur's salary should be set at a level so that he can continue to live as he has before. Only rarely has salary become an issue in negotiations I have conducted. I would wonder about the entrepreneurial qualities of someone who seemed overly interested in salary. He may be more interested in the perks and trappings of a corporate life than he is in creating an important company.

EMPLOYMENT CONTRACTS

Employment contracts typically benefit the employee and seldom the company. In general, they ought to be avoided by the investors, particularly when they relate to new companies. On the other hand, compensation agreements can be useful to define the basis for compensation. A compensation agreement of this kind is very different from an employment contract that agrees to employ an individual on certain terms for a specified period of time.

An employment contract should not be necessary when dealing with an entrepreneur who has a continuing interest in the form of equity in the company, except when the contract may be used in conjunction with the shareholders' agreement. For example, certain equity givebacks from the entrepreneur to the company will result in the event of certain objectives not being achieved.

Stock options, phantom stock plans, profit shares, royalties, bonuses, and so on, are all valid incentives to be used by the owners of a business to reward employees. These corporate lollipops should always benefit the money-investing owners of a business and not dilute their interests.

SUCCESS AND FAILURE 6

THE SUCCESSFUL VENTURE

Success cannot be judged solely in the amount of dollars earned. It must also be judged by the achievement of projections upon which the investment was premised. This means that the entrepreneur gets where he said he was going within the framework of time originally laid down. Thus, in the rare case of an accurate projection, the success was really achieved when the projection was made. The result can be that the actual profit in dollars can come as an anticlimax. Success for the investor is the achievement of maximum gain with minimum risk. But it is not for maximum gain alone— it's not just a matter of making a great deal of money. Success should always be evaluated as risk-related, and profit is not always quantifiable as the monetary return on investment. Also, the investment, which is frequently more than money, can be difficult to define.

With successful private companies, money is mostly made through patiently staying with the company. The wise investor is in to stay, except in cases where the public or other buyers anticipate greater success for the company than is realistic. In general, when a private company becomes successful, the investor will regret in future years having sold out early.

Investor strategy may require selling off part of the holding, somewhat like cashing in the chips of one's original stake in a gambling casino while one is ahead and playing from that point on on the house's money. An investor running a portfolio of private company investments is more likely to do this than an investor in a single company. There are all sorts of emotional and psychological reasons for not wishing to sell one's holdings in a successful private company. After all, in part, it's the investor's baby.

WITH SUCCESS, FURTHER OPPORTUNITY

Assume that a private company venture is not only successful but is making a lot of money. Assume also that the investor has either control or an ability to substantially influence the management of the company. What should he do to maximize his success? Should he do anything at all? I like the farmer's advice: "If it ain't broke, don't fix it."

Going public and becoming paper-rich is an enormous temptation and frequently a very good idea. Besides this, there will be ever-present opportunities to sell out, and there is nothing wrong with a ringing of the cash register. The more dollars an investor possesses, the more progress he can achieve in both personal and societal enrichment. See Appendix H for the valuation of a business.

Bill Berkley said, "The best time to sell a company is when it is doing well and you are predicting it will do better. Never wait for a downturn. However, when earnings are increasing is the hardest time to sell, because things look as if they will go on like this forever."

However, there are some other possibilities to consider. The success of the investor's venture probably indicates the presence of a superior management team. This success presumably also brought about the establishment of significant executive-benefit programs. Such benefit programs can in themselves be an important part of the investor and entrepreneur reward of success. For an investor to be included in these benefit programs, he or his wife should be a director or consultant. The entrepreneur should be willing to include the investor in the executive-benefit programs to ensure his cooperation and generosity in situations where the investor has sufficient control or influence. The benefit plans may include pension, profit sharing, stock repurchase, and so forth and are all capable of playing a vital role in the estate planning of both investor and entrepreneur.

What about using the successful private company as an investment vehicle? The investor in a thriving company will continually have other investment opportunities presented to him. Should he decide to invest in a new venture, he can probably now finance it independently and with greater ease and probability of success due to his experience with the already successful venture. But why not bring the opportunity to the already successful company? The singular advantage in doing this would be that the investor has already identified, and perhaps played a role in creating, a group of proven successful managers who can not only assist in the evaluation process but also be of enormous assistance in helping the management of the new company.

What about the possibility of buying real estate or other assets through the successful company? Why not? Losses can be charged against the earnings of the company for tax purposes—most of the time—and whatever leverage is required may well be easier to obtain through the successful company. The critical consideration, however, in all these issues is whether or not the effort will prove to be a damaging distraction for the managers of the business. Nothing should be considered which will jeopardize that wonder of wonders—the truly successful privately owned company.

Highly successful private companies possess personal relationship strengths upon which further enterprises can be built. Such a company also has an invisible structure of professional advisors and availability of finance. While this cannot be valued on a balance sheet, nevertheless it is a very real asset and one which can be used.

The successful private company may invest in other ventures by becoming a joint venture partner. Such a company can also invest through loans, guarantees, and technical assistance programs.

The essence of being a good private company investor is to find truly capable people and to develop a mutually good working relationship with them. The more good people an investor has on his team, the larger will be his estate. My advice is to *use fully the efforts of the few motivated and capable people you can identify and attract. Such use will be to your and their advantage.* That's what venture investing and being a great entrepreneur are all about.

TIME TO GET OUT

As George Jessel used to say, it's not just a matter of deciding to sell—it's a matter of to whom. Buyers are easy to find for 100 percent of highly successful companies but will probably be difficult to locate for presently marginal or downright unsuccessful companies. Disposing of a minority position will probably be almost impossible. Thus, opportunity may well be the trigger to sell. Certainly, an investor should try to sell when his association with the company no longer brings him pleasure and satisfaction. If you're not enjoying it, get out if you can. Also, an investor should have the ability to compel the sale of an unsuccessful company in order to salvage a part of his investment.

Since the investor in a private company does not have the luxury of calling his broker with a sell order and can get out only where a situation permits it, he should extricate himself as soon as possible when he loses confidence in the entrepreneur, if the investor is unwilling or unable to replace him. Private company investment requires a much greater degree of uninformed reliance on management, by and large, than does investment in a public company, because of the greater information output a public company must give its shareholders. Once his trust goes, so too should the investor.

Declining profit margins are a tipoff to seriously consider exiting. The private company investor must be aware of profit margins on a monthly basis, not merely quarterly or annually. An effective way to do this is to keep a chart, which can also include a number of other operational elements of the company, such as order backlog, sales, cost of sales, profits, square feet used, number of employees, employee expense as a percentage of revenue, employee expense as a percentage of earnings, executive expense as a percentage of other staff expenses, rate of incoming orders, and debt maturity. Using a monthly updated chart and the notebook in which he has recorded the entrepreneur's projections, the investor can readily see where he has been and probably where he is going.

Who has the right to sell the company is another thing the investor must keep in mind. Without a contract stipulating to the contrary, management or the board of directors is the group that determines when a company should be sold, to whom, and on what terms. Although the investor may hold a 51 percent interest in the company, frequently a two-thirds or three-quarters vote of shareholders is required to sell. One of the safeguards investors should consider writing into either the shareholder or loan agreement is that, under certain conditions (these conditions would be basically protective, such as failure to achieve earnings or failure to maintain a current ratio), the investors have the right to sell the company or to sell their shares in the company to the company. Depending on the provisions of the contract, management that has failed to meet certain projections can be excluded from voting.

Management may be given the opportunity, or first opportunity, to buy the investors' stock. Indeed, in a troubled company, management may be the only market for it. Under these circumstances, the investor may retain an appraiser or investment banker to estimate the value of his holdings. If the company has been successful, he will probably already have been the recipient of a number of offers and will have a fair, though perhaps exaggerated, idea of the value of his stock.

The investor should remember also that offers may have been made for the company of which he has not been fully informed. If management holds little or no stock, they may correctly see the sale of the company as a threat to their positions and turn down the bids, or bid overtures, without passing them on to the shareholders for consideration, or management may inform the shareholders only after the bid has been discouraged or rejected.

The value of a new company's shares will be affected by how far along it is toward its projected success. Obviously, the shares of a company that expects to be in the red for another three years will usually be sold (if they can be sold) more cheaply than the shares of a company which has shown a little profit in its fourth year and expects to show a big profit in its fifth.

Competitors in the same business are clearly one group that may be interested in buying out a company. The same business in a different geographical location may wish to expand by buying out the firm. Suppliers and customers may be interested. Personal contacts made by the investors can be buyer candidates. Over the time period he is in a particular business, the active investor opens himself to many contacts in that and allied businesses.

Finally, the investor who wants out may consider making a deal with management. In exchange for his stock, he may accept a certain sum and, say, 2 percent of sales over a specified period. He may prefer to be paid as a consultant to the company over an agreed time span in order to be entitled to certain corporate benefits.

DEALING WITH FAILURE

Failure can be defined simply as not achieving projected results. From the investor's viewpoint, a failed venture and a failed company are not synonymous. The investor may even be able to get out at a profit in the case of disappointing results if the deal was well structured. Since it is essential to the investor to recognize a failure before it becomes common knowledge, he should rely on monthly updated charts to indicate danger trends. When a trend becomes set—that is, when it continues beyond the third month—it typically becomes difficult to reverse.

The investor's corrective action will depend upon what element of the company is in a downtrend. The radical surgery of a complete sellout may not be required. The trend may not be irreversible. Management or product may be changed. A plant may be closed or opened. Another important factor will be the investor's own freedom of movement. With success, he has significant control over his destiny; the absence of success limits the amount of his control and increases that of others over his destiny. Thus, an investor using borrowed funds may find his options severely limited.

The investor's primary concern in the event of failure must be to salvage as much of his investment as possible. Ideally, the contract should provide a means for this. It is my view that the private company investor should always be in a preferred position until he recaptures his investment with a time value for the period he has been investing. In negotiating an agreement on the future distribution of company assets to the interest holders, the point at which all interest holders rank equally must be identified. It's not necessarily from "dollar one." For example, if the original investor had put $150,000 into the company over four years, he might qualify for a $200,000 settlement before anything was paid to the other interest holders.

If the company is to be sold, the investor had better understand what salaries and perks the management of the company are going to get from the new buyer. A little conspiracy, or pseudo-conspiracy, can easily develop between the new owners and old management, particularly when management is advising the selling investors on the fairness of the deal. The manager of a troubled company, aware that the investors are anxious to sell, may approach a potential buyer and say,

> The investors are really fed up with this thing because it isn't going as expected. I think I could persuade them to take 10 cents on the dollar. Let me

tell you, with another $150,000 in there, I could really turn this company around for a new owner. What about letting me stay on as president and giving me 20 percent of the profits?

Nothing is more frustrating for an investor than to end up having gotten out of a deal only to see some of the same people who were in the deal with him make a profit where he lost. The investor must retain control over the sale negotiation for his protection, and never simply act as a ratifying agent for whatever management negotiates.

If a company still has any vitality and potential, its own management may be its most likely buyer. Certainly, the entrepreneur/manager is in a position to be most helpful to an investor who wishes to get out. He can most easily arrange to have the investor paid either all or part of his money back or some of it now and some at a later time. The investor cannot demand much more than he is entitled to, and that will usually depend on what is in his contract. Management should be informed of the investor's intent to exit and be provided with a chance to structure it to everybody's mutual benefit.

Circumstances other than failure may prompt the departure of the investor. Thus, an investor might purchase a small plant from the company for a $100,000 note. He might exchange his interest in the company for the patent rights to a single product manufactured by the company. The investor may wish only to change his relationship with the company; for example, he may wish the company to continue manufacturing a product, sell it to him at an agreed price, and give him exclusive servicing of a certain number of accounts. Management will often redouble their efforts to buy out an investor they think might sell his interest to a competitor. The parting does not have to end in screaming and crying. It can be a very amicable arrangement and mutually constructive.

If a company does close its doors, who gets the tax benefit? My position is that the entire tax benefit should go to those who invested money, not to those who invested talent and effort. Again, this is something which must be spelled out in the purchase contract.

Most people lose all of their money when a private company fails. I think this is unnecessary in a lot of cases. If they did a better job of structuring their withdrawal, they would not lose so much. It can also be a matter of when the investor decides to throw in the towel. The earlier he recognizes the result of a downtrend, the greater is the probability that he will be able to salvage something. The longer a business continues to lose money, the greater its losses, leaving less available to the investor and entrepreneur. And the longer an investor is in a losing business, the greater is the likelihood that he will believe it in his best interest to put more money into it.

The alert, intelligent investor learns from his failures, and *all* investors have failures. These failures need not necessarily include a company's bankruptcy—any investment which generates less than the results anticipated, which justified the original assumption of risk, constitutes a failure. Every investor will have his own set of rules: Never go into a company unless it is adequately financed. Never invest in a company unless its management has had prior success in running a business. Never invest in a company that is dependent upon a small number of customers. Never invest in a company that is dependent upon a narrow range of technological developments. Never invest in a company in a geographic location which is not prosperous. Never invest in a company which is labor-intensive and unionized. Never invest in a company which is dependent upon government regulations. Never invest in a company which is dependent upon financing from a single financial institution. Never invest in a company in which an inventor is the chief executive officer. Never invest in a company that is in a business in which unsavory individuals are present. There are a lot of lessons to be learned, and the investor learns a new one with each experience.

NECESSITY FOR INVESTOR'S ACTION ON DOWNSIDE

From the investor's position, a critical point is reached when a company's trend toward failure seems set and the probabilities for failure outweigh those for success. The investor will not have time to argue with the entrepreneur at this critical point—he must have already put himself in a position to take direct action. Typical of the measures which the wise investor will have taken are: control of an increasing number of the company directors in inverse proportion to the rate of company success; an irrevocable proxy which takes effect at a critical point, ratifying the sale of the company or its dissolution or whatever the investor requested; and, a signed but undated letter of resignation from the entrepreneur to be activated only at the critical point.

Although these measures are tough on the entrepreneur, the investor who asks these contractual concessions knows that most investments like his lose money, and he has no assurances that his will be an exception. Also, being in possession of these rights does not mean that an investor must exercise them. In practice, the investor often feels sorry for the entrepreneur and in spite of his better judgment, allows the entrepreneur to continue running the company. But the investor must have these powers—restricted to the downside—if he is to be in a position to grant largesse.

WHEN A COMPANY CLOSES

Lots of things happen when a company closes. The reputation of everybody involved is damaged. The reputation of the product being offered is damaged. Competitors come in and fill the void left by the failed company. Creditors have to be dealt with if money is owed.

Does the failed company own the patent on the product, or does the entrepreneur own the patent and license its use by the company? Is it an exclusive license? Is it a limited license or a full license? Is the license terminable by the company's failure or by certain guaranteed ratios not being maintained? Is the license dependent on a certain level of sales being attained and maintained by a certain date? The entrepreneur frequently gets his holdings in the company through assignment of either the license to the patent or ownership of the patent. The intelligent investor will probably take the patent interests or an assignment thereof as part of the collateral for a loan, or certainly as part of an overall transaction which may be triggered by certain events, such as failure to maintain certain ratios.

The investor should not think that the company can pass from the scene this year and come back at a future point. More likely, the assets of the company will be sold to satisfy creditor claims. If the investor has done a worthwhile job in structuring the original agreement, he will be one of the creditors who has to be satisfied—perhaps the primary creditor who has to be satisfied.

LITIGATION

Most investors are reluctant to become involved in lawsuits, and, in most cases, that reluctance is well founded. However, there are exceptions. A loss can be considerably minimized by litigation or the threat of litigation when the investor's loss is someone else's fault. Investors are considered to be fair game by many, and most investors do not take sufficient action to ensure that other people treat them fairly. It may take only a couple of hours of a lawyer's time to investigate whether there is any liability on the part of someone for the investor's loss in a failing company. In many cases where this need not have been the result, the investor is the only one to take a loss. Frequently, the greatest remaining asset of a failing or failed company is the potential liability of its directors and others who may have contributed to the loss. The investor is often too embarrassed to sue, having not listened to the advice of friends not to invest in that company, fearing that his reputation will be damaged by publicity, and wishing to forget this bad investment and move on to a good one.

The decision whether to litigate frequently depends as much on the defendant's ability to respond to a judgment as it does on the merit of the investor's case. The vast majority of cases are settled out of court rather than litigated, and these settlements often involve the faults of others being translated into lesser losses for the investor. Attorney fees for litigation of this nature are probably best handled on a contingency-fee basis.

The following will indicate to the investor facing a loss the type of questions he should be asking. Did the entrepreneur have the assets he claimed to have before the investment was made? Did the entrepreneur spend the investor's money in the way the investor was told it would be spent, or did the entrepreneur spend it in a manner designed to benefit him in a way not disclosed to the investor? As an inducement to purchase goods or services from him, did a supplier lead the investor to believe that he could deliver his product at a specific point in time, and was the investor's lack of success caused by this supplier's inability or unwillingness to supply in time the product he had contracted for? Have the employees leaving to start their own competitive company stolen data which are the property of the investor's company? Is the investor's loss a result of bad legal or accounting advice?

A lawsuit cannot be brought by an investor against an entrepreneur who has honestly tried and failed to accomplish what he set out to do. However, inexperienced entrepreneurs are taken advantage of by other companies, and to the extent that the investor has suffered damage by someone taking advantage of the entrepreneur/manager of the company in which he has invested, the investor can do something about it.

WHEN YOU ARE THE LEAD INVESTOR

7

Before an individual decides to become the lead investor in an enterprise, he should carefully review whether he is willing to assume the responsibility of the role. As the lead investor, he will in fact be inducing other investors to assume risk by his very presence in the transaction and relationship. He will also be assuming a responsibility for most appropriately structuring the transaction to gain maximum benefit for the investors. When the terms of the transaction are subsequently to be modified or additional funding is required, he can have another problem to contend with—that of finding himself aligned with the management group, frequently almost becoming a part of the management team by virtue of the ongoing monitoring that he has been performing. He has probably become more aware of the company's problems than the other investors, and certainly more of a believer in the entrepreneur's view of its potential. It is also possible that the investor will have experienced such significant frustration in dealing with the entrepreneur that his judgment regarding the whole business opportunity will be distorted. Therefore, the possibility, or rather the probability, exists that his perspective and overall view of the company will diverge from those of the other less involved investors.

Arthur Little, chief executive officer of the Narragansett Capital Corporation, had this advice for the lead investor:

If there are going to be others investing along with you in a venture, warn them to use their own judgment before committing themselves. When some people in Rhode Island hear that I am investing in something, they decide to do it too. Sometimes that works out well for them, and sometimes it doesn't. I am very careful not to recommend ventures to people, but in spite of that they often go ahead and invest anyway.

On balance, I would recommend against the informal or individual investor becoming the lead investor of an investment group, unless the other investors are more sophisticated than he is, or unless the other investors have the ability to make more than simply a financial contribution to the company.

Bill Berkley had this to say to the lead investor:

In attracting or selecting appropriate partners or participants for investing in a venture, deal with people you think have the resources to invest and the knowledge to be able to make a decision. Knowledge is the greatest problem, because it is very hard to talk with someone who has no comprehension what the business really involves. When you try to discuss a supermarket proposal with someone who is knowledgeable only in the insurance business, you end up having to teach him the industry. My criteria for selecting partners would be, first, financial resources and, second, at least some knowledge of the business involved.

ATTRACTING PARTICIPANTS

The individual or informal investor has already been advised not to accept the responsibility for soliciting investments from other nonprofessional investors, even though he may be tempted to tell his friends about this wonderful new company he has discovered and even offer them the same terms he is getting himself. Apart from the inadvisability of being gratuitously responsible for the other people's money, the investor is assuming that the deal will work out as predicted. If the deal does work out as anticipated, and few deals do, the investor will be a hero to his friends. If the opposite occurs, he may reasonably expect an opposite reaction from his friends. If the outcome of deals could be anticipated so easily, instead of asking others to join him, an investor should borrow from banks and mortgage his property in order to provide all the money himself. The nonprofessional investor is not likely to understand all of the risk areas inherent in private company investment.

However, if the informal investor, as lead investor, can interest a successful provider of venture capital, someone with a wide business knowledge, or, ideally, a person with knowledge of the field in which the new company is situated, he should not hesitate to do so. The lead investor himself will be called upon to contribute more than money to the enterprise, and all other sophisticated investors he finds, who can make contributions over and above their financial commitments, will serve as an enlarged resource for the company.

THE BOARD OF DIRECTORS

The significance of a board of directors in a private company depends upon how the voting equity is distributed and upon shareholder and purchase agreements surrounding the financing transaction. If, in fact, the entrepreneur holds the vast majority of the voting equity, a board of directors per se is not particularly important, and many of its functions can be adequately provided by a board of advisors. After all, one of the primary functions of a board of directors is to evaluate the performance of the management of the company and to decide, when necessary, if management must be replaced. Therefore, if the management of the company controls the vast percentage of the shares and can elect their own directors or appoint themselves as directors, it does not make a great deal of sense to look to the board for investor protection other than as a source of entitled information. Also there are meaningful personal liabilities associated with being a director, of which the investor should be aware.

The qualities of a director which can be of value to a company are those of wide business experience. By and large, it does not make a lot of sense to put a scientist on the board of directors, particularly that of a private company, because his contributions of skill and experience can be equally well made by him as an advisor. A director should have a sense of humor and perspective, the former being desirable and the latter important. Experience is the key word.

The number of director appointees an investor has is critical when a board votes. The board of directors is important in a company's life when there are controversial decisions to be made; then votes become very significant. Among the critical decisions that a company commonly must make are: whether to embark on a new project; whether to seek a financing; whether to accept the terms of a proposed financing; whether to buy another company; whether to sell or merge with another company; whether the compensation paid to the managers of the company should be increased; and whether the managers should be removed or transferred. As a rule, the directors representing investor interests will usually agree with management proposals during periods when the company is doing well. It is during those periods when the company is failing to achieve projected results, or when things are otherwise not going well, that investor interests and entrepreneurial interests are likely to become divergent. At that time the natural adversarial relationship, which has been lurking below the surface all the time, will tend to become obvious to all. Then votes can be critical. For this reason, in structuring financings, I frequently include provisions that grant to the investors the ability to appoint an increasing number of the directors upon nonachievement of projected results.

Investor interest can also be protected by the creation of bylaw provisions requiring approval for certain acts of an amount of outstanding shares which would have to include those held by the investor, and thereby providing at least an effective veto ability. For instance, if the investor holds 25 percent of the voting shares, shouldn't authority for borrowings, in a small company, exceeding $100,000 require the affirmative vote of 80 percent of the outstanding shares? Of course, it should not be possible to change the bylaws with less than a similar percentage of the shares being in favor of the change. Mergers, acquisitions, and so forth should require similar levels of shareholder approval. Therefore, it is not only through board memberships that elements of control can be created and maintained. Much the same control, negative or positive, can be worked into a shareholders' agreement. Needless to say, the level of control exerted by the investor can, and should, lessen with the positive achievements of the entrepreneur. There is little reason to rein in a clear winner—let him run his heart out once you have confidence in him, justified by results and not based upon hopes and expectations. Authority has to be earned by deed and not promise.

Investor interests, as opposed to entrepreneurial interests, must be protected, since it is the investor who typically takes the financial risk, whereas the entrepreneur benefits, and I believe appropriately so, in the case of success disproportionately to his dollar investment. The equitable offset to that position is that the investor should be protected on the downside considerably more than the entrepreneur. This protection will in part take the form of increasing control by the investor of the company the entrepreneur has started. When to sell, when to close down the company, when to stop a particular product line, and when to accept financing which may be opposed by the entrepreneur as being too dilutive are all areas in which investor interests and entrepreneurial interests will diverge.

People with wide and relevant business experience should be invited to serve on the board of directors. That experience may be acquired either through having started new companies themselves or, in the case of an academic, through having observed a large number of companies in similar stages of development. I think that academics, typically professors or associate professors from business schools, can make very worthwhile directors, even when they are not investors in the company. Lawyers similarly are in a position of observing and being involved with a large number of companies, and are, therefore, able to frequently make contributions. However, I question having the same lawyer who represents the company on the board of directors. Clearly, the lawyer representing the investor would, from the investor's point of view, make a good director candidate.

I recommend that the board of directors of a private company, particularly a startup or development-stage company, be limited in number to perhaps five. As in the case with most committees, an inverse ratio exists between the efficacy of the unit and its size. The larger the board, the longer will be its meetings and frequently less will be accomplished. Five directors is a good number. In a situation where the investors put up all the money and receive approximately 50 percent of the equity of the company, which by the way seems to be a more or less typical situation, the board could be composed of two directors from the entrepreneur's side, two from the investors' side, and a fifth director who is agreeable to both sides and an adherent of neither camp. However, should the projections not be achieved, one of the entrepreneur's seats on the board, and possibly both, should be transferred to the investor group.

Hired management need not always be represented on the board, but the entrepreneur should be represented, because he is an equity owner or has, in some form, an equity or profit related interest. I believe it is a mistake to view, as many young companies do, placement on the board of directors as an honor to bestow on members of the management team. The company can obtain from those same managers all of the contribution they can make without placing them on the board of directors or even a board of advisors. From the board of directors or a board of advisors, the company obtains benefit of the advice and experience of those not involved in the day-to-day management of the business and even of those who are not involved as direct investors.

The investor should have a right to appoint directors but need not necessarily serve on the board himself. However, the investor must recognize that there is liability associated with serving on any company's board of directors and that, in all probability, he may, and certainly the company will, have to offer an indemnification to anyone serving at his request on a board. Director and officer liability insurance is not generally available to new companies; anyway, the premiums are extremely high.

This report from the June 1982 issue of *Venture* is an extreme example of director liability.

> In a decision handed down by the U.S. District Court for the Southern District of New York, the court found Roy Furmark, a former director of the Newfoundland Refining Co. (NRC), a privately held Canadian corporation, personally liable for $11 million when the company went bankrupt. Although there was no claim of fraud, Furmark was held liable because, according to the decision, "for a period of two years preceding the bankruptcy, NRC loaned $30 million to its sole shareholder and owner, John M. Shaheen, and other companies owned and controlled by Shaheen."
>
> Furmark appealed the decision, claiming that it means not only personal disaster, but disaster for corporate directors everywhere. The U.S. Court of Appeals for the Second Circuit did not see it that way, and upheld the District Court's decision. At present, John Shaheen, the primary defendant, is petitioning the Supreme Court to review the case.

In the Furmark case, the court is taking the position that the director had a fiduciary duty to the creditors. This is based on the old English law concept that creditors, uninformed of a company's true state of finance, can look to members of the board of directors to personally make good the creditors' losses on the grounds that the director theoretically could have halted the acts of commercial deception. All of this assumes that the director had perfect vision and that he himself was adequately informed as to the true circumstances of the company.

I suggest that directors be appointed and asked to serve for a two-year term. As with most consultants and advisors, a director will make the major portion of his contribution in the very early state of the relationship. It is always difficult when the controlling shareholders or management of a company determine either that a director is no longer serving a useful purpose or that there is another person they want in his seat. Someone then has the embarrassing job of suggesting to the director that he not stand for reelection or that, perhaps, he should retire. It is much easier to ask people to serve for a specific period of time and, if they prove unsatisfactory, simply not reinvite them. One can, of course, issue another renewal invitation to those one wishes to continue. But all find it easier when they know they are serving on the board for a specific period of time and it is not something that will go on forever. Of course, directors are always elected to serve for specific periods, but the election is a formalization of an invitation made informally. My suggestion relates to the issuance of the invitation by the controlling party.

Compensation for directors is understandably a consideration which should be focused upon. Whether independent directors should be compensated with equity, warrants, options, or anything that relates to equity, as opposed to simply receiving a per diem fee or retainer, is open to debate. Heidrick and Struggles, the executive recruiting firm, have prepared much survey material regarding the compensation of directors, as have Deloitte Haskins & Sells (Appendix I) and a number of other accounting firms.

The real issue in the compensation of directors is whether they should have a vested interest in the rapid growth of earnings and, therefore, rapid appreciation in price or valuation. I believe it is better that the directors be in a position to act as a restraining influence on an aggressive management, continually taking the side of prudence against that of overly ambitious expansion. Similar in concept to this problem is one whether an investor should pay his attorney, in part or in whole, in shares, warrants, or some other interest in the company. If the investor gives him a holding, that attorney will have as his central focus the growth of the company, or the growth of the company's earnings, and the enhancement of his vested position—as opposed to functioning as a traditional lawyer by indicating the areas of danger and risk and the problems associated with any transaction. The investor may be putting his board of directors in a similar position by giving them stock. If the directors will all benefit from increase in earnings and the price of the stock, then who will take the position of caution and prudence? All things considered, I think that directors representing investors should be paid with fees on a per diem basis. If they choose to invest themselves, that opportunity should be made available to them on, perhaps, the same terms as the investors. But it is probably a mistake, from the investors' standpoint, to offer the investor-appointed directors incentives similar to those of management.

The members of the board of directors often serve as window dressing for the company. The composition of the board of directors is one of the things a prospective customer, a sought-for employee, and even a prospective supplier looks at. At such time as the company is negotiating with an underwriter in terms of going public, the composition of the board of directors becomes more important. Everyone likes to see on the board, particularly that of a young company, names of independent directors which are recognizable, either because of individual accomplishment or because of the individual's associations. A senior vice president of a bank, a vice president of General Electric, an astronaut, or a professor of business administration at a well-known university adds much luster to a private company's board of directors.

In terms of the contribution of the individual at board meetings, a distinguished name or title is less significant than the experience that the name or title *may* represent. If the individual serves on a number of boards of directors, the chances are he will be in a position to make a meaningful contribution. If he serves on no other or only one other board, he is less likely to make contributions based on wide experience and observations of other companies.

One can usually rely on the integrity and intelligence of an experienced director not to permit himself to be appointed to the boards of companies in direct competition with one another so that he would be placed in a position of having a conflict of interest. A more difficult issue is where the director of a company is also affiliated either with a supplier of goods or services to the company or with a customer of the company. By and large, I believe that directors on the board of a company should not be either vendor- or customer-affiliated any more than they should be affiliated with a competitive company. However, in many cases, a key supplier or an important customer may wish to have a director on the board and may even be an investor in the company.

SELECTION OF THE BOARD OF DIRECTORS

Legally, directors represent all of the shareholders without distinction. In practice, directors have special loyalty to those shareholders or corporate officers responsible for their appointment to the board. In private companies, a *we* and *they* situation frequently develops—we the entrepreneurs, they the money; or we the investors, they the managers. Accordingly, directors often wear team colors.

While directors' votes reflect their views as to that which is in the company's best interests, what those best interests are can be a matter of viewpoint. These problems are resolved in real life by certain individuals and factions retaining the right to appoint a certain percentage of company directors to protect their own interests. Thus, it is well understood by all concerned that when an investor has the right to appoint 50 percent of the board and does so, those directors will be primarily representing that investor's interests, since he has the ability to replace them with those who will. In most cases, there is a commonality of shareholder interest, and it is usually only during periods of stress that the interests diverge.

However, directors should not be mere puppets. They should not be totally controlled, or at least should not usually be, by the interests they represent. Some of their decisions occasionally will be in opposition to the wishes of the individual who appointed them. They have legal obligations to all of the shareholders, and, as intelligent people, they must vote what they believe to be in the best interests of all of the company's owners. Their obligation is, however, only to the owners, and not the managers, of the business.

The following report was published in the April 1982 issue of *Venture*.

"No one around here ever asks the boss a tough question—so I decided to form a board of directors to give myself a few peers to talk to," says Ray Peterson, owner and president of Industrial Fabricating Co. in Stratford, Conn. If he worked for a large corporation he says he'd have six or seven "equals" to swap ideas with; his board helps provide similar feedback.

Peterson formed the board in spring, 1981. Last year the maker of metal casings had sales of slightly over $2 million, only a small improvement over the previous year's $1.8 million. Yet Peterson is enthusiastic about the board's impact on the company and he expects the board's suggestions to eventually help earnings. "The best thing about it is it makes me think," he says. His board has already made an important contribution to savings; in response to board probing, Peterson was forced to admit one of his products was unprofitable. He dropped it immediately.

Any question can be brought up at a board meeting, but it's wise to concentrate on business objectives and performance. A wisely chosen board will give your business expert guidance in areas where your own knowledge is weakest. "Most small businesses are started by people with technical or service expertise who don't know enough about business and finance," says Robert A. Howell, clinical professor of management at New York University's Graduate School of Business Administration. "I've seen cases where a board has taught an owner to multiply earnings 10-fold," he says. Most states require all corporations to form a board but companies often create boards "in name only" that seldom meet and don't make serious contributions to the firm.

In order to find the best board members for your company, you should isolate your weaknesses and look for people who are strong in those areas. Howell recommends that you choose five to seven members; (if you have an odd number of directors, you eliminate the possibility of a tie vote) too many people can stall a decision with too much discussion.

A hypothetical board might consist of a venture capitalist, an investment banker, a business school professor, and an owner of a small business that is similar to yours, provided there is no conflict of interest. You may want to find someone with a strong background in accounting, although this person will most likely not be a CPA—most members of "big eight" firms are forbidden to join corporate boards. Some owners also find it useful to appoint an attorney well versed in business law. Select directors who are likely to serve for an indefinite length. "The longer, the better," says Howell. "Look for commitments of 10 to 15 years, so that they get to know the company." Peterson advises that you look very carefully at the prospective members' personalities too. "Make sure that they're straightforward," he says. "Get people who can be counted on to ask tough questions."

There are a number of ways to make board membership attractive. Money alone rarely serves as a major incentive. But many companies hold annual or semiannual all-expenses-paid conferences at posh vacation spots. Others give their board members equity in the corporation. But even if you can't offer either of these things, you may be surprised by how many people accept your offer. "I only pay my board $200 a meeting—but they do it for the experience," says Peterson. "They gain as much knowledge and insight as I do."

Most important of all is to learn to be completely candid with your board and accept its contributions. Howell says that too often owners of small businesses are used to making all important business decisions by themselves and can't break the habit. "After having spent a lifetime being self-reliant, a lot of business owners find they can't open up as much as they would like to," Howell says. "I've seen a lot of unnecessary problems occur because of this, and it's always sad when someone who could have prevented the difficulties was sitting on the board all along."

ADVISORS AND CONSULTANTS

For the purposes of this discussion, a differentiation is made between advisors and consultants. Advisors tend to serve on a long-term basis; they will probably form an advisory board and have a lasting concern with the company. They may be investors, people with banking or technological experience, or retired members of a board of directors or of a management group. Advisors, of course, may also perform consulting functions. Essentially, advisors are continuously available to the management of a company to give advice.

Consultants are typically retained on a per diem basis to address a very specific area of the company's activities or to solve a particular problem. The professional consultant is essentially a butterfly that flits from company to company in an act of cross-pollination, taking experience gained in one company and applying it in another. Although a consultant will often try to establish a long-term relationship with a company, the attempt should probably be rejected in favor of a number of short-term consultants. The consultant will probably settle for periodic assignments. As with directors, the company is likely to get the major percentage of the consultant's total contribution very early in the relationship. Although consultants are extremely useful sources of information as to what is going on in the industry generally, and as to what is happening in other companies of special interest, small-company management is conspicuously backward in making use of them. Investors may be useful to the managements of companies by suggesting, or perhaps even imposing, specific consultants with whom they have had prior experience.

MANAGERIAL CHANGE AND INTRIGUE

No one likes to enter a marriage with a prenuptial agreement. However, recognizing that more than 50 percent of all marriages end in divorce or separation, such an agreement may be appropriate when there is a disparity of financial assets prior to the marriage. The relationship between investor and entrepreneur is a marriage of sorts, with the investor almost by definition having the greater personal asset base. Added to this is the fact that the investor most frequently will end up eventually investing more than had been originally expected at the time of the initial investment. Finally, there comes the time, all too frequently, when the investor believes that the company will fare better with a new manager and that the very protection of his capital in fact requires a change in management. At this point, the investor will find it extraordinarily useful if he has provided the necessary protection for the owners of the business of a contractual agreement stipulating that, upon the nonachievement of projected results, the entrepreneur/manager will resign some, or all, of his positions. The investor or the board can always decline the resignation or reappoint the entrepreneur.

In practice, most entrepreneurs will not want to stay with the company if not in the top position. The entrepreneur rarely recognizes the situation where a developing company requires new or different skills in its management than the entrepreneur himself possesses. The entrepreneur ideal for the initial startup may be totally unsuitable to the company at later stages in its development, especially during periods of stress and disappointment.

The agreement as to role change can, of course, be part of a buyout package where the entrepreneur has agreed to sell *all* of his stock to the company or to the investor at, say, book value under certain conditions. In startup companies, this in effect means that the entrepreneur will simply surrender his stock under certain conditions, because the stock will probably have little or no book value or net worth at the time the agreement is triggered. The triggering of the agreement might be a third consecutive quarter in which projections of revenues have not been achieved. The trigger might also be a shortfall by 50 percent or more over a given period of time of the cash flow, or a combination of sales and earnings. Whatever the trigger point, the period to which it is related should be relatively short-term. This protective device for the investor should be used much more often than it is.

In many new companies, management struggles result in intrigue, some against and some for the investor. With entrepreneurs, the investor is dealing with people who have enlarged egos, since otherwise they probably would not be entrepreneurs. The entrepreneur, in turn, has to deal with an investor who is fearful of losing his investment and who will quickly seek to blame someone other than himself when something goes wrong. The entrepreneur is the logical person to blame. Thus, it is not unusual for a private company to have struggles, intrigues, secret meetings to which not all of the board members are invited, meetings within the management group, meetings among investors, and meetings between various parties and their attorneys. These things have a way of escalating as the groups tend to panic with impending problems.

On the subject of investor protection, I suggest that the investor recognize that the position of secretary of the company, so frequently thought to be titular, has at crucial moments a real significance. The investor's attorney is the most advantageous person for him to have as secretary of the corporation. Similarly, the investor might consider having the company use his attorney as corporate counsel or certainly as co-general counsel. A further precaution would be for the investor to arrange for the selection and appointment of auditors, rather than the company or entrepreneur.

WRITING OFF STARTUP COSTS

Almost all businesses lose money in the beginning. This article, by Jim Ostroff, appeared in *Venture* in June 1983.

The Miscellaneous Revenue Act of 1980 contained an amendment that was designed to help new businesses write off startup costs. Three years later, it's obvious the measure is a flop. You may gain some cash-flow assistance from the provision, but don't count on a windfall. That, tax experts say, is more likely to go to established companies that spin off subsidiaries. The Treasury will lose revenues of $1.055 billion for the fiscal years 1982 through 1987 because of the measure, according to the House-Senate Joint Committee on Taxation.

The law permits companies to write off over five years the costs of researching and planning either a new business or the expansion or acquisition of an existing business, training employees, and advertising. Previously, these expenses had to be maintained on the books as unrecoverable capital costs. But many entrepreneurs argue that the 1980 law does little for small businesses, since its five-year write-off period is too long to help cash-pressed ventures.

William Winquist, president of Sunnyvale, Calif.-based Intelligent Systems Inc., says the measure is almost worthless to high-technology startups. "For companies like ours, most startup costs involve just planning, which costs virtually nothing," he says. Winquist says his company—whose sales for fiscal 1983 are projected at $2 million—spent about $200,000 for equipment after its "official" startup last April. Therefore, it was nondeductible under the above startup rules.

Startups can depreciate capital expenditures over three, five, or 10 years, just as an established business can. But under present law, the equipment can't be depreciated until it is placed in service. Thus, a startup may be forced to carry heavy capital investment costs for a year or two before it can begin to depreciate them. Established companies, Miller points out, have the resources to buy equipment and buildings before the official startup date, enabling them to write off expenses faster than startups can.

The law also suffers from hazy definitions. The description of the startup date is clear enough: the date of incorporation. But how do you determine the precise time you began to investigate and plan for a startup? The best explanation: as soon as you show your interest is more than a hobby. The law states only that you must be actively investigating the creation of a new venture. "A key point is to prove that you have a specific business in mind," says Ronald Fleming, tax manager with Price Waterhouse, Washington. "In this way," he adds, "you not only strengthen your startup case, but if you are unsuccessful in entering a business, you can use other tax provisions and write off your costs in one year."

Since there's no limit on the time you can spend investigating and planning a startup, you should document all startup costs and "act in a businesslike manner in all your dealings," according to Lee Weinberg, a partner in Granet and Granet, a Union, N.J., accounting firm.

Creative entrepreneurs have found ways to take advantage of the law as it stands, its drawbacks notwithstanding. Winquist, for one, delayed investing in capital equipment. "We contracted an order and produced it at a client's facility," he says. "This saved us capital expenditure expense during the crucial startup period."

KEY-MAN LIFE INSURANCE

In the event of the entrepreneur's death, key-man life insurance can spell the difference between a recovery of the investor's investment and a certain loss. This article, by Kathleen Mirin, appeared in *Venture* in June 1983.

Whether it happens with a plane crash, an automobile accident, or a heart attack, the sudden death of a company's founder can also mean the death of the company. But young companies can be protected from an early demise by life insurance policies for the key employees who make the business run.

Key-man insurance, as it is called, is a high-stakes insurance policy purchased by the company, which is also the sole beneficiary. If a top executive should die, key-man benefits—often amounting to several million dollars—buy valuable time to adjust to a new scheme or to find a successor, provide funds to buy out the stock of the deceased partner, or reduce debt while the company reorganizes. "The purpose of key-employee insurance is to keep the business in business," says Michael L. Abruzzo, corporate vice-president with New York Life Insurance Co.

Key-man insurance is also standard in venture capital contracts. "The venture capitalists' reward for backing an enterprise is the growth of the company," says Stan Meadow, a small corporation specialist with McDermott, Will & Emery, a Chicago law firm. "That type of growth depends on the entrepreneur."

How much should an entrepreneur be insured for? The central question is, what would it cost to replace the founder or key executive? Formulas based on a multiple of the person's salary or a percentage of the company's profits—common measures in established companies—are useless in the case of a startup, where the founder may take stock in lieu of a big salary and the company may not turn a profit for several years.

The most common way to gauge a founder's worth is to "calculate what it would cost to bring in someone of equal skill," Meadow says. In most startups, that almost always means a six-figure salary, since the newcomer will lack the personal commitment to the company and will not receive as much compensation in equity. "If you have to go out of the house to hire, it's almost inevitable that you have to pay a higher salary," Abruzzo says. "And it may take a number of years to bring that person up to the level of the lost employee."

Most young companies opt for term insurance rather than whole life policies because term policies are lower. For example, a $ 1 million term policy from New York Life on a 45-year-old, non-smoking executive in excellent health would cost $1,400 the first year. A comparable whole life policy would cost $21,500. "In the early years, they buy term," Abruzzo says. "When the picture gets rosier, they convert to whole life so they begin accruing equity."

Jim Liautaud, a Chicago investor who has started four high-technology firms since 1968, says he also considers the company's rate of growth in deciding how much key-man insurance to buy. "The faster the company grows, the more critically it depends on one man," he says. "Every time I start these things up, I have a high horsepower guy who is vital to the company. During the first two, three, or four years of the company, these guys are critical."

Liautaud founded American Antenna, a Chicago-based manufacturer of CB antennas and other consumer electronic products, in 1977. Subsequently, he purchased a $1 million term policy for $4,500 a year on Doug Mele, the 24-year-old president who was making

$100,000 a year. By last year, American Antenna's sales had grown to $15 million—from $2 million in 1977—and its management staff included vice-presidents of marketing, advertising, engineering, and purchasing. Ironically, the very success of the company had made Mele less indispensable. "When you start out, everything is in your head," he says. "The biggest thing I have done in the past three years is to delegate responsibility." With the safety of shared responsibility, Liautaud decided to cut Mele's key-man policy to $400,000, "because the company is mature now and we have management depth." The premium dropped by about 50 percent, Mele says.

In his interview with me, Arthur Little told me,

"I always insist on very substantial life insurance—for a million or 2 million dollars—for key people in new private companies. The insurance is taken out in favor of the company in order to protect my investment, even though this is not a tax-deductible expense."

STRUCTURING THE DEAL   8

Before the investor can structure a deal, he has to make an attempt to really understand the motivations and needs of the parties to the agreement. Just how high a money motivation does the entrepreneur have? How much risk can he stand? What are his long-term goals? Is he an empire-builder? Does he want, and perhaps actually need, complete control over his life and, therefore, over the company? Can he accept direction? Does he need social status? Is innovative management something the entrepreneur enjoys? Does he want to prove to a prior employer or associate that he was right and they were wrong? Is making the most amount of money using the least important to him as a game? How will he work under stress?

I, as the investor, must review my own objectives in this project. Do I truly want to hold control, and is that my principal objective? How much involvement do I really want in the company? Is the product or service area one which I find interesting or fun? How much risk can I really accept? Do I want to take a total risk in this particular venture? What if some of my other ventures need additional financing at the same time as this new pet needs a second feeding? It always happens that way. Do I have the capability to manage the company if something happens to the entrepreneur or if I have to replace him? Are his talents readily found elsewhere and at similar cost? What other investors could make this a better and safer investment for me? How much board of directors representation do I really want or need? What is the best return on investment I am currently earning, and what is the best currently available to me? What is the minimum return on this investment necessary to make it attractive to me? How balanced in terms of risk is my overall portfolio? How much do I know about the entrepreneur or the business he is proposing I get involved with? Am I interested in heightened visibility in the community? Do I want to have my spouse or children involved?

As indicated elsewhere, I believe strongly that investor funds take precedence over promotional or entrepreneurial interests. The only question in that area is whether or not investor funds should earn while waiting for the business to be successful. This is not to say that the actual payment for the use of the funds cannot be deferred until the company can afford to make the payments. Since the entrepreneur in all probability will be paid a current wage, it seems reasonable for the investor's dollars to earn a wage for their owner while they are being put to work.

Risk level assessment and containment by the investor must be considered next. If the investor wishes to limit risk—to the extent that it is ever possible in a private company investment, let alone a startup—he should be willing to accept a lessened upside potential. It is only fair to recognize that the investor cannot have it all his own way. He cannot expect to be fully secured and to have 100 percent of the equity. Once the investor accepts that fact, it is only a matter of establishing the appropriate tradeoff points. How much risk is fair for how much profit potential?

My view is that the investor is better off in early stage investments in taking a heavily secured (to the extent possible) and senior position. In other words, he should let the entrepreneur have more of the initial equity and take a lesser profit play but on a maximally secured position. My reasoning is that the investor will likely get a chance to improve his position once the company develops further, since the entrepreneur has, in all probability, underestimated the amount of funding required. The investor, therefore, will be in a natural, and perhaps inevitable, position to improve his potential profit participation later, with little sacrifice of ranking. The golden rule of business becomes increasingly operative as businesses need additional funding. Also, the more senior the investment position of the investor, the more deals he can do as he can then use leverage more effectively himself. Therefore, investing through providing the use of assets, to which title is held, might be the best way to invest in a private company. The ownership of the assets can always be exchanged for equity later in the company's development.

Since it has been concluded that the investor's investment should outrank that of the entrepreneur, and that the investor should initially take a lesser reward potential in exchange for a lesser risk potential, the questions remain of how much, and of what. In many cases, the question of what is more difficult than that of how much. What is the reflection of the investor's interest in the project? Stock or profit shares or royalties? My own preference is for a share of revenues which can be converted to equity, either by the entrepreneur under certain circumstances or by the investor. My least favorite reflection of investor's interest is that which relates to profits.

I have two reasons for my aversion to profit-related inducements to invest in private companies. First, the *reported* net profit, in the instance of success, of a privately owned company is highly controllable by the management. It also may well be in the best interests of the company, or its managers, to take actions which reduce current profits for the sake of either increased future profit or for other reasons. Second, I see no virtue in any investment structure which unnecessarily places the company management in the position of having to report for tax purposes the highest amount possible.

The way I like best to share in a business is through a royalty on revenues. I do this through the medium of revenue-participation certificates.

REVENUE-PARTICIPATION CERTIFICATE

The revenue-participation certificate (RPC) is an instrument reflecting a royalty which provides a means of participating in a business through a royalty on its revenues. I believe that someday RPCs will be publicly traded and used a great deal by successful and otherwise still private companies. The private company investor today can use RPC techniques as his inducement to finance ventures. Revenue-participation terms can be as flexible and ingenious as the parties to the agreement choose.

RPCs can be acquired by purchase or as the inducement to make a loan or provide a guarantee. They can be used to pay for services and, although I have not done so myself, goods. In real estate, the concept of RPCs is accepted and manifests itself in the form of participating leases.

RPCs can be secured, unsecured, or guaranteed by third parties. They can have a minimum or maximum annual payment and can be for an infinite or a fixed period. They can scale up or down, can terminate upon reaching a certain level, and can be convertible into some other security. RPCs can have a termination payment price, can be assignable or nonassignable, and can require payments to be made only by or to a specific bank or by or to any bank chosen by the RPC holder. They can be in any currency and can be paid to non-U.S. entities. They can require personal services or only the availability of personal services by the holder (this is for tax purposes in order to assure deductibility by the company).

The company will of course wish to deduct for tax purposes the payments, and the holder will, therefore, be receiving ordinary income. There is a danger of the IRS claiming that the RPC payment is a form of dividend, and, therefore, both in form and substance such IRS concern will have to be recognized.

My approach to negotiating the RPC is to negotiate the terms of the deal as if it were going to be a debt plus free shares or straight-equity arrangement. In so doing, the earnings projections are reviewed. The pretax profit on sales is usually the area of greatest focus. If the originally proposed deal was that I would receive 40 percent of the shares of the company for having made the loan or issued the guarantee, then I would translate that into 40 percent of the amount of projected profit on sales and fix payments to me to that percent of sales. In other words, if the company was projecting an average pretax profit of 5 percent on sales, the RPC would be for 2 percent of sales, which is the same value as 40 percent of the company shares. It does not have to be done on a basis of averages, since the RPC percentage of revenues can track the projections year by year into the far future or up to a point when the projections become fixed as to percentage profit on sales.

The reaction of the entrepreneur on hearing the investor's suggestion is likely to be one of immediately becoming more conservative and modifying the projections, claiming that he "needs some room" for the vagaries of business and so forth. This will not affect the investor, since his legitimate demand for an increased percentage of equity, and, therefore, RPC interest in sales, will naturally follow the less rosy projection. In other words, if the total projected profit is going to be smaller, the source of finance should be entitled to a larger share of the smaller pie in order to maintain the investor's risk-related return on investment objective. The negotiating process will then restart, and a balance of accepted (perhaps with mutual resignation) fairness evolve. The translation from equity percentage holdings to RPC percent of sales can then be accomplished. It is important that the entrepreneur accept that there is comparability between giving the financier 40 percent of his business in exchange for the money (or its use) and giving the financier forty percent of the profit on sales, in the more predictable form of 2 percent of sales, while the entrepreneur retains 100 percent of the business.

There are a number of other advantages to the RPC arrangement from the standpoint of the investor. These include the fact that the investor can be paid daily, weekly, monthly, or whenever the company itself receives revenue payments. The company must agree to deposit all revenue payments in designated banks, and it is possible to arrange for the bank or banks to automatically split the deposit between the company and the RPC holder, on irrevocable instructions from the company. An advantage for the company is that there is no need for the RPC holder, in that exclusive capacity, to require audited financial statements, since all the RPC holder is concerned with is an honest count of revenue. Therefore, a gross, or net if that is how the RPC is structured, audit or third-party attestment of revenue is all that is needed.

I am surprised the RPC technique is not more widely used (I know of no other financier using this technique as often or broadly as I do, although it is used in various forms in the oil, real estate, entertainment, and publishing businesses), because it has so many advantages from the perspective of both the company proprietor, who can retain all the very real benefits of full ownership, and the investor, who is isolated from the problems of profit margin maintenance.

Among the disadvantages of RPCs from the entrepreneur's viewpoint is that they tend to develop into too good a deal for the investor, because the entrepreneur tends to overestimate the projected profit levels upon which the RPC percentage of revenue is based. Also, the RPC must, in most cases, be eliminated in the event the owner of the business decides either to sell out or to go public. However, terms for the termination of the RPC are easy to work out since the original point of departure in the creation of the RPC was equity-related. Therefore, if the company goes public and if the RPC holder is offered registrable shares having a market value of at least an agreed upon amount, he can be required to exchange the RPC for shares. The same exercise is applicable if the company is going to be sold, since the issue then is only one of allocating sales proceeds.

The RPC holder can usually extract a premium for agreeing to any termination that has not been negotiated as part of the original deal. The premium would be in the allocation of proceeds of more than solely the percent of profits represented by the money paid the RPC holder which the company would have earned if the RPC payments were added back and which are to be included in that which was acquired by the new owner. This is due to purity of return, unadulterated by normal margin pressures and the disease of mediocre management. Of course, it is possible that the RPC can be maintained under new owners or public participation in the company.

I truly believe RPC investing is a win/win situation if properly structured and that most entrepreneurs are much better off enjoying the life of the successful business owner rather than being a public company chief executive officer or even controlling shareholder of a privately owned company with other owners.

DEAL STRUCTURE CAN BE MORE IMPORTANT THAN PRICING

The structure of a deal can be much more important than the apparent or stated pricing. The example here is real estate, but the approach is equally applicable to private company investment.

BUYER: I'd like to buy your house. How much are you asking?

SELLER: $90,000.

BUYER: You have a deal.

SELLER [*taken aback*]: Aren't you going to negotiate?

BUYER: No, I never negotiate price. But *we* have a problem.

SELLER: What's "our" problem?

BUYER: I don't have $90,000.

SELLER: What are we going to do about that?

BUYER: I have $15,000. I'll go to the bank this afternoon and find how much of a first mortgage they'll give me, and you're going to give me a five-year second mortgage on the difference.

SELLER: I am?

BUYER: You are, since we both want me to buy this house for $90,000.

The deal was struck for $15,000 in cash from the buyer and $55,000 from the bank, with a five-year second mortgage of $20,000 from the seller.

All that may be needed in a deal is a single element of initial agreement:

ENTREPRENEUR: My company needs a million dollars for 90 days, until the public offering becomes effective.

INVESTOR: I like you people and I like your company. What do you want to give me?

ENTREPRENEUR: A 5-year warrant on 25,000 shares. The stock will be offered at 16.

INVESTOR: I'll take that. But you're also going to give me, as well as the 5-year warrant, a put so that at the end of five years I can put the stock back to you 20 points higher. In other words, I am going to both buy the stock at 16 and have the right to sell it to you at 36 at the end of five years.

ENTREPRENEUR: That's a $500,000 profit over five years!

INVESTOR: You say the price of the stock is going to climb, that earnings will increase significantly. Won't the stock be selling at way over 36 in five years' time?

ENTREPRENEUR: Of course, it will be. Our earnings are going to quadruple.

INVESTOR: Terrific. So what do you care then if I have a right to put the stock to you at 36?

This agreement was based on the entrepreneur being willing to accept a single element around which a deal could be constructed. The investor did not argue with the entrepreneur about the number of shares being offered. He simply took what was offered to him and locked the entrepreneur into what the entrepreneur himself proposed.

Thus, an investor can let the entrepreneur propose the deal as he sees it and then take the elements he can work with from that proposal.

LIPPER EQUITABLE DISTRIBUTION FORMULA FOR FINANCING STARTUPS

In many cases, the entrepreneur approaches the investor with an excellent idea for a business and appears to be qualified to manage it. There is only one problem: The entrepreneur does not have the money and chooses, typically out of concern for his family, not to incur personal obligations. Otherwise, everything seems great—the idea, the market, the product, the staff, everything.

My proposal in such a case is that the investor receive 100 percent of the initial equity of the business (perhaps structuring to qualify for the benefits of Section 1244 and S corporation status) and that the entrepreneur receive an option from the company to acquire within 5 to 10 years 50 percent of the then to be outstanding shares at 150 percent of the investor's cost, with of course the money going to the company. The investor could permit a lower exercise price if the option was exercised earlier than agreed or could adjust the exercise price to the performance of the company. The important feature is that the investor initially owns all the shares and the entrepreneur none.

If the entrepreneur suggests that this (or any other proposed deal) is too tough a deal, I usually ask if he has any friends or family members who would like to participate with me in this overly unfair deal favoring the investor. They can have any part or all of it. I also suggest to him that it probably *is* too tough a deal if he is only going to build a small company, but that it is a great deal if he is going to build a big company, since the company is getting well funded at the outset. The entrepreneur can subsequently borrow money, sell some stock, or sell some of the options (they may even be registered if the company goes public) in order to buy the rest. Thus, for example, he could have an opportunity to buy half of a company worth $8 million for $300,000—the ultimate value of the company being dependent upon his own efforts. I also point out to the entrepreneur that if the investor owns all the stock initially, the investor will likely be less reluctantly forthcoming with more money when it is needed and will be all the more motivated to contribute whatever assets he has.

This arrangement does not affect entrepreneur salary, employee stock option plans, or any other conventional means of motivating the entrepreneur and management.

There are a number of variations on this approach. The option price and/or number of shares optioned can vary with projected result achievement levels. The arrangement can, and should be, structured to recognize additional shares issued for capital or acquisitions. The investor should think through what he wants to happen to what may become a block of shares equal to, or by that time, larger than his own in the event of the entrepreneur's death or divorce. Should the shares be equally voting if held by other than the entrepreneur? Any restriction on voting will, of course, reduce the value of the shares and, therefore, of the option. I always provide an incentive in a deal for the entrepreneur to invest earlier than the option's maturity.

PROFIT MARGINS

The essence of business planning is estimating future revenue levels and accurately determining the cost of being in business at various levels of volume.

In reviewing projected financial results, the investor is obliged to constantly challenge assumptions in order to understand the dynamics of the project's profit margins. Are the profit margins realistic in terms of other companies in the same field? Will they be maintainable once competition enters? Can they be attained with the funding being sought or that which is available? It is in this area of profit margin analysis that the investor's accountant can possibly be most helpful. I would not ask an accountant for general business advice nor would I seek his counsel regarding the reasonableness of the projected revenues. I would, however, want to have the benefit of his experience regarding the likelihood of the projected profits evolving if the revenues were as projected. The accountant is more likely to be blessed with the "pessimism of reason" than either the entrepreneur or the prospective investor.

When the investor reads the business plan for a venture, generally it should be the profit margin attainability upon which he focuses. The accountant can be most helpful in this area.

Many of us read business plans, hundreds each year, by glancing at the summary and quickly reviewing the five-year projections. If the business concept seems at all reasonable *and* if the five-year projections are of sufficient magnitude to be interesting to me and appear reasonable in relationship to the various elements, then, and only then, do I think about reading the entire thing. This may be a little like reading a murder mystery by looking at the last chapter first. I want to know what "happened" and then go through the drill of reading to see (1) how it happened and (2) if it was a reasonable conclusion to reach based on the facts presented.

STOCK VERSUS ASSETS

The investor is most frequently offered an opportunity to invest in or lend to (if there is a difference) an existing corporation and, thus, does not have the flexibility and comfort of forming his own corporation for the project. He is specifically being asked to buy stock rather than assets.

What is the difference between stock and assets if the values are comparable? The answer is known and unknown liabilities. Although liabilities can also be stated as being comparable, the investor does not know how fully stated they are in the case of the already existing corporation. An ongoing business can present the investor with many unwelcome surprises; for example, the entrepreneur may have promised to give the finder (of the investor) a lifetime consulting contract at $2,000 per month, or there may be a dispute about the creation of the product or ownership of the patents, or a claim may be threatened by an ex-associate or employee for damages of some kind. The pending action may not even have reached the stage yet where the company has become aware of it.

The investor is much safer from unknown or underdisclosed liabilities in a completely new corporation where future claims involving the entrepreneur, for acts committed previously, will probably focus on, or likely can be contained within, the entrepreneur's interest in the new corporation. Of course, a reader of this book will have learned to obtain an indemnification from the entrepreneur for legal actions relating to his prior acts.

Investing in assets, rather than stock, in the form of buying shares of a newly formed corporation which acquires the assets and none of the liabilities of the predecessor corporation, is better than investing in the original corporation, because of the unknown liability issue. Included in such a transaction are the assumptions that the assets can be cleanly transferred for consideration—the consideration being available in a form satisfactory to the owners and known creditors with prior interests in the assets—and that there is not a significant tax-deductible loss being left behind in the original corporation. It is also being assumed that suppliers and customers will not be upset by a change of ownership—the business being the ultimate asset— even though the name of the enterprise has remained the same (being one of the acquired assets).

With a new corporation, the investor can create bylaws and structure the company to suit his purposes, rather than undertake the sometimes more difficult task of altering and amending an already existing situation. Another benefit of forming a new corporation is being able to produce a net worth statement for lenders which without question can fairly and completely identify assets and liabilities. (There may, however, be a question as to the valuation ascribed to any particular asset or liability.) The investor is comforted to know there is no skeleton in the closet, because the closet was just built today.

For a short article on this subject, see Appendix J.

ENTREPRENEUR GUARANTEES

Most venture capitalists require some investment on the part of the entrepreneur in the venture being financed. The individual investor similarly has reason to feel more comfortable if the entrepreneur has something tangible to lose if the investor is likely to be faced with financial loss. The question is the amount and form of the entrepreneur's risk and what the investor should do if the entrepreneur is without financial assets. After all, some of the best qualified and most creative people—the very kind an investor wants to run a company in which he has a major interest—have no money available for investment or other significant unencumbered assets. However, these same people will be making the projections as to future events on which the investor will be relying both as to the basic decision of whether to invest or not and the appropriate valuation to place on the business.

James Bergman, of DSV Partners, pointed out,

> The investor largely has to force the entrepreneur to attach his signature to his representations. At this time, the investor may discover that the entrepreneur has not done all his homework; for example, he may not have completed a thorough search to ensure that his patent will be accepted and does not infringe on the rights of another. This is the time for the investor to make such discoveries. When something incorrect is discovered after a closing, the investor's money is gone.

The normal way of handling the issue of projections is through the investor discounting them in reaching a decision as to whether to invest or not, through valuation and in the allocation of rewards (equity). Yet, what can be done to spread the possible pain in the event of investor loss?

Why be concerned with sharing the pain of loss. The reason is to equalize the risk/reward relationship. The entrepreneur should not have only upside potential. If he has nothing to lose, he has every reason to gamble and not bother with taking a measured view of management decisions and their likely results. Always betting to win is not prudent, and prudence is a requirement in the management of other people's money. Too few entrepreneurs consider these responsibilities, perhaps because too few investors make the point to the entrepreneur that he is in a fiduciary position and must act accordingly. This is not to say that risk should not be accepted, since that is the expectation of the investor. It is to say that the risks taken should not be total. One does not "bet the farm" on a single hand of cards, unless *all* of the owners of the farm agree and understand the possible consequences.

The basic question remains of how to have the entrepreneur share present and future risk intelligently. One way I have done it is to require the entrepreneur making the projections to personally guarantee the same bank loan I am guaranteeing to the extent that the retained earnings or book value results fall short of his projection. In one case, I provided a $100,000 bank guarantee in consideration of receiving 10 percent of revenues of a service business. The business had a number of contracts from major customers in hand and was growing rapidly. The money was to be used for increased marketing efforts, such as having more salesmen and producing a brochure describing the company services. The entrepreneur represented that the contracts already in hand were certain to produce minimum revenues of $1 million the first year, $2 million the second and $3 million the third. Therefore, I could expect to receive a guarantee fee of at least $100,000 (which, of course, is income to the guarantor and fully taxable) by the end of the first year. I told the entrepreneur, "you are making these projections while having no personal liability to me or to the bank, since the bank is lending your company money on my guarantee. You will have to guarantee that I will receive the fees anticipitated or, in the event of a shortfall in fees paid to me, co-guarantee the bank." The significance of having the personal guarantee of the entrepreneur/manager is that the investor-guarantor of the corporate loan will, if called upon by the bank to make good on his guarantee, inherit through subrogation all of the assets, including the personal guarantees of the entrepreneur, held by the bank to secure the loan in the first place. This assumes the bank is fully guaranteed and has agreed, as has the borrowing entity, to have the pledged assets subrogated to the guaranteeing party. The entrepreneur then owes the amount guaranteed to the bank to the investor-guarantor.

It is also possible for the investor to require of the entrepreneur that he obtain, under certain conditions, the guarantees or investment of others. If the entrepreneur is without friends or acquaintances who, for profit expectation or friendship, will not expose themselves to *any* risk, the investor might have some second thoughts as to why this should be so.

As a matter of principle, I believe the entrepreneur should be at some risk. However, I am flexible as to quantum, timing, and circumstance.

MORE ON ENTREPRENEUR GUARANTEES

It is all well and good to conclude that the entrepreneur will manage a business more prudently if he has something tangible to lose if the business fails or even if agreed-upon objectives and projections are not met. The question is how to structure the penalty payment, or penalty risk assumption, which may never result in any payment. A guarantee of a portion of the investor's potential loss is an appropriate means of accomplishing risk sharing. The entrepreneur now says (commits) that he "will make up half the investor's loss if sales are not X by Y date." Now let's assume that sales are less than X, and the investor looks to the entrepreneur for compliance with his undertaking. As the entrepreneur often has little, if any, real money, the statement was empty in the first place and there never was any real sharing of risk. As there was not the risk reduction anticipated by the investor, there was in fact an increased risk over that which the investor had agreed to accept.

The fact that the entrepreneur says "sorry investor, I just don't have the money to make good on my promise" does not mean that the investor is necessarily out of luck or permanently out of funds. There is always the future; entrepreneurs have a way of making repetitive tries for the gold ring and frequently—for periods, at least—succeeding in gaining wealth. Also, because entrepreneurs are very human, they frequently forget the pain for which they were previously responsible. Therefore, a point to consider is that the investor's return of capital may come from a future business enterprise. Accordingly, the terms of the entrepreneur's obligation should not be an unchangeable impediment to the entrepreneur's future. It may make sense for the guaranteed investor to subordinate his future interests in the profits (or whatever) of the entrepreneur to those financing the entrepreneur's new venture in the future. The guaranteed investor wants the entrepreneur to get into business again and to succeed. Similarly, the investor has a vested interest in seeing that the entrepreneur's credit rating is not damaged more than the facts justify. In a surprising number of instances, people who have gone bankrupt (and legally, therefore, have no further obligations to creditors) have repaid in full all previous creditors from money made in subsequent businesses. Investors, however, will not be hurt by attempting to "insure the conscience" of the entrepreneur by obligation. Incidentally, I would almost always back an entrepreneur who made good on prior obligations when he was not required to do so. Successful private company investors invest in good people.

Therefore, I suggest taking the entrepreneur's note as evidence of his intention to pay at a specific date in the future or whenever possible. The earlier the investor attempts to get the note, the easier it will be. The correct time is before the investor's money passes to the entrepreneur's control.

One last thought regarding promises to pay investors by the entrepreneurs: The investor can treat a note or promise to pay as a sort of foreign debt or even debased currency because as an asset it has a possible or probable value, but it may not be easily ascertainable by either the holder or the party to whom the investor is trying to assign or sell it. A note is like a large yacht: the more people you have on it the more fun it is—for the holder of the asset. Of course, depending on the situation, the investor can properly seek or insist on third-party full or conditional endorsements on the guarantee or note. These endorsers (or co- or sub-guarantors) can be the spouse, the brother, or other family and friends of the entrepreneur, or just those from whom the entrepreneur bought an endorsement for a fee or for the prospect of reward sharing. The endorsers can have a limited or full liability for the amount involved. Also, the personal obligation being undertaken in an unendorsed guarantee can be, for, say, 10 percent (or more) of the entrepreneur's future earnings over Z amount per year, up to some amount. All of these protective devices should be instituted before the investor permits the seduction to be consummated, as afterwards ardor wanes and reality sets in—that is, few entrepreneurs assist investors in subsequent fund recapture unless so obliged.

The very idea of the investor (or lender) requiring (extracting) the guarantee of the wife of the entrepreneur will offend some readers. I do not suggest that obtaining the wife's endorsement is always a must. However, there are at least two reasons why it is a good idea.

The first is illustrated by the story of the advice given by a London merchant banker to the King of England during one of the bleakest periods of World War II. The advice was, "put Canada in your wife's name." Business owners and entrepreneurs frequently, and at times with perfectly valid reasons, separate assets between themselves and their wives (and children). This asset division should be reflected in the personal net worth statement the entrepreneur is required to prepare for the investor. An understatement of assets (where there is an obligation) can be just as misleading, and therefore fraudulent, as an overstatement. The investor can never really be certain if he has been fully informed or if the situation will remain constant. The wife could inherit money after the execution of the guarantee, as could the children (from their grandparents, perhaps). If the investor is intent on recapturing his money to the extent "possible" then he must think through all of the disaster scenarios and position himself accordingly. The investor must remember that after the honeymoon, attitudes and perspectives change; the investor is not likely to be in as good a position to protect himself after the check passes as before. If the reason for the guarantee is to get money back, make sure the document is drafted and executed appropriately.

Second, the wife is an integral part of the total picture, or makeup, of the entrepreneur. She will share in the rewards of success whether or not she remains married after the success is achieved. To assist in achieving success, she is going to have to continue to positively motivate the entrepreneur and make personal sacrifices of attention. She will be more understanding of the pressure the entrepreneur bears if she is a direct participant therein. She may also hold an initial interest in the company and most probably will as a widow. Although a co-signer is sometimes described as a "fool with a fountain pen," I believe that the act of co-signing between married partners can be a relationship-strengthening indication of confidence and participation. Let the lady sign. As with all of the other protective devices suggested in this guide, the holder is not required to use it even though he holds it.

JUSTIFICATION OF PENALTY FOR NONACHIEVED PROJECTION

Since it has been stated that projections are almost always wrong, or at least highly suspect, the thought may have occurred to some that the purpose of requiring entrepreneurs to provide them is to trap the entrepreneurs into a performance-based deal. This is absolutely not the case.

The purpose of investors' requiring entrepreneurs seeking funding to prepare and provide projections is twofold.

First, the reason for being in any business is to earn profit, and the amount of profit believed possible justifies the amount of the investment of time, talent, money, and risk of loss. Whether or not the entrepreneur actually puts a business plan on paper, every successful entrepreneur who has built a business has had a plan. The purpose of committing a plan to paper is to better share it with others. Projections of results are an integral part of such a plan and must be developed to determine the steps the business manager will take. A business plan is simply a road map used to plan a trip. Without such a map, getting lost is almost inevitable. Getting lost can sometimes be fun, but it can also prove fatal. In starting and running a business—any business—the investors, entrepreneur, and managers must know what is expected around the next turn. To know this, they must also know where and when the turns are placed along the path they intend to travel. As the Dun & Bradstreet business failure statistics show conclusively, and as has every other study I have heard of, it is lack of adequate planning which is the major reason for business failure. Therefore, the entrepreneur must prepare a plan and make projections in order to come to a conclusion himself as to whether he has a valid business venture or just an idea for a new product or service which might well be attractive to some company already in a business having many of the required elements in place. By seriously studying the plan with the entrepreneur, the investor will come to understand (1) the business being proposed and (2) something of the entrepreneur and his talents and weaknesses. The entrepreneur must be able to defend satisfactorily, to the investor, all assumptions and premises made which have an effect on the financial results projected. If it doesn't make sense on paper, it won't work in practice.

Second, the investor can estimate a projected return on his possible investment in the project only through learning from the entrepreneur or through the entrepreneur's business plan and its projections. Only after calculating such a return on investment, assuming that the entrepreneur has fairly presented the facts and assumptions, can the investor compare the return on the private company investment with that available by investing in publicly traded companies, which may be in the same area of business activity and, thus, have a similar potential from the same macroeconomic trends predicted or assumed by the entrepreneur.

A thought which presents itself here is that investors would be well advised to specifically identify those publicly traded securities which are most directly related to the private company being considered. A detailed study of these several publicly traded companies may yield ratios and performance measurements applicable to the private company. It may also be a very good idea for the investor to invest in the public companies, since it is very possible that the private company entrepreneur's knowledge of the industry and his predictive capabilities concerning new developments are superior to his ability to run a business or even to obtain the necessary funding to start one. Such a public company investment could yield much information and insight and possibly offset the results of the private company investment if that does not work out as hoped. Certainly, the added intelligence gained from studying and coming to know the competition can only help in the decisions the investor will be called upon to make. Of course, if both the idea and the private company investment work out, the investor will really have a great parlay.

I believe it to be a fair supposition, and a basis for negotiation, that the entrepreneur knows more than the investor about the proposed business. Therefore, it seems only fair to burden the entrepreneur with the responsiblilty for his statements and projections, since the investor is forced to rely on them for the prospect of profit and apprehension of loss. I would agree that the entrepreneur should not be penalized if he is also risking capital on the same basis as the investor, or if he will place himself in financial risk in the event that that which he has projected is not achieved. In the absence of a financial risk undertaking by the entrepreneur, penalization through withdrawal of reward seems a logical offset.

MOTIVATING THE ENTREPRENEUR

Since most entrepreneurs are motivated by a need to achieve, to be recognized, and, most importantly, to prove something, money tends to be more important to them as a symbol than as buying power. Most of the successful entrepreneurs I know do not live at the level their income or net worth would permit. Thus, the investor who wishes to motivate the entrepreneur must consider how best to do it and not simply throw money at him by way of reward.

In structuring the deal, the investor has to be clear in his own mind how the entrepreneur's greater effort can accomplish the desired goal. Does the investor want sales to increase overbudget, or does he prefer that expenses be kept to an underbudget level or to a set percentage? Does the investor want debt levels reduced, or does he want an increased subordinated debt which does not have to be guaranteed by him? Does he want a new group of executives? A reduced unit cost in some manufactured item? A merger completed? The sale of a division? The completion of a certain task? Once the investor has decided what exactly it is that he wants and how the entrepreneur can best help him get it, he should set up a bonus plan which can involve cash or stock or stock equivalents.

The investor has to understand the business well before he can expect to know where the efforts of the entrepreneur/manager are best focused. As a partner, the investor may well be in a better position than the manager of the business to point out the areas that most need improvement. It is the investor's money which is being used to pay people, and it is his profit which is either being increased or diminished by more or less attention to specific areas than would otherwise be the case.

I believe in specific project bonuses and not in general performance rewards. The entrepreneur is already motivated in the general performance area by virtue of his holding an interest in the company and receiving a salary. Specific project bonuses mutually agreed upon by the investor and entrepreneur/manager can be highly constructive for a company. When a management team is involved, its key members should be included in the bonus plan.

You, as the investor, can think of your dollars as green slaves—the more you have of them, the less you have to do yourself and/or the more you can accomplish. Thus, the interest on your money is equivalent to rental of your green slaves in the form of more green slaves. It seems reasonable that the owner of these green slaves should be willing to pay a premium for their early release for reassignment to other jobs. After all, the owner of the green slaves is going to be paid more proportionately for their showing up for work on the first day than for any other part of their effort. In venture capital terms, I structure deals in such a way as to give the entrepreneur a benefit if he can replace and thereby free up my money at an earlier than anticipated date.

The wish of an investor to recapture his money for redeployment in this way must be distinguished from the approach of most professional venture capital investment managers. They are paid to employ the money undermanagement rather than to achieve the highest possible total return. The normal venture capital money manager is not financial-leverage-oriented, because if he is successful (in raising money), he already has all the money he can use for current investment purposes. This is not the case with the individual investor investing in private companies. He needs his green slaves back as soon as possible . . . and in good condition. He cannot, somewhat smugly, take the position that venture capital investing is a process which requires seven years to know performance results. If you ever wish to upset a venture capitalist, suggest the need for a performance measurement service, such as those I created in 1967 for mutual funds.

Paying the entrepreneur a cash bonus or reducing the revenue-participation-certificate (royalty) rate, either in percentage or maturity, are other ways the investor can motivate the entrepreneur to replace his money.

The individual investor fortunate enough to have a flow of deals to consider should be willing to pay a premium for earlier than contracted fund recapture. The more sophisticated entrepreneur will probably, of his own accord, suggest such an arrangement if more attractive funding becomes available to him. However, it is more advantageous for the investor to offer the entrepreneur an incentive early on, because his offer will appear more attractive in the early stages of the business before actual profits have been generated.

Bill Berkley told me,

> By and large, I don't think that partnerships are the best form of structure for a new or very young company. A corporate structure that involves a convertible redeemable voting preferred stock held by the investor often provide a big incentive for management when the conversion ratio is tied to the achievement of objectives. If the entrepreneur/manager does not redeem the stock, the investor ends up with a big piece. If the entrepreneur/manager meets certain objectives, the preferred stock gets redeemed out and the combined equity ownership balance changes. I do not give a particular incentive for early redemption, and there's no penalty for late redemption, either in the cost of the interest or the accrued earnings.

Dan Lufkin had this suggestion to make. "One very useful formula goes like this: the investor puts up all the money and gets 100 percent of the equity; if the entrepreneur pays back all the money in one year, he gets 80 percent of the business; in two years, 60 percent; in three or more years, 40 percent."

DANGERS OF OVERCAPITALIZATION

If I were writing this book for the purpose of advising entrepreneurs rather than investors, I would advise them to seek the maximum amount of money they could get while keeping as much equity as possible. The advice I offer to investors is not the reverse image of this. I do not believe that investors should necessarily invest as little as possible in return for the greatest amount of stock they can get. Entrepreneur and investor must not lose sight of the fact that there is a business to be built and managed. The real issue is the very difficult job of estimating the true amount of investor funds which will be required and the timing of the need for the funds. The scheduling of investment, with appropriate go/no go points, is a large part of the art.

The question of how much money is required must be answered by the added question of from what source. It is overly simplistic to answer "from the investor." Which investor? The one who took the seed-capital risk, or the one who came in for the startup phase? Then, there is also the investor who at the time of seeking seed and startup money decided that although the project interested him, it was too early for him to come in. He may be the one to put up the money now. It is understandable for the entrepreneur to want to put the painful, tiring, and disagreeable chore of money raising behind him once and for all. Nevertheless, investors have different risk tolerances and greed-level thresholds, and the entrepreneur will retain more of his company if he raises the money in tranches. He will also be able to maintain more control over his investors if he has different investor groups rather than a single one.

The early investor should have the right to provide additional funding on terms negotiated by other investors. The early investor should also be delighted if and when other investors make committments on less advantageous terms than his own and should not feel a need to participate simply to maintain his position in the company. So what if the investor's percentage holding declines? The purpose of the investment is not for the investor to be able to tell his friends that he owns 33 percent of Robby Robot Corp. The purpose of the investment is to make money for the investor, to have each of his invested dollars work as hard as possible for him, and for at least the minimum returns he has established.

The dangers of overcapitalization will readily be seen in the similarity of the investor's giving his teenage son too much of an allowance or granting any young manager of a division too much of an operating budget. Once funded, the entrepreneur is off and running. Being goal- and achievement-oriented and not necessarily profit-oriented, he is likely to become a walking example of the laws of Northcote Parkinson.

The point is that in the case of startup investing, the investor is most often financing someone who has not previously built a business or made a lot of money himself, and, of course, therein lies a major part of the risk and the reason for high startup failure rates. It is up to the investor to supply some of the missing experience which often translates into restraint. The investor should challenge the entrepreneur's stated initial personnel and equipment requirements, with particular emphasis on the timing of the need for them. I do not really accept the premise—although I have been persuaded many times into accepting and financing it—that good people should be hired when they become available and that business will follow. If they bring business with them (salesmen, for instance), that would be different.

In the act of "growing" a company from little to big, the measured growth will likely be profit growth. The investor will remember that entrepreneur enthusiasm is catching and that the wish is often the parent of the thought. A Lipper rule for the investor who is in a position to influence the entrepreneur: "Do it smaller at first, then do it larger when you know enough to do it better."

The typical entrepreneur needs to prove something. This results in his being more concerned with being the biggest and best at something than with being a conservative and prudent manager. Being biggest and best at almost anything is an expensive undertaking. As an investor, and frequently sole financial risk taker in young ventures, I opt for a lesser early growth. As with a sports car, it's easy to get going so fast that operating control is jeopardized. Perhaps a good road sign for entrepreneurial investors would be: *go slow—learning curves ahead.*

For a review of an actual case affected by overcapitalization, along with other mistakes, see Appendix K.

VOTING TRUSTS AND PROXIES

Under certain conditions, more frequent than many suspect to be the case, the entrepreneur can become a serious hindrance to the business and the investor. At times of corporate stress and problems, the entrepreneur is frequently motivated differently than the investor. Also, the entrepreneur may act irrationally (1) if "his baby" is being threatened, or (2) if he feels he must vindicate his original judgments. In either case, he needs, and the investor needs, a mechanism which permits decisions to be made in a non-emotional, businesslike manner. The establishment of a voting trust, into which all or a significant portion of the entrepreneur's shares are placed, is a worthwhile consideration.

The trustee can be a person unaffiliated with either the entrepreneur or the investor or can be chosen by the investor. The trust can terminate on the achievement of certain objectives, such as four consecutive positive earning periods, sales reaching a certain level, or net worth reaching a stipulated level. Any number of termination points can be used other than simply a moment in time. Of course, if the company goes public or if the investor is offered an agreed upon minimum amount for his investment, the trust can also be terminated.

Some of the benefits of a trust can be created, with less formality, by the investor holding the proxy on the entrepreneur's shares to vote either on all matters or on specific ones, such as merger, liquidation, or recapitalization, in the event of certain things having occurred or not occurred. The problem of holding a proxy versus establishing a trust is one of the mortality of the proxy holder. When the individual invests through the medium of a corporation, the investing company holds the proxy. The immortality of the corporation conveys benefits frequently worth the administrative expense and possible double taxation concerns. Of course, the use of S corporations ameliorates the concern for double taxation.

The private company investor can invest through trusts established for his own benefit or for that of others. One very wealthy family that has been highly successful in entrepreneurial investment has invested principally through the medium of trusts. I have been told that in terms of tax management, it has worked out wonderfully well for the family.

INTEREST

Most private company investors lose sight of the reason why they are investing when it comes to interest on their money as the form of return on their investment. If maximum current return coupled with apparent safety of principal are an investor's true objectives, second mortgages may be his best investment. He might also consider the factoring of accounts receivable. Indeed, in both of these areas, it is at times possible, in the case of commercial borrowers, to work into the loan equation some sort of equity or warrants to buy equity participation.

The investor who wishes to participate in building a new company must structure his deal so that the rent the company pays on his money will not stunt the company's growth. By all means, he should calculate the interest return he expects as being necessary to justify the private company investment. An investor must be aware at all times of the value of his money. But, he should not extract interest from the company at the stage where the money is worth more to the company than it is to him. If the investor needs the income currently, he should not be investing that money in a private company in the first place.

There are a number of ways in which an investor can defer or offset the rent due on his money. The simplest way is for him to accept notes evidencing the accrual of corporate obligation. This technique unfortunately gives rise to an income tax obligation for the investor. Another technique is for him to add the amount of money rent to an exit or a buy-back formula, which will be discussed. He can also accept the rent in the form of additional equity or warrants to acquire equity.

The point the investor has to remember is that it would be silly for him to deprive an infant of nourishment if he expects it to grow and develop into something which can serve him in the future. He can structure a fair deal while recognizing that growing a company is an exercise in the allocation of resources. To use another metaphor, don't drown the plant with money and don't let it die of thirst. The investor can think of funding as a water-feeding device that provides water as the plant needs it but only as much as the plant needs.

The problem with a buoyant new issue market can be that too much money is made available to entrepreneurs, not that prices are too high or bad deals are being financed, but that instances of great waste occur as entrepreneurs get too much money without sufficient restrictions or controls on their use of the funds.

Since the private company investor is in a position to dictate the terms of the deal to his advantage, he should make a special attempt to understand the company's cash flow projections, instead of concentrating on projected profits. Cash flow is the critical issue in young companies.

ACCELERATION OF PRINCIPAL PAYMENTS

Acceleration of principal payments—if installments are not paid when due, then all money owed becomes due—is an important clause to have in any investment purchase agreement (loan or stock repurchase), since it gives the investor an opportunity to gain more control, more quickly, when the situation arises of the company not being able to meet an obligation to him or others. The investor must remember that the creditor who gets in control fastest is the one most likely to achieve the greatest recovery. Investors have to remember, and entrepreneurs recognize, that the investor's gaining of control does not in itself mean that it will be used unfairly or adversarially to the entrepreneur. A company being obliged to accomplish something difficult or even impossible, such as paying the investor all of the money it owes him, gives the investor power he would not otherwise have, but that power is a result of the investor's being placed in unexpected jeopardy.

CONTRASTS IN PRIVATE AND PUBLIC COMPANY INVESTING

Figure 1 is an effort to graphically display the three most critical considerations in the rational investment decision-making process. Of course, far greater reliance on the investor's predictive abilities are required when dealing with private companies, particularly early development or seed capital stage companies than when comparing mature, publicly traded company shares. These comparative analysis elements are:

1. The period of time it requires for a company to "earn back" the amount originally invested. In other words, if a company's stock is purchased at $10 per share and the shares earn an aggregated average of $1 per share for the next 10 years, then there would be a 10-year earn back period. A price earnings ratio is simply another way of expressing a similar concept in that the P/E indicates the number of years of the current (or a projected) year's earnings which are represented by the current price of the stock. An earn back estimate is used by anyone buying 100 percent of the shares of a business in determining whether

FIGURE 1

Number of Years of Projected Earnings Required To Equal Amount Invested in a Private Company on a Comparable Basis as Company Having Similar Projected Earnings and Trading Publicly at the Price Earnings Ratios Indicated.

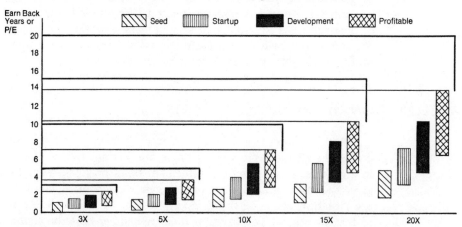

Price Earnings Ratios of Publicly Traded Shares Using Projected Cumulative Earnings for the Same Period as for the Private Company.

Note: Assumes required ROI increased to recognize illiquidity of private company investment on basis of: Seed 5–10X, Startup 3–6X, Development 2–4X and Profitable 1.5–3X.

or not the price asked for the company is reasonable. In other words, the buyer of a company must have a view as to the future levels of cumulative earnings, and not those of only the current year or the year ahead.

2. The value of liquidity is reflected in normal securities markets pricing by the magnitude of the discount applied to various price related ratios. The more liquid the security, the more generously will the market usually value the comparable ratios. In other words, if a widely held and broadly traded issue sells for 12 times current earnings shares of an otherwise comparable private company should logically be valued at a lesser price earnings ratio level. There is "exit safety" in liquidity and the absence thereof usually justifies, and normally imposes, on price related ratios a discount from that of a comparable company which has the investor benefit of marketability or liquidity.

3. The earlier the stage of development in a company the further in the future are normally the earnings which may be expected to earn back the original investment. The fact of business that "time is money" is represented by either interest charged (or paid) or in the discount factor applied to the price earnings ratio based upon current or projected earnings. Very significant cumulative future earnings are required to analytically justify paying a high price earning ratio based upon current earnings. The buyers of stocks selling at low current P/Es usually have better longer-term investment results than those who buy high P/E stocks because predicting future events accurately is so difficult.

Clearly, these comparative factors, as they relate to one another, have to be thought of as ranges and not as absolutes. The purpose of Figure 1 and the following exhibits is to indicate possible appropriate ranges when relating the elements.

The exhibits will force a user to consider the three factors of comparable earn back period (price level), liquidity premium or discount (exit value), and proximity of earning power (predictability). It should be recognized that the further in the future the projected earnings are the more that can go wrong in achieving them. Also, the further away the cumulative earnings are, the greater the money cost factor (interest or discount) which has to be applied to make the investment comparable to currently available and already profitable liquid investment alternatives. Of course, that is what professional investing is all about, the constant comparing of available capital use alternatives. That which the successful investor must focus upon is his assessment of ultimate, time-related risk and reward-related elements. Use and study of these exhibits will, it is hoped, be found of value in comparing dispassionately price related factors once there exists the basis for an assumption of future earnings for the companies being compared.

For example, were an investor using Figure 1 to gauge the comparability or attractiveness of a private company investment, the investor would determine the level of cumulative earnings which are expected to develop over, say, the next five years for the publicly traded comparable company. Let's assume that amounted to $12 per share and that the shares were currently selling for $36. Therefore, the stock is selling at a multiple of cumulative earnings of three times. If we assume that a currently profitable private company should be valued at a discount to yield the investor between 1.5 to 3 times as much as the investor would receive by investing in the publicly traded shares, then the private company would be valued at 1 to 2 times the cumulative five-year earnings level whereas the shares having the benefit of liquidity were valued at three times. Such range is indicated by the bar at the lower left. Note that the line immediately above the group leads to the left scale at the three times or three year level.

Now let's assume we are comparing a private investment with a publicly traded share selling at 20 times (also if current earnings and not cumulative earnings are used then 20 years are required to achieve earn back). Of course, a multiple of 20 implies the expectancy of future earnings increases. Actually, much of the securities analytical "science" involves the projection of *rates* of earnings growth. In this example, we will assume that we are considering investing in a development stage private company which is not yet profitable. If the appropriate premium to the investor is 2 to 4 times the return the market anticipates for the publicly traded share, then only 5 to 10 times the projected earnings should be paid for the private company. Note that the discount is greater for earlier stage (than the already profitable company used in the first example) and that the range is greater in absolute terms.

By studying the table which appears on page 102, the investor can determine the arithmetic basis for the Figure 1 graphic presentation and also calculate the specific values derived from the table which may be applicable to a specific investment opportunity.

As a further example for use of the table, assume that the investor requires a minimum earnings yield (the inverse of a price earnings ratio) of 12.5 percent (a P/E of 8) as that is the amount the investor believes he could earn with only the acceptance of a minimum amount of risk. In this case, the investor would have to convince himself that the current per share earnings level of at least $1 per share would increase by 5 percent for each of the next 6.9 years as this is necessary to earn back the price paid for the stock if purchased at $8 per share. It is also true that the earnings would have to increase at an average annual compound rate of 10 percent for 6.2 years, or at 15 percent for 5.6 years, or 20 percent for 5.2 years, or 25 percent for 5 years . . . all to provide an earn back assuming a cost of $8 per share and a current level of earnings of $1 per share.

The above simply "follows" the line across at the "8" level and indicates that the longer a compound annual average growth rate is assumed to continue the lesser may be the annual rate of growth to achieve a required level of cumulative earnings.

The art of investing requires an appreciation of compound interest tables . . . and this is a fact which should not escape any student of the market or investment opportunities.

DEFINITIONS AND INVESTMENT RETURN GUIDELINES FOR USE WITH TABLES AND FIGURE

Seed Capital

The idea stage, frequently preincorporation. Money used for feasibility studies, business plan development, product investigation, and marketing surveys.

As this is most speculative stage, at least a 500 percent better return than that expected from publicly traded securities is warranted. In other words, if an investor expects to double the value of his publicly traded securities portfolio in five years, then seed-capital investments should have the realistic potential for a 10-fold return in the same period.

Startup Phase

This is the stage where money is used for renting offices, hiring personnel, developing products or services, and initiating sales. A 300 percent improvement in projected return over publicly traded securities is warranted by the illiquidity and usual risk levels assumed.

Development or Second Stage

This is the stage where the company is in business but not yet profitable. Additional funds are used to further the activities of the business. Depending on the financial assets and liability relationships, a level of return of 200 percent of that available from liquid investments of a similar nature is reasonable.

Profitable but Private

Funds at this stage are needed to expand the business At least a 50 percent premium seems warranted to compensate the investor for the illiquidity inherent in private company investment.

The Price of Illiquidity

What is the fair or appropriate relationship between the price one is willing to pay for the future earnings of a private company versus that of a company the shares of which are publicly traded? The question assumes that the investor recognizes that a current or projected price earnings ratio, or earnings yield, is a reflection of the number of years of future earnings

Stock Price	Current per Share Earnings	P/E	Earnings Yield	Years to Earn Back*					
				0%	5%	10%	15%	20%	25%
6	1.00	6	16.7	6	5.4	4.9	4.6	4.3	4.1
7	1.00	7	14.3	7	6.2	5.6	5.1	4.8	4.6
8	1.00	8	12.5	8	6.9	6.2	5.6	5.2	5.0
9	1.00	9	11.1	9	7.6	6.7	6.1	5.6	5.3
10	1.00	10	10.0	10	8.3	7.3	6.6	6.0	5.6
11	1.00	11	9.1	11	9.0	7.8	7.0	6.4	5.9
12	1.00	12	8.3	12	9.6	8.3	7.4	6.7	6.2
13	1.00	13	7.7	13	10.3	8.7	7.7	7.0	6.5
14	1.00	14	7.1	14	10.9	9.2	8.1	7.3	6.7
15	1.00	15	6.7	15	11.5	9.6	8.4	7.6	7.0
16	1.00	16	6.3	16	12.0	10.0	8.8	7.9	7.2
17	1.00	17	5.9	17	12.6	10.4	9.1	8.1	7.4
18	1.00	18	5.6	18	13.2	10.8	9.4	8.4	7.6
19	1.00	19	5.3	19	13.7	11.2	9.6	8.6	7.8
20	1.00	20	5.0	20	14.2	11.5	9.9	8.8	8.0
22	1.00	22	4.5	22	15.2	12.2	10.4	9.2	8.4
24	1.00	24	4.2	24	16.2	12.8	10.9	9.6	8.7
26	1.00	26	3.8	26	17.1	13.4	11.4	10.0	9.0
28	1.00	28	3.6	28	17.9	14.0	11.8	10.4	9.3
30	1.00	30	3.3	30	18.8	14.5	12.2	10.7	9.6

* Number of years required for earnings to equal price paid if earnings increase at annual percent compound rates of growth shown.

which are represented by the current price of the shares, or valuation of the company. The following table may be instructive.

In order to provide the private company investor with a possible scale of comparability, the following matrix is presented. The illiquidity penalty is for illustration purposes only as there are many factors to be considered before reaching any conclusions as to the level of penalty to be applied. The only point of which to be certain is that the returns anticipated from the illiquid investment must far exceed those available from marketable securities.

Private Company Investment Stage	Expected or Required Increased Return (or Illiquidity Premium)		Public Company Cumulative P/E for Same Number of Years*				
			3X	5X	10X	15X	20X
Seed	5 to 10 times	=	1.6–0.3	1.0–0.5	2.0–1.0	3.0–1.5	4.0–2.0
Start-up	3 to 6 times	=	1.0–0.5	1.67–.83	3.33–1.67	5.00–2.50	6.67–3.33
Development	2 to 4 times	=	1.5–.75	2.50–1.25	5.00–2.50	7.50–3.75	10.0–5.0
Profitable	1.5 to 3 times	=	2.0–1.0	3.33–1.67	6.67–3.33	10.0–5.00	13.3–6.67

* Range of price/earnings ratios (based upon cumulative projected earnings) for marketable securities which a private company investor could use in calculating appropriate private company valuation or p/e.

PERKS AND REWARDS FOR THE INVESTOR

Perks as a return on investment is an area not generally contemplated by investors or entrepreneurs, or even by many professional venture capital investors. (However, some underwriters approach this area of reward through imposed management consulting contracts.) After all, one of the advantages of having one's own business is the exercise of personal discretion over the spending of monies in a manner beneficial to the owners of the business.

The entrepreneur/manager of a business will expect to have funds available for travel and entertainment. He will also expect to be able to use discretion as to the hiring of staff. He may expect the company to provide him with a car and, as the business grows and prospers, even with a plane. But what about the investor? To the extent that these expenses are really nontaxed dividends and are not truly "required" in the daily running of the business, shouldn't the investor also have some available to him?

The investor can discuss openly with the entrepreneur his feelings on the subject of perks. Whose son is hired for the summer? Shouldn't the investor have a company American Express card with an understanding as to charge limits and purposes? Shouldn't the investor have the use of a company car when on company business? Should annual meetings, or even quarterly meetings of the board of directors, be held at resorts? I have pointed out elsewhere that the investor may be served when the entrepreneur's wife is involved with the business. Similarly, the entrepreneur may be well served if the investor's wife is interested and well informed about the business. Therefore, shouldn't consideration be given to naming the investor's spouse as a director or an advisor of the company? After all, if the investor were to die and be succeeded by the spouse, the entrepreneur will fare better with a widow well informed about the business and its demands and potentials.

Perhaps the best approach is for the investor to discuss with the entrepreneur the level of travel and entertainment expense allocations expected and then to assign some percentage of that amount to the investor for him to spend in promoting the interests of "his" company. When a company prospers, it is not only the entrepreneur who should benefit from its success in ways generally associated with the owning of private businesses. The private company investor should think of himself as a partner or owner of (a part of) the business and not as a shareholder. The connotation of the term shareholder is, or should be, one of being able to sell to an ever-present buyer, such as is usually the case with publicly traded securities and rarely with private companies.

Consideration may also be given to the company hiring the investor as an advisor or consultant on terms known at the time of the investment. It is not unusual for underwriters to insist on an agreement by the company, as part of their underwriting package, that the company retain the underwriters, or their designees, for advising and consulting services at $1,000 to $5,000 per month for 1 to 5 years. Professional investors also at times charge fees for consultation. The private company investor is advised to read the prospectuses or offering documents of low-priced and speculative offerings to obtain an idea of the amounts extracted from company owners for access to other people's money. The reading of many prospectuses is a good education for the private company investor, and he should pay close attention to the sections headed "underwriting compensation" and "certain transaction." He will remember too that the underwriter is typically getting the stated rewards without having to assume the risk of investment. Other rewards for the underwriter may include added undisclosed compensation areas, such as pension fund management and brokerage business derived from the employee benefit plans of the underwritten company.

One great reason for investing in a private company seldom gets attention in print—to obtain a job. This way the investor has the opportunity to employ *both* his skills and money. If this is one of the investor's motivations, he should get it out on the table quickly to gauge the reaction of the entrepreneur. The investor should not be surprised if the entrepreneur is less than enthusiastic about the idea. From his standpoint, he is being saddled with another personality with which to contend, and one which is unlikely to be as receptive to his commands as others. The entrepreneur may also have no reason to believe that the investor really has anything more than his money to contribute. From the investor's standpoint, he gets a chance to participate fully in the new company and watch how his money is being utilized. The investor must understand that such an investment can be very expensive and result in a less than great job. On the other hand, it can be a great investment and a great job—if it all works out as projected.

Investor employment is a difficult area. One of its basic aspects is that the investor understand his own motivation. In making the investment, is he simply putting his dollars to work for him? Or, is he willing to accept a lower return on his dollars in exchange for employment and recognition? Two questions can be asked as a measure of such a situation. Would the investor have put his money into this company without the promise of employment? Would the entrepreneur have hired or associated with the investor if he did not have money to put in the company?

An agreement can be reached that the company will retain consulting services from the investor (or the investor's company) once the company has reached a certain revenue level or achieved certain profits or some other agreed upon measure of progress. A prior understanding should be reached of the services to be performed and the amount of time to be devoted to providing these services. The duration of the services should also be discussed. Perhaps the services will continue until dividends are paid, until the net worth of the company reaches an agreed upon level, or for as long as the entrepreneur/manager receives a salary above a certain amount.

Although investor employment can be very constructive, there is a good chance of misunderstandings. There is a risk too of IRS claims of "dividend" declaration, whereby they deny deduction of amounts paid by the company but still require the individual receiving payment to treat it as income. This situation is only likely to arise if the compensation is unwarranted by effort or excessive in amount.

INVESTMENT THROUGH THE PROVISION OF PROPERTY

Although I have touched upon this subject elsewhere, I cannot stress enough the logic of the approach. Leasing property to the company is so much simpler than lending the company money and then having to worry about security on the loan or fighting with other unsecured creditors in the case of loans made to the company or payments due for one thing or another.

Suppose a company with which you are favorably impressed asks you to invest equity money to build a plant. Tell them that instead of giving them the money, you will build a plant for them and lease it to them for a consideration which will include an ability to acquire an agreed upon interest in the company. Suppose the company wants to use the money for the development of a new process. Have all rights to the new process assigned to you in exchange for your money, and give the company back conditional rights to use the process for an interest in the company. One of the conditions might be for the company to be profitable or have a stated level of sales or net worth. Whatever the proposed use of proceeds, the investor can find elements to own. That ownership can be structured in such a manner as to make the benefits, as long as everything is going well and as projected, accrue to the company much as if the company had simply gotten the money from the investor and then itself acquired the assets.

The difference in the arrangement becomes apparent only when the company runs into trouble. In a troubled company, the burden of debts and other pressures tend to confuse and make difficult the life of the entrepreneur and any unsecured creditors. Having unencumbered title to tangible assets provides protection for an investor in such a situation. The investor in this position of strength has *options*, and it is this availability of options which permits private company investment survival and capital enhancement possibilities.

Much of commercial life is a zero-sum game in which for every winner there must be a loser, as in the commodity trading business. Things are not always that way, but they are frequently enough to make the investor aware that he is the one who must protect himself, since no one out there is going to do it for him. Anyone who doubts the reality of this should observe some creditors' meetings (particularly the first one) and witness an enlightening display of greed and fear, righteous indignation, and jousting for position and advantage.

ASSETS AS LOAN SECURITY FOR COMPANIES IN DEBT

Investors are frequently requested to advance funds to companies already in debt. Most often earlier lenders have acquired as protection the traditional asset classifications of the company such as property, plant, accounts receivable and inventory. In many cases, the lenders have also obtained the personal guarantees of the entrepreneur and, perhaps, even a pledge of all the shares of the company. Thus, the lack of available assets to secure a loan can be a major problem for new investors.

Another problem for investors in lending to companies already in debt is the possibility that the debtor will resist payment at the time the loan matures. It is also possible that other creditors will be claiming the same assets as the investor and that at the very least there will be a delay in collecting monies due, as well as an incremental expense of legal action.

The investor should always try to lend through the medium of asset acquisition and contributed use thereof with the thought that he will make a profit on the sale or subsequent use of the acquired property if the loan is not repaid.

One technique for avoiding the necessity of getting a "judgment note" (though that is not a bad idea for the investor) and of obtaining a claim on assets is to purchase them at the time the loan is entered into. The purchase can be made for a nominal amount and other good and valuable consideration—namely, the making of the loan. The assets purchased may include the right to use the name of the entrepreneur's company, his patent or the rights to it, exclusive rights to use his customer list, full distribution rights to his product, and the rights to any product improvement—the list can be as long as one's experience and imagination permits. Obviously, the entrepreneur will not be willing to sell these rights to the investor for a nominal amount unless he can also recapture them for a nominal consideration. Thus, the entrepreneur is given the right to reacquire these assets for the same sum as he was paid for them *if prior thereto the loan has been repaid.* A profit can be built into the arrangement by increasing the exercise price of the option with the passage of time, thereby providing the entrepreneur with an incentive for early repayment of the obligation. These techniques should not be considered foolproof and may be attacked by creditors. Therefore, whenever possible the contracts should be executed prior to there being any other creditors. His answer to the entrepreneur who questions the amount of the loan in relation to the value of the property is that the relative value is of no consequence *if the loan is repaid* as the entrepreneur has promised. To protect the entrepreneur from the possibility of the investor having his own financial problems which might prevent the exercise of the purchase option, an escrow agent or trust may be used.

In looking beyond traditional asset classifications, the investor may have to do his own creative thinking. I was asked once to provide funds for a heavily leveraged hotel project in Singapore. Having been told that every conceivable asset of the hotel was mortgaged, I proposed to the owner that I would provide funds through acquisition of two assets were they to be unencumbered. One was the elevators. My thought was that I could control all convenient access to the floors above ground level if my loan was not repaid, regardless of who had claim to all the other assets. Clearly, if anyone was going to operate the hotel, my claim would have to be satisfied. The second asset I wanted to acquire was the large neon sign on top of the hotel and unrestricted use of that sign. The owner was puzzled. Why did I want the sign? The name on the sign was very well known, being associated with more than 20 other hotels in Asia, and I told the owner that if my loan was not repaid, I intended to take the sign off the roof of the very imposing hotel and place it on top of a squatter's hut on the airport road, visible to all using the airport. As it happened, we were able to arrange a full refinancing of the property without my acquisition of either the elevators or the neon sign.

As with all techniques discussed in this book, the investor should check with his lawyer before proceeding. The laws of the land are frequently drafted to "protect" the borrower (and differ from state to state) and, therefore, may disadvantage the lender. In lending through the acquisition of assets, the investor must be certain of his rights to the title and use of the acquired asset. The same acquisition techniques can be used to gain or secure equity interests in houses and companies. The investor should ensure that the costs of registering title and the possible tax consequences are well understood by all concerned and paid for by the seller/borrower/entrepreneur.

Investor acquisition of assets, with a leaseback or license to the selling company, is frequently a good way for the investor to participate in the developing company. The lease payments can be geared to reflect revenue levels or unit throughput as well as the fixed minimum rental. A capital gain may also be anticipated if the terms are such that the company leasing the assets has an incentive to reacquire the assets at a premium price to avoid the payment of high and/or increasing lease payments.

USURY LAWS

"You charged me and I agreed to pay an amount that I now find to be too much, so I won't and don't have to pay back anything at all."

Usury laws, which vary from state to state, can frequently be accommodated by providing for the payment of services which the investor is prepared to offer and which are reasonable in terms of the size of the payments. The investor may also buy property from the company for a nominal consideration and lease it back to the company; of course, the investor has to be sure the property acquired is vital to the continuation of the business. Such vital items could include patent rights, customer lists, key pieces of equipment, property essential to the company, or the rights to certain developments of the company.

EXIT FORMULAS

Exit formulas or prearranged takeouts are the private company investor's equivalent to a prenuptial agreement. Their importance is probably the least understood and least focused upon element of informal investor dealmaking. Why is the recapture of the investor's funds so frequently left to chance? Just as it is hardly the most optimistic (though possibly realistic) of attitudes a loving couple demonstrates before marriage in executing a prenuptial agreement, perhaps many investors think of exit formulas as bad luck or self-fulfilling predictions of failure. There is no room for such queasiness in the business world. The investor must have the option of recapturing his funds under certain conditions.

What are those conditions? They are time- and/or progress-related. The investor, and perhaps the entrepreneur, should have a means of breaking the relationship on a least painful basis. Equity investments of course are being discussed—debt repayment scheduling is a different matter, although some of the techniques are similar in both areas.

As an approach to exit, the investor can (or be required to) tender or put to the company some percentage of the shares of the company held at a price which relates to either book value or a multiple of earnings or cash flow. Revenue levels can also be used as a determinative of value for shares repurchased or put. As previously indicated, the entrepreneur may wish to have a call at, say, a multiple of book value, but he should be required to have achieved some level of earnings or cash flow for the call to be exercised. In most cases, the investor should get, and not grant, the options.

An agreed upon percentage of a company's earnings can be dedicated to purchasing an agreed upon segment of securities issued by the company. Further, the company can also agree to use a portion of earnings for the redemption of preferred stock; this preferred stock can also be convertible or have common stock purchase warrants which are attached and which may be detachable initially or at a later stage.

Overall, the most effective exit formula is no formula at all, if there is in place a buy/sell agreement which permits either party—or perhaps only the investor—to initiate the offer to purchase. The recipient of the offer can either accept it or require the initiator to accept the same deal as he proposed.

It is important to remember that the existence of a binding agreement does not require its application, since the parties to it can modify it or cancel it at any time. The purpose of agreements protecting the investor is solely that of protection. Such agreements do not have to be put into effect. Just because one has a loaded shotgun in the closet does not mean one has to take it out and use it. One can, but one does not have to.

RIGHT OF FIRST REFUSAL

The investor should insist on a right of first refusal to reinvest in the company on the same terms, and up to an agreed upon amount, as any other subsequent investor making either a new or follow-on investment. The reason for the investor to insist on this right is that subsequent investors in the company will probably drive a harder bargain than will one of the original investors. Added to this is the fact that all investors seek good investment opportunities and, thus, the original investors should retain the right to make new investments. The entrepreneur will almost certainly not resist the investor's requirement for a right of first refusal.

However, Howard Stevenson of the Harvard Business School presents another point of view:

> An investor's right of first refusal very often prevents good negotiation with a new buyer. The buyer is put in the position of having to spend his time and effort on what he knows may end up as the investor's deal. A right of first refusal denigrates the value of any property. I think people forget that a preempted right to invest has a cost.

Recognizing the validity of Professor Stevenson's observation could cause an investor to insist only upon a right to participate in new financings to the prorated extent of his original interest. Professor Stevenson's point is, and was, more directed to the possibility of a sale of property than to financings.

Most new issue underwriters will ask for a right of first refusal as to future sale of securities by the company, and even by the company's shareholders. My advice to companies is not to give such a right, because the underwriter will probably do the deal without it and, hopefully, the company will grow sufficiently to be able to attract a larger and more prestigious underwriter in the future. Also, why should the company commit itself to deal with a firm which may itself change and be controlled by different owners, which may suffer financial or reputational reverses, which may simply be less attractive than another underwriter who then wants the company's business? As the investor will probably have to agree to the terms of the underwriting, he has a veto, which can be used effectively at times.

BUY/SELL OPTION

I always insist on a buy/sell option in situations where I am providing funds to an individual or buying into a deal and where I will end up with an equal number of shares as, or an interest of equal proportion to, the other player(s) in the game. The buy/sell option is indeed a thing of beauty in that it keeps all players honest.

It works as follows. The initiator can at any time (or at a previously agreed upon time—for example, two years into the deal) propose the purchase of the other participant's stock on any terms and for any price. The other participant then has the right, within a specified period of time, either to accept the offer or to compel the initiator to sell to him all of his interest on the terms and at the price the initiator originally proposed. A six-month delay in closing (with extreme penalty for nonclosing) may be provided to give a less wealthy party time to arrange financing of the transaction, if necessary. Of course, if the recipient of the offer chooses to take over the property on the terms bid, he can elect a shorter period to closing.

The buy/sell option's great attraction is its mutuality and symmetry. What's fair for one is fair for the other. Having said all that, I must admit to never having used a buy/sell option in the form in which it appeared in the contract. Since both sides know that the option is there, they negotiate around it and propose something that does not permit or require it to be put into effect.

Years ago, while negotiating a deal with COMSAT, for one of the companies I owned, I proposed a buy/sell option and the financial vice president involved said, "Oh yes, a Texas option." I have not heard it called that before or since, but whatever you call it, it remains an effective safety valve in many 50/50 deals.

DO THE DEAL—THEN INVESTIGATE

Jack Whitehead negotiates the deal before investigating the opportunity. As one of the very shrewdest venture capital investors, he regards time as one of his most valuable assets. In order to avoid wastefully investing his own time and that of his associates, he establishes a preliminary understanding with the entrepreneur before the time-consuming process of investigation is put in motion.

The nonprofessional investor should be aware that many entrepreneurs seek funding from more than one investor at a time. On occasion, an entrepreneur will also "shop" the deal finalized between him and an investor with other potential funding sources. Whitehead and the entrepreneur agree on the basic terms of the deal "should Whitehead Associates decide to proceed within 30 days." In other words, the entrepreneur offers Whitehead a 30-day option in return for Whitehead's seriously investigating the deal. Of course, only a person with the experience, knowledge, and reputation of Jack Whitehead could (1) know by limited exposure to an investment opportunity and only a few meetings with the principals if the deal has sufficient potential to make the investigation effort worthwhile, and (2) legitimately persuade the entrepreneur to tie up his deal for 30 days without a commitment.

One benefit to the entrepreneur is that other venture capital investors will view any deal on which Whitehead has "bid" as being sufficiently attractive to pay slightly, or even significantly, more than what was originally offered.

A slightly different approach designed to achieve the same result as the prenegotiated deal (which the less experienced investor in private companies may not be ready to make) is as follows. The applicant for funds agrees to pay the investor's cost of investigation and review if the investor in turn "offers" him a deal, within certain broad parameters, within a specified time period, and this deal is then rejected by the entrepreneur. In a way, this is a better arrangement for the entrepreneur, since he is still free to continue his money-raising efforts while the investor is doing his research. All that the entrepreneur is committed to do is pay for, and perhaps purchase, the work product of the investor's investigation if the investor decides to go forward and the entrepreneur has found a better deal. Of course, an entrepreneur's simple agreement to pay an "investigation fee" to the investor may be sufficient insurance for the investor.

Entrepreneurs must beware of the payment of investigation and commitment fees, and frequently prepaid expenses, to con men who masquerade as investors or financial agents and who have neither the intention nor ability to make investments. Blind ads in the classified sections of publications offering money on terms which appear to be overly generous may be bait for unsophisticated or overenthusiastic entrepreneurs.

Certain underwriters of speculative public offerings also make money by requiring the up front payment of fees "to cover expenses" without a commitment to provide funding for the entrepreneur. This practice is also found in the case of some "best efforts" commitments if that is not a conflict in terms. My problem with this unattractive practice is not related to legitimate underwriter expense reimbursement but rather the profit element frequently bundled into the arrangement. Specifically, the company agrees to the payments being for "non-accountable" expenses and that leaves room for the functioning of rampant greed. Higher quality investment banking firms do not usually have this up front payment requirement as they are dealing with established companies. There is a positive correlation between the fairness of the arrangements and the strength of the securities issuing company. Such is the way of the financial world, and it should surprise no one that weaker companies pay more for less.

REFINANCING AND ITS NEAR INEVITABILITY 9

ARE THE INVESTOR'S POCKETS DEEP ENOUGH?

In creating his original business plan, the entrepreneur frequently under-projects the amount of money the proposed company will need. Being a born optimist, he does not allow sufficient room in the business plan projection for the almost inevitable delays. The entrepreneur is also aware that the more money he asks from the investor, the less likely the deal is to get financed. He realizes too that in exchange for large sums of money, his own interest in the company will be diminished. The entrepreneur projecting a need for a million dollars may suggest that he get half the stock of the company and the investor the other half, whereas the entrepreneur projecting a need for $5 million clearly cannot suggest with the same degree of confidence that he should get half the stock with little or no investment. Thus, there is a strong tendency for the entrepreneur to minimize continually the amount of money that is going to be necessary in the development of his project.

A consultant, perhaps an accountant, can be of assistance to both the investor and entrepreneur in studying the basis for business plan projections as they relate to the need for additional investment.

Arthur Little told me, "When it comes to refinancing, the investor has to let the entrepreneur know he is someone who must be reckoned with. Then, the entrepreneur will be willing to negotiate and make a bargain. But the investor should not be objectionably tough with him; otherwise, he will go elsewhere first the next time."

If the investor puts in only a quarter of the funds he has available for private company investment, he most likely will find himself in a position to adequately refinance his holdings in a new company. Thus, and investor who sets aside 20 percent of his available investment funds for the purposes of private company investment uses only 5 percent of his available investment funds in his initial investment in the new company. He thereby avoids the principle mistake made by many investors—getting in too deep too early.

WHEN TO SAY NO

For an investor trying to salvage part of his investment in a situation that is not working out as anticipated by the entrepreneur, the critical decision is when to stop the game. Who must take the initiative? If things are allowed to drift, a point will be reached where the payroll cannot be met or suppliers cannot be paid, bringing the game to a stop. However, there is almost certainly a point prior to this when most dispassionate observers would realize that the game has to end. This is the point where the probabilities of failure far outweigh the probabilities of success and is certainly the latest time at which the investor should begin to terminate his risk exposure and view investment salvage as his primary and overriding objective.

Left to his own devices, the entrepreneur will typically run the company right up to the moment they take out the telephones. After all, he has enormous investments of ego in the project and frequently cannot bring himself to admit to himself or others the failure which is so apparent to those not involved. There is likely to be much conflict between the investor and the entrepreneur who still believes in the project and in his ability to pull it off. Here comes into play the investor protection mechanism of having a preponderance of the board of directors, of having a proxy from the entrepreneur on whatever stock he possesses, and of having the contractual right to sell or terminate the business.

When the call for more money comes, the first question the private company investor must ask himself is whether this is a chance for genuine reinvestment or simply a financial contribution toward delaying almost inevitable failure. The answer should be clear. The investor should only invest more money when the balance of evidence suggests success, and this success should be achievable with the amount of money the investor is prepared to invest anew in the situation, as opposed to only the possibility of the new investment bringing success. I suggest making a list of the possible good things and bad things that may occur within the period of time the new investment permits.

In the absence of clear indications of failure—such as the fact that the invention did not work or the contract did not come through—management often comes to believe that the only obstacle to success is the reluctant investor. Management may readily admit that they have incorrectly projected their need for money but point out that success is within their grasp with a new infusion of funds. If only the investor would have confidence in them.... He may very well *cause* the failure of the project by his fears and stinginess. Nothing has gone wrong, in management's view. It's simply that they have run out of money. At such a point, the investor must realize that, in all probability, neither he nor management has the ability any longer to make dispassionate judgments regarding the situation.

Yet, the investor has to make a determination. He must deliberately seek to make a rational, rather than emotional, decision. One mechanistic approach would be: If the management of the company cannot persuade any investor not already involved in the company that an investment should be made, be it for only a part of the money that is needed, then the present investor probably should simply take his loss, or cause the loss (if that is the way management presents it) by failing to put in the additional funds.

Such subsequent or involuntary investment, made in part for the purpose of vindicating earlier judgment, is frequently the worst kind of investment—one which causes the investor disproportionate pain, because he is in further than he wanted to be and because it seldom works out. The original investor is probably best served in not investing more money in situations where the required reinvestment is caused by disappointing results.

The best kind of reinvestment to make in a private company is that which is required because the company has grown either according to plan, or better than planned, and needs the money for expansion and delivery of goods and services. This kind of second-stage investment is what all venture capitalists seek; indeed, some venture capital organizations are only interested in making second-stage investments, because so many companies die after the initial investment without ever getting to the second-stage level.

AN INCIDENT

The entrepreneur had already started, using his own resources, a company manufacturing office partitions. Prospects were bright, but he was having some cash flow problems and needed an infusion of new money. He asked the investor to guarantee a $25,000 bank loan in exchange for a 40 percent holding in the company, with an agreement that the company would buy back that 40 percent holding in two years for $25,000. The investor said to himself that all he had to do was guarantee the note, put no actual money in the company and collect $25,000 in two years' time—a 50 percent annual return on money he did not even have to invest!

When the investor went to the bank, he found he had to put up $25,000 worth of Treasury bills as collateral. He signed the loan guarantee without worrying about the clauses that said he was also guaranteeing interest on the $25,000 loan and costs of collection. The business began to fail, and the investor decided to cut his losses by getting out. At this point, the bank refused to demand full repayment of the loan, thereby shutting down the business, as the investor requested. The bank had made a guaranteed loan, was collecting interest, and had no incentive to terminate the arrangement. The investor found himself liable for $50,000, double his original guarantee, when the company finally closed.

Dan Lufkin says,

> What hurts people is that they make a distinction between a guarantee and actual investment of money. They think it's much easier to make a guarantee, that it's not money out of their pockets. Never sign a guarantee without having in mind that you are signing a check. And as you would when writing a check, look closely at what you sign.

REALISM IN CASH FLOW PROJECTIONS

The entrepreneur and management team who lack a great deal of experience in projecting the time period, and, therefore, funds required to reach and maintain positive cash flow are in for a difficult task. The investor should be aware of their level of expertise, and he must remember that most things take longer than originally anticipated and that this extra time is going to cost money in salaries, rent, insurance premiums, and so forth. The chief cause for the underestimation of monies that will ultimately be required by a new company is the inability or unwillingness of the entrepreneur, in preparing his business plan and its associated projections, to make allowances for an adequate passage of time.

The investor can take a mechanistic approach by substantially increasing the amount of estimated expenses and pushing back the date of income receipt expectation, or he can halve the amount of income he expects to receive. However, none of these approaches are truly satisfactory. The investor, therefore, must study and question all of the key numbers in the projections themselves.

It is not wise simply to look at the profit figure projected for the fifth year, assume the company will be worth, say, a multiple of 10 times earnings at that point in time, and feel that a position acquired today at a fraction of that sum is an investment bargain. I suspect that this is a normal series of events with many informal investors. They take the highest earnings figure, apply a price/earnings multiple to it, and then regard their investment as the price of admission to that wonderfully high figure.

The investor can evaluate a situation only by taking the time to understand the numbers generated by the entrepreneur. Are the salaries full and complete? Is the office or plant space requirement realistic in size and what has to be paid for it? Are professional fees realistically portrayed? Has an adequate time allowance been made with provisions for delay? Have interest and financing charges been adequately provided for? Will sales be as projected in the time frame projected? Are sales commissions and discounts adequately reflected?

I suggest that the investor spend a minimum of several hours with the entrepreneur and have him defend, month by month and year by year, the projections presented. The investor could have someone, perhaps, more knowledgeable than himself attend the meeting with him to question the entrepreneur further on each of the numbers used to reach the projected bottom-line result. Notes should be taken by the investor and his representative during this meeting. These projections are really the inducement to make the investment, and it is important for the investor to have a record not only of the projections but of how they were put together by the entrepreneur. These notes may be of great assistance to the investor later in strengthening areas of weakness in the company and in reaching reinvestment decisions.

UNDERESTIMATING FINANCIAL NEEDS

All investors and entrepreneurs would like to make a lot of money by having to use only a little. Entrepreneurs in making projections, and investors in reviewing and evaluating them, often permit the wish to be the parent of the thought. The making of money usually requires time and money, and time is money.

One unpleasant result of underestimating the need for finance in a new company is that the need for more money will arise before the company has achieved clear success and that, therefore, the new investor providing the needed funds will impose terms unattractive to the previous investors. Also, it is at the time of such an unexpected refinancing requirement that the relationship between entrepreneur and investors is most likely to become strained. The only solution to this problem is to do a better job of estimating the financial needs of the company.

The entrepreneur and investor, once involved, must provide for the needs of the company, since estimating them alone is not sufficient. The company's future financial requirements can be met by pledges from investors or from others pending certain developments or achievements. Whatever arrangement is used, the predictable needs of the company should be provided for during the initial period of buoyant optimism, before reality sets in. It is always easier for the entrepreneur to raise funding before he has a shortfall on projections to explain away.

ACTIONS PLANNED IF SCHEDULE SLIPS

As anyone who has been through the military understands, contingency plans are vital to ultimate success and, frequently, to survival. Although no one expects things to work out exactly as planned, most people find it difficult to make constructive alternative plans. For the investor, contingency planning should focus on assuring himself that his control and influence in the company will increase, rather than decrease, as problems develop. With increasing failure of original plans to materialize, the role of the investor should increasingly change from that of observer to that of controlling factor. This shift in the balance of power, if it does not save the company, can greatly reduce loss to the investor.

A contingency plan is normally made to anticipate a lower than projected level of revenues and profits but can equally well be made to anticipate a level of revenues greater than had been projected, resulting in a strain on production facilities and delivery mechanisms or service aspects of the business. Contingency plans include cutting back overhead unless revenues reach a certain point and closing a plant or aspects of an operation if revenues fail to reach a certain point. Contingency planning really involves scheduling the use of resources, which is perhaps what business is all about, in that it is the meshing of resource and opportunity.

CONTINGENCY COMMITMENTS OF OTHER PARTICIPANTS

In some companies, investments are staged. Sometimes, they are staged simply by time, and this is frequently the case with research and development limited-partnership tax shelters. Perhaps, a third of the money goes in at the time of the original investment, a third is due in January of the following year, and the final third January of the next year. The wise entrepreneur seeks a letter of credit to represent the commitment of the investor, since the entrepreneur must assure himself as to the availability of the committed funds as scheduled. The wise investor keeps a string on his investments and has some sort of trigger, or measure, which warrants the incremental payments, such as the completion of a development, the attainment of a level of sales, or the obtaining of a customer order—something to evidence progress. Should the investor become dissatisfied with the progress of the enterprise, he may refuse, if performance standards have been previously agreed upon, to make his incremental payment.

In a company where there is a group of investors, one investor who fails to provide the monies committed, for whatever reason, can jeopardize the position of all the other investors. Therefore, the investors should have an agreement whereby failure to perform as committed, which in itself places a burden on the other investors, entails the immediate loss of interest of the defaulting investor. Of course, unless agreed otherwise, the defaulting investor has liability for damages to the other investors.

Perhaps, the most equitable way of handling such a default is that the defaulting investor gives up that portion of his equity, or whatever form the original investment has taken, to the extent needed by the remaining investors to obtain a new investor to stand in his place. In other words, if the original investor has a 5 percent interest in the company and defaults on a $20,000 incremental payment that would have entitled him to another 5 percent of the company, the remaining investors should, by agreement, have the right to use part or all of the original 5 percent holding as an inducement to a new investor. In order for the investors to avoid having to threaten or plead with a defaulting investor at the time money is needed, contingency arrangements should be worked out in advance.

NEGOTIATING THE INVESTMENT

10

TECHNIQUES OF NEGOTIATION

I do not intend to give advice such as "Always sit with your back to the window or light source" or "Arrive first at the meeting and take the chair farthest from the door so that your opponent has to walk to you" or "Put your watch on the table to let your opponent know that you have only a limited amount of time for this matter" or "Spread out your papers to intimidate your opponent with the depth of your study and knowledge of the matter." Incidentally, *Power,* by Michael Korda,[1] is a very funny book on negotiating and power plays. It should be read with Woody Allen in mind as the practitioner of what is being advised.

That the other party is an *opponent* is the key word and thought of most how-to-negotiate books. While this is always true to some extent, an investor in private companies must not lose sight of the fact that he is entering into a partnership and will probably not be able to extricate himself (or his money) unless it works out well for all concerned. Because of the intensely personal nature of most private company investments, it is a mis-

---

[1] New York: Random House, 1975.

take for the investor to think in terms of buying a security. He should, however, know the elements he must have in a deal to make it work for him. The making of a list of such points can be helpful.

A technique of negotiating with entrepreneurs I have found to be effective is to view and, perhaps, present yourself, the prospective investor, as an intermediary or investment banker responsible for investing your own funds. In other words, think of representing your interests as a professional and not of being the investor. Think of your being held accountable by the owner of the money for the deal you are negotiating and subsequent developments as they affect the company and, therefore, the investment. Think of having to answer to the owner of the money as to why you made the investment and why you permitted the terms as they developed. Note the use of the term *permitted* in reference to contractual terms. Since the investor does not have to do the deal, any concessions he has made during the negotiation are there only because he has permitted them to be. He must always remember that he is not required to invest, that there will be other opportunities for him to employ his dollars. He should remember the golden rule of business: The man with the gold makes the rules.

The investor must never allow himself to be hurried into a deal. He should beware any deal which must be closed at short notice, remembering how much easier it is to get into a deal than out of one.

In response to a question of when life begins, a priest said "at the moment of conception," a minister said "at birth when the first breath is taken," and a rabbi said life begins "when the dog dies and the children leave home and go to college." There is no question as to when an investor's involvement and risk exposure begin. For an investor, the life of his investment starts *only* at the closing. All of the negotiations that go into the decision-making process are unimportant, in terms of risk exposure, until that point where the investor commits himself.

BEING REPRESENTED IN NEGOTIATION

Several schools of thought exist on whether the investor should negotiate directly with the entrepreneur or should use a representative. If the investor uses an attorney, the entrepreneur is likely to use one also—so that at least four people are now involved in the negotiation, which will be expensive and take a longer time to complete. If the investor and entrepreneur can agree upon a single attorney, he can play the role of arbitrator in working out a fair agreement.

Needless to say, it is important to have an attorney put on paper the agreement reached between the principals; the attorney also ensures that the principals understand the consequences of their agreement as to possible developments in the future. After all, much of the boilerplate in a contract is a result of experience in prior transactions, and few people are better qualified in this regard than seasoned lawyers. The fact that the boilerplate typically favors the side that prepares and presents the contract is something which should be remembered by the investor.

Apart from the attorney benefiting the investor through his experience, the use of an attorney to negotiate a deal can also give the investor a second bite at the apple in that the investor can moderate or change what the attorney has negotiated or enhance his position by insisting that certain terms be renegotiated. However, the investor must bear in mind that in private company investment, he is in effect entering into a partnership, and it may not be to his ultimate advantage to deal in a manner which might be considered unfair by his future partner.

The following opinions were given independently.

Howard Stevenson said,

> An attorney's fundamental role in negotiating contracts is to make sure that the deal which is agreed upon is the deal which in fact gets down on paper—that there are no time bombs sitting there in what has been termed *just boilerplate*. Every investor has to remember that boilerplate is put in documents because it closes loopholes in favor of the one who put it in, which can have important consequences. Anytime someone says to me "It's only boilerplate," I grow wary.
>
> An investor who uses an attorney as a negotiator will generally wind up in a much more adversarial position than he would if he had used a neutral middleman or negotiated for himself.

Harold Bigler, of Bigler Investment Management Company in Hartford, said,

> Rather than have attorneys negotiate on their behalf, I think the investor and the entrepreneur should do their best to understand what it is they want to accomplish, put that in writing and then go to a lawyer to have him draw up a term sheet. It is a mistake to get lawyers in the negotiations too early, because you'll get lost in trivia.

And Howard Arvey, my friend of many years and senior partner of one of Chicago's most competent and powerful law firms—Arvey, Hodes, Costello & Burman, said,

> For an upcoming negotiation, I recommend that the investor go over the base parameters with his attorney or consultant or advisor and review the transactions principle by principle. If the investor is the type of person capable of negotiating for himself, then he should do so, after first having gone over the ground in consultation.

The investor is not striving to strike the hardest or toughest bargain. He is striving to create a fair deal, but fair favoring himself: Fair favoring the investor means that his interests are protected during periods of disappointment.

It has been suggested that any experienced businessman, or indeed any intelligent individual, can serve as an umpire in a negotiation. An investment banker or a professional dealmaker, neither burdened nor blessed by a law degree, may serve both parties equally well. Nevertheless, an attorney should always be used to prepare the final documents. Appendix L shows a term sheet used by Whitehead Associates.

Howard Stevenson added, "Negotiation is always easier with some sort of middle person. He helps avoid a clash of egos, and such clashes are a characteristic difficulty of negotiations. The role of a middleman can be very important here."

WARRANTIES FROM PROMOTERS

One of the first things an investor should ask the promoter or finder of a private company investment opportunity is how much of the deal the promoter is taking himself. And if the promoter is not himself investing in the deal, the investor should ask why not. The investor should also seek terms equal to, or superior in protection of capital than, those of the promoter.

Promoters and agents of deals need the ability to make their opportunities sound attractive, and one of the simplest ways to attract an investor to a deal is to make it sound like a sure thing. If the promoter of a deal plays down its risk to the investor, the latter is entitled to suggest that the promoter give him a warranty in exchange for his cash investment. For example, an investor is told that if he invests $200,000 in a company, it will earn $100,000 next year and $200,000 the following year. This clearly is an investment opportunity that could be structured into an attractive investment—whether it is a good investment will depend on the deal the investor negotiates. The investor should ask the promoter for an affirmative warranty regarding the $100,000 guaranteed profit the next year. If this is not forthcoming, the investor can test the promoter by asking for a lesser amount, say $25,000, guaranteed by the promoter and undertaken as a personal liability. My guess is that the finder will decline the opportunity to warrant any earnings, and there may be a message in that for the investor.

In the case of the entrepreneur being also the promoter or finder, the investor could ask for a warranty in the form of additional stock. Suppose the investor's $200,000 investment originally entitles him to a 25 percent holding in the company; the warranty might provide the investor with an additional 50 percent holding if the $100,000 "guaranteed" profit next year fails to materialize.

Another form of warranty is one which requires the guarantor to make up the shortfall to the company rather than directly to the investor. Thus, if the shortfall amounts to $50,000, the guarantor, instead of writing a check to the investor, is required to buy $50,000 worth of common shares in the company. This assumes the investor holds a senior convertible security which has anti-dilution protection. The advantage of this form of warranty is that it provides the company with additional working capital. The disadvantage is that it provides the guarantor with a block of shares which may be a nuisance in the event votes become important. Of course, nonvoting shares might be issued to the guarantor. A warranty requiring the entrepreneur or promoter to lend money, subordinated to interests held by the investor, interest free to the company, in an amount equal to the shortfall, may be even more advantageous to the investor than one requiring the promoter to buy equity.

The forms that warranties take vary enormously from industry to industry with the financial circumstances of the entrepreneur, with the size of the company, whether it is early or late in a company's development, and so on.

Most of these warranties intended to be protective of the investor's capital should disappear when the company becomes profitable or when it has attained its projected level of activity for two or three consecutive periods, since it would not be fair to have the investor protected from unforeseen developments forever. In my view, the investor should be protected from unforeseen developments, vis-à-vis those holding promotional (not paid for with money) interests, only during the early stages in the development of a company.

It is easy for the promoter or entrepreneur to let his enthusiasm run away with him and persuade the investor that his project is a sure thing, almost risk free, with the result that the investor puts in more money than he can afford or even borrows funds in order to invest them. This is the scenario which is frequently the cause of much money being lost, perhaps unnecessarily so in many cases, by private company investors.

FEES

When a finder's fee for finding the investor is paid by a company, in effect the investor is paying the fee, or at least his proportionate share of it. The investor should not object to the company in which he is considering an investment paying a finder's fee to someone who brought them to him so long as (1) the fee is reasonable in terms of the total, and (2) the fee does not significantly increase the amount of money necessary for the investor to provide. For example, a company-paid fee of 20 percent of the investment, leaving the company only $80,000 out of a $100,000 investment, would certainly be looked upon unfavorably by any experienced investor. Likewise, a fee that gives the finder (who performs only that service) a 20 percent holding in the company, compared to the private company investor's 50 percent and management's 30 percent, is clearly unreasonable. Of the reasonable standards of fairness for a finder's fee, the five, four, three, two, one formula has stood the test of time: 5 percent of the first million, 4% of the second million, 3% of the third million, and so forth.

A distinction should be made between the simple finder and advisors or consultants to the company. My use of the term *finder* refers strictly to the introductory agent between the entrepreneur and the money and not to the individual who is providing other services on an ongoing basis to the company or who may have provided services to the company before the financing. That individual is really just another part of the management team that the investor is acquiring.

The consulting fee charged the issuing company in many low-priced new-issue underwritings is frequently not a consulting fee at all, but rather an element of incremental underwriter profit taking the form of a contractual relationship between the National Association of Securities Dealers member underwriter and the issuing company. I believe it is outrageous for underwriters to propose that they or their designees be paid, say, $4,000 per month for a period of 36 months after a deal has been completed. This is frequently a way of attempting to avoid NASD regulations that limit the amount which can be charged by an underwriter in a public offering. It is unfair to the investors and equally unfair to the management of the company. I strongly believe that, between the underwriter and the company, there should be a strict limitation on, or possibly even exclusion of, contractual commitments entered into prior to the receipt of funds which require services to be rendered after the receipt of funds.

If, in fact, the management of the company wants the advisory services of the individual or firm which has been responsible for having raised the money for the company, they can acquire those services or contract for their provision after they have the money in hand and not as a condition of their receipt. I suspect that few companies would otherwise retain these services on the very steep terms described in many new-issue offering documents.

Incidentally, investment bankers and intermediaries frequently charge on-going management consulting fees to companies for which they raise funds from private investors. Investors, therefore, should be aware of all the profit elements which may affect the judgment of the party recommending the investment to the investor.

EXPENSES OF REVIEW AND NEGOTIATION

Investigating investment opportunities in private companies is an expensive pursuit. One needs lawyers, accountants, and technical experts. The question of who pays for the investigation is best divided into the two subsidiary questions of who pays for it in deals that close and who pays for it in deals that do not close. The investor is always best served by an agreement that the company will pay the expenses of investigating the deal and his attorney's fee. This is becoming much more usual than has been the case.

In the case of a deal that closes, it, perhaps, should be agreed that the company pay the costs of negotiation and investigation, considering these expenses to be part of the deal. In the absence of the company's undertaking to pay these expenses, the investor should probably increase his expectation of the amount he is to receive from the company, either in equity or some other form.

In the case of a deal that does not close—the assumption being that it does not close because the investor has decided not to go forward—certain expenses should be borne by the company. For instance, if the company makes a projection of earnings of $100,000 and the investor, in analyzing all the projections, reaches the conclusion that the earnings projection is absurd and without basis, then this investor should receive reimbursement for his expenses if he is clearly in the right. Certainly, the investor should be contractually entitled to reimbursement if any material statements made to the prospective investor are found to be inaccurate.

Most frequently these days, underwriters of low-priced issues require a company for which they have not issued securities before to present payment in advance for a certain percentage of the underwriter's compensation and to be responsible for all the underwriter's expenses. In one case I recently negotiated, a $25,000 payment was expected at the same time as the underwriter's nonbinding letter of intent was executed; this sum was simply to cover the underwriter's legal fees involved in the early stages of prospectus preparation and the underwriter's "due diligence" research.

In the case where an investor retains an advisor or a consultant, the fact that the company pays the expenses does not mean that the company selects the professional retained to assist the investor. The company is simply the one he sends the bill to. The consultant or advisor can have only one master, and that must be the investor. However, if the company pays the bill for a feasibility study and the investor elects not to proceed, clearly, the feasibility study should become the property of the company. They then will have the right to use the study again as they see fit and as is permitted by its author.

WHEN TO SPEND ON INVESTIGATION

The costs of investigating a private company for the purpose of investment are high and may vary little in relation to the size of the company. Thus, investigation of a small investment costs about the same as investigation of a big one, which is one of the reasons why venture capitalists shy away from small deals. The investor who sees a high flow of deals cannot afford to investigate more than a small percentage of them, since each serious investigation can easily cost him a minimum of $5,000–7,000.

The wise investor waits until all other elements of the deal are in place before actually spending any real money on the investigation—that is, the investor should have already made up his mind, on the basis of other factors, to go ahead if the investigation results turn out to be favorable. It is reasonable for the investor at this point to seek an agreement from the entrepreneur that if the entrepreneur cancels the deal from this point on, the entrepreneur should pay the costs of the investor's investigation. If the deal is closed and the investment made, then it is an open question as to who pays for the investigation. Typically, the business pays, which, of course, amounts to the investor indirectly paying some of his own expenses.

WHAT IF . . .

All investors, and most particularly private company investors, should understand that anything which can go wrong, will go wrong. Especially when it comes to keeping to a schedule.

Therefore, the compilation of a "what if" list of things which can go wrong can be gone over, item by item, by the investor and entrepreneur. The corrective actions agreed upon should find their way into the shareholders' agreement or memorandum of understanding in order that they may be implemented if the circumstances arise. Not all contingencies can be envisioned, and one certainly does not wish to have a team of lawyers preparing a 100-page document. This is meant as nothing more than a suggestion that it is constructive for investor and entrepreneur to try to look forward into the future together. Anything agreed upon can later be changed with the consent of all parties. The investor should not be afraid to get it on paper. Even an informal note or memo of an agreement, initialed by both parties, is better than no "paper" agreement at all.

The entrepreneur's reaction to these questions, or others like them, will provide the investor with insights into that entrepreneur's personality. How the entrepreneur handles the stress of answering "what if" questions can provide the investor with insights as to how he will handle the stress of being faced with a real-life problem. In fact, the investor should keep in mind that the entrepreneur will probably make better decisions in the simulation than he will in real life. If he cannot respond intelligently to the following sort of questions, in all probability he will not be able to handle such problems.

1. What if the company fails to achieve projected results for four consecutive months (or quarters or years)?

2. What if the product on which the business depends cannot be produced at anything like the cost anticipated?

3. What if certain executives are found to be incompetent?

4. What if the investor is unwilling or unable to fulfill future funding committments to the company?

5. What if the chief executive officer dies or becomes incapacitated? Incapacitation must be defined to the satisfaction of both parties. Is a stroke incapacitating? Is alcoholism? What about a spinal injury that keeps the CEO in a hospital for more than 3–6 months? What about a psychiatric report showing advanced paranoia (not an uncommon affliction of both entrepreneurs and private company investors)?

6. What if the company is sued for patent infringement and counsel advises that the company's case is not strong?

7. What if three of the top engineers or scientists on whom the company depends leave to start their own competitive company?

8. What if a competitor makes a bid for the company? At what price and under what conditions will the investor and entrepreneur agree to sell out? (A buy/sell agreement can resolve this.)

9. What if the financing promised by the bank (or underwriter) fails to materialize? What fallback financing positions exist, in terms of both source and the deal, which might be acceptable under the worst conditions? How much interest can the company really afford and remain a viable business entity? What is the maximum amount of equity that can be given up as a sweetener and still leave enough to justify the participation of the investor or entrepreneur or both.

10. What if the plant burns down or a flood sweeps the office records away? What other natural disasters can be jointly imagined and planned for?

11. What if a divorce takes place and either the investor or the entrepreneur is faced with a hostile ex-spouse as major interest holder? Do shares become nonvoting in the hands of an ex-spouse? What about widows? Does the control of the company change, or only the profit participation, with change in personal circumstances of the investor or entrepreneur?

12. What if the investor (or entrepreneur) files personal bankruptcy?

13. What if embezzlement is discovered? Is it company policy that where a law is broken, the authorities are informed?

14. What if a union attempts to organize the workers?

15. What if a competing company becomes available for purchase?

16. What if the use of drugs by executives or workers becomes prevalent?

17. What if supplies of raw materials become hard to obtain?

18. What if a competing company already has some of the dire problems being considered possible for the new company?

19. What if an underwriter suggests taking the company public?

20. What if a competitor has a problem with production or integrity of executives? Will the new company publicize the problems of its competitors?

21. What if the entrepreneur intentionally exceeds budgeted expenses?

CHECKS AND BALANCES

After the entrepreneur has presented the company budget to the investor, and the investor has approved it, the question remains of who will ensure that the budget will be adhered to. One answer is monitoring by the investor of all major expenditures and of all borrowings. As suggested elsewhere, the investor can have the right to co-sign or at least review all company checks made out for more than a certain amount, for example, $1,000. The entrepreneur should not have the right to borrow additional funds without the investor's prior approval.

The initial budget approved by the investor may have to be changed to reflect changed business conditions. The investor should retain the right of approval of all budget changes over a certain amount.

WHO SPEAKS FIRST?

I usually insist that the other party in a negotiation set forth their side of the deal first. Whoever speaks first is merely suggesting an initial point of departure. He may not realize this, but that is all it amounts to. For me, it is mandatory that the entrepreneur put out on the table what he thinks the deal consists of and what he thinks his relationship with the investor should be. This then becomes the point of departure for the investor to improve upon.

This way the investor finds out quickly what the entrepreneur's parameters are. If the entrepreneur is overestimating the value of his company by 50 percent, perhaps he and the investor can solve their differences through discussion and deal structure. But, if the entrepreneur is overestimating his company's value by 500 percent, it would probably be a waste of time for the investor to discuss it with him. Rather than hurting the entrepreneur's feelings by speaking his mind, the investor is better off sending him to speak with other investors, telling him to come back after he has had some specific offers.

A DIALOGUE

ENTREPRENEUR: I've no money but I've put a lot of time and energy into this project.

INVESTOR: Certainly, you have. Just as I've put a lot of time and energy into making the money you need for your project. So I don't think your prior effort is any more significant than mine. But I recognize that this business is your idea and that there would be no deal if it were not for your efforts. How much money do you need?

ENTREPRENEUR: $150,000 for a year.

INVESTOR: Why don't we do this then—I'll take 80 percent of the company and you'll take 20 percent and I'll lend $150,000 to the company. The day that you repay me my money, if it's within the next fifteen months, our positions will reverse. You'll own 80 percent of the company and I'll own 20 percent. Does that sound fair?

ENTREPRENEUR: [*Pause*] What happens if the schedule slips a bit?

INVESTOR: You said you wanted the money for a year. I've already given you fifteen months—three extra months. What do you mean by the schedule slipping a bit? Give me the number of months.

ENTREPRENEUR: Maybe two years instead of one.

INVESTOR: In your presentation of the enterprise to me, you said I'd get my money back in a year. That's what I based my thinking on. Now you're saying two years . . .

ENTREPRENEUR: I'll pay you interest the second year. Maybe both years.

INVESTOR: That isn't always a fair trade. How are you going to get me paid? I think I should have some form of guarantee. Initially, you will own 20 percent of the company, and I will put in $150,000. Can you guarantee $30,000 of that personally.

ENTREPRENEUR: After two years, you will have all your money back and have 20 percent of the stock. I won't have all my time and energy back.

INVESTOR: Isn't your 80 percent holding going to be worth a great deal of money then?

ENTREPRENEUR: Yes, I guess it should be.

Note how the entrepreneur was attracted by the symmetry of the investor's deal, which may or may not have turned out to be fair. In dealmaking, symmetry frequently gives the appearance of fairness and can result in increased equity for the investor.

Of course, the two-year deal, even with interest payments in the second year and a $30,000 guarantee, is not nearly as attractive as, though it may be more realistic than, the one-year deal. Therefore, a greater equity retention by the investor would seem fair.

AN ENTREPRENEUR'S UNREALISTIC OFFER

ENTREPRENEUR: I need $50,000 to establish my restaurant business, and I'll contribute my services free for a year.

INVESTOR: But that's not a good deal for you. How can you live without income for a year? Since you would need at least $30,000 to survive for a year, your offer indicates to me that you already have at least this amount in a bank or in your wife's name or whatever. Yet, here you come asking me for money. If it's such a good deal, why aren't you putting your own money into it?

ENTREPRENEUR: I have no money. My wife works. We'll live on her income.

INVESTOR: Your joint income will be reduced for that year. Are you sure that you're one of those very remarkable people who can go back to living on much less than what they earned the previous year?

The investor must be warned against the entrepreneur who is contributing his services for free or making other offers the investor considers too generous, because this can lead to a wholly unrealistic set of financial projections. A business must be viewed on the basis that the investor is paying a market price for all the necessary elements of the business. The investor must be able to lure a replacement for the entrepreneur should he die or become disabled.

WHEN THE ENTREPRENEUR THINKS HE CAN FIND A BETTER DEAL

ENTREPRENEUR: I have to consider looking for someone else who will give me the money I need in exchange for a smaller amount of equity than you demand.

INVESTOR: Go right ahead. By the way, how many people have you gone to for money before you came to me?

ENTREPRENEUR: I went to the bank. They turned me down. After them, you're the first person I came to.

INVESTOR: It's very reasonable for you to want to have alternatives. Why don't we end this meeting now. I'm interested. You look to me like a winner. I think I'd like to be in business with you, but I must suggest that you go out and spend some time talking to other investors and other sources of money. Come back and talk to me when you find what other sources are available to you. Without your making these comparisons, you will probably think that whatever deal we might agree on now is unfair to you if the business is successful.

The investor here is not trying to rush the entrepreneur into a deal, anymore than he would wish to be rushed into one himself. The investor realizes that if his future partnership with the entrepreneur is to be harmonious, the entrepreneur must not feel coerced by the investor's terms. If the entrepreneur said he had seen several investors previously, the investor here should ask him what was their reaction, had any made him an offer, and had any asked to check into his background.

DEALS PASSED OVER

At some time or another, every investor will pass up what later turns out to be a good deal. Yet, he must remember that, for any number of reasons, that deal might not have turned out to be a good one for him. One common way of missing out on a deal is to be uncompromisingly negative on the whole deal, because certain parts are unacceptable. An example of this occurred to me recently. I took a deal in which a company was seeking a million dollar guarantee in return for a five-year warrant on 25,000 shares to an investment banking firm, which I will call Smith & Co., suggesting to them that I would participate jointly with them. Smith & Co. liked the company but not the deal and turned it down on the grounds that the rewards for providing the million dollar guarantee were not lucrative enough. I offered to pursue this with the company to see if I could get a higher level of return, but Smith & Co. were not interested in considering under what conditions they would change their decision, and, thus, they decided to simply pass.

I went back to the company and told them what Smith & Co. had said about the rate of return they were offering, telling them that Smith was a knowledgeable firm whose opinion I respected and which had to be reckoned with, which was true. The company immediately offered another 15,000 shares of free stock, and, thus, we picked up $240,000 worth of stock at no change in risk simply through an improvement in the deal. If Smith & Co. had asked for a change in the deal instead of simply saying no, they would have obtained a better deal.

Instead of saying no, the investor should tell the entrepreneur under what conditions the deal would be acceptable to him. I never say no to someone I want to do business with, because I know that in reality I am investing more in people than in businesses. I say "Not on these terms" or "Not in this business," but I finish by telling the entrepreneur, "Come back to me again, because I want to do business with you. Together, we'll find a basis that makes sense to both of us."

If you like the person and have confidence in him as an entrepreneur, invest something with him—even if you do not like the deal. If he asks for $100,000, suggest that you will participate with others to the extent of

$10,000 on whatever terms are negotiated. He will almost certainly run out of money and need a refinancing, and, by that time, you will know more about the venture than you can now. You can always then come in on the second stage financing if it looks good. Sprinkling money amongst talent is a good program for entrepreneurial investors.

The entrepreneur may be initially disappointed in being offered a $10,000 participation instead of $100,000 but will usually accept, realizing that with one investor committed, for whatever amount, others will be easier to attract. Even if you lose this deal, the entrepreneur will come back to you with his next project.

Obviously, the investor putting in a small fraction of the whole is not in a position to dictate terms to the entrepreneur, although he should try to get the same terms as the major investors. If he does not get the same deal as the major investors, perhaps he can get a different deal rather than a lesser one.

MENTIONING SPECIFIC CASH AMOUNTS

The investor should not make an offer of a specific amount of money or percentage to an entrepreneur, unless he feels they are close to making a deal. If the investor has suggested a particular sum of money for an agreed upon interest in the company and the entrepreneur then asks for a delay in their discussions, the investor should make it clear to the entrepreneur before he leaves the room that this sum of money is not a firm bid, that it is not something the entrepreneur can always return for and be assured of getting, and that it most certainly is not a sum the entrepreneur can quote to other investors in hope of raising the bidding. This is not to say that the knowledgeable entrepreneur should not seek a firm proposal for a set period of time. He is certainly entitled to seek the best deal possible. But why should the investor give away such an option when he can sell it? It is not unreasonable for the investor to propose to the entrepreneur that, in return for an agreed upon dollar amount or interest in the company, the investor will agree to be committed to a specific deal for, say, 30 days.

ENTREPRENEUR AS INVESTOR'S PROTECTOR

The highest rate of return available to an investor is in the predevelopment, or seed-capital investment, stage. The earlier an investor goes into a company, the more equity he can demand in return for his investment, since the risk is greater at this point than later in the company's development. While it is true that later investors often take priority over the original investor, the original investor can structure his deal so that he does not suffer a dilution relative to the entrepreneur—that is, so that the entrepreneur cannot dilute his interest relative to his own along the way. The original investor can be given the benefit of sharing in the entrepreneur's compensation (over an agreed amount) and warrants, shareholder appreciation rights, phantom stock plans, and so on. He can have a contractual relationship with the entrepreneur that in the event the company is sold or its control changes hands, the entrepreneur will share pro rata with the investor the benefits of the shareholder-appreciation rights, stock plans, and employee stock-option plans. The investor can force the entrepreneur to be a guardian of his equity interests in the future—in other words, give the entrepreneur fiduciary responsibility in preserving the position of the investor—not as a percentage of the total shares outstanding but vis-à-vis the shares or interests of the entrepreneur. This approach on the part of the investor can be of assistance to the less financially sophisticated entrepreneur, who may not be thinking in terms of protecting his original holding in the company. Such a relationship preserves the concept of partnership, even though one party is more directly involved in the day-to-day affairs of the company.

WORST CASE PROJECTIONS

When an entrepreneur comes to see me with his business plan, I tell him,

Give me your worst case projection. Don't give me your middle or best case. We'll negotiate the deal from the worst case, because any shortfall is going to be from your pocket and not from mine, since you are the one making the projections. Now, if you do better than your worst case projection, you should have a bonus. But I shouldn't have to pay you anything for achieving the projections you tell me you are going to achieve, because I'm already paying for those in the terms of whatever deal we may make today.

Projections are not a matter of symmetrical percentage variance—in other words, if the projection is 100 and the best case is 120, the worst case is not necessarily 80. The basis for arriving at worst case must be an analysis of individual elements that can go wrong, causing a halt or a delay in the production process: a delay of three months in this department, a delay of five months in another, shortage of a raw material periodic, and so on. These realistic elements must be used in working toward the bottom number. Thus, a business plan in which there is symmetry between the best and worst cases is probably not based upon realistic or seriously contemplated factors.

QUESTIONS BY ENTREPRENEUR

The investor should not have to prove himself to the entrepreneur. The entrepreneur has typically come to the investor simply for money. The entrepreneur has not come to the investor, though he might have been more successful had he done so, as a money partner. When the entrepreneur approaches the investor with the attitude that the investor's only value is his money, he has no justification to demand personal data about the investor.

However, entrepreneurs often approach investors with the line, "Your money is incidental, what I really want is you as a partner in the business." Investors beware!

If the entrepreneur has other, approximately equal offers, it is reasonable for him to determine which of the investors is going to be easy to live with. Is the investor's motivation to increase his visibility and influence? Is his purpose really to grab control of the business? Is the investor a user, in the negative sense, of people? What has been the investor's history of dealing with people?

On a moral basis, the entrepreneur should be concerned with how much of the investor's net worth is being invested in his enterprise. There are obvious issues of morality when an entrepreneur persuades an investor to invest more than he should in a venture which is clearly speculative.

The investor should look upon the entrepreneur's questions with a view to having a balanced relationship with him. The entrepreneur has a right to know what will happen if the investor dies. Also, the investor may have skills, contacts, or so forth that could help the entrepreneur in the business and, thus, give the entrepreneur more to work with in his efforts to make the business successful.

DISCLOSURE OF INVESTOR'S NET WORTH

On occasion, I have been asked to provide a net worth statement to a lender. This has come about either because I was borrowing directly or because I was guaranteeing the obligations of some borrower with whom I had a relationship. I have always declined to provide the requested data, because I only borrow on a fully secured basis, pledging collateral. I do not seek unsecured credit. If unsecured credit is sought, personal net worth information is clearly a valid request by the lender. My reason for declining the request mostly has to do with my not wishing to have on record the extent (or lack) of my own wealth or that of a private company which I control. Such information on an investor in the files of a financial institution, especially in this country, can be, and frequently is, made available to the institution's many employees and to its officers and directors, and possibly their friends, without the investor's permission or even knowledge.

In any case, the reason why lenders want the information in the case of secured or guaranteed company loans is not so much to form a judgment as to creditworthiness as it is to have something to which the supplier of the information can be tied in case of a default. If a lender can show, even remotely, that a misstatement was made by the seeker of credit, the latter can find himself in a much more difficult situation than otherwise. It may be almost impossible for an active businessman to accurately describe *all* his assets and liabilities. An assessment made to the best of his ability at one time may appear incomplete and even intentionally inaccurate years later, when in all probability his assets and liabilities will be much changed.

Years ago, Dr. Henry Jarecki, chairman of Mocatta Metals, provided a direct, simple, and fair solution to the problem. I was at the time seeking a line of credit in commodity dealing for a company I controlled. He asked me for a financial statement for the company, and I told him that we did not, as a matter of principle, distribute them. He then asked for my personal net worth statement. My answer was the same. He next asked if the current net worth of the corporation was in excess of a certain amount. I said that it was. After that, he asked if my personal net worth exceeded a certain amount. I said that it did. Then he simply asked if (1) I would attest to those statements and (2) I would agree to be personally responsible for informing him if either the company's or my net worth fell below 80 percent of the amounts stated in order for him to take steps to protect his company in terms of the credit being extended. Henry knew that as long as he had me personally liable, without (please note) my technically guaranteeing any obligation, he had all of the real benefits of a net worth statement and personal guarantee. I have used his brilliant solution many times since learning it.

MONITORING AND MANAGING THE INVESTMENT

11

SCOPE OF INVESTOR INVOLVEMENT

One assumption made in this book is that the investor is going to be active rather than passive. Another assumption—when it is not being spelled out as a warning—is that the entrepreneur's projected results will not be achieved and that the investor's degree of involvement in the new company will probably involuntarily increase as he becomes more concerned with the protection of his capital than with its enhancement. If the investor is not prepared to be involved with the company and to spend at least several hours a month, and perhaps considerably more time than that, in monitoring the progress made by the company in absolute terms, as well as progress made by the company relative to its projected rates of progress, then the investor is well advised to seek capital and income opportunities in publicly traded securities.

Private company investing requires time, diligence, and intelligence—but lots of time. This is not to say that the time invested has to be viewed negatively, because working with private companies can be extremely rewarding, both in terms of the ongoing process of learning and of the satisfactions to be derived from helping someone create a successful and viable enterprise. Nevertheless, lots of time is required—weekends and nights usually, because a private company investor normally has his own business affairs to look after during working hours.

The amount of time required to look after his investments may cause friction in the family life of the investor. In extreme cases, the investor's family come to resent the private company investment and the entrepreneurs and management involved in the private company. This resentment can result in pressure on the investor to take actions which he might not otherwise have taken. More frequently than not in these cases, the investor's family brings pressure on him to disengage himself from the private company.

I think it important that the wife of the private company investor be fully aware of the potential of the company, as well as the problems as they develop. Investing in private companies, particularly within smaller communities, is very much a family affair. There are going to be a lot of hard feelings and resentment if the investment does not work out well, and, sometimes, they are there even if it does. However, pressures can be minimized by the family having a better understanding of what is involved.

It is a fact that the successful entrepreneur, and also I believe the active entrepreneurial investor, creates the additional time necessary to be successful in his commercial pursuits at the expense of what some describe as the "quality" time spent with his family. The emotional demands, let alone physical demands, on the individual building a business are urgent and frequently all-consuming. The private company investor, not having the ability to take his loss (or profit) whenever he chooses, has this additional anxiety over that of the investor or speculator in publicly traded securities. The private company investor is burdened at times with a feeling of impotence and loss of control. He may not be able to get out of an investment which threatens his financial security, because he has put more money in than he had anticipated or was prudent by making follow-on investments to protect that which was already invested. His wife in the meantime may well have suffered the natural fear of loss of family assets and security, combined with having been ignored or at least having received less attention than previously.

When a company or investment works out well after a period of anxiety, the spouse is mindful of "her sacrifice" and can be resentful of the success of her husband. Thus, family pressure can result from success, just as it does, in a different and more intense way, from failure. I am suggesting here that the successful entrepreneur, and often the successful active investor, pays a generally unrecognized price for his success.

The private company investor who is not burdened with his own domestic troubles may have to contend with those of the entrepreneur. A point worth noting is that with success comes a financial incentive for separation due to the increased wealth available for division. In some cases, the investor may have to consider the entrepreneur's ex-wife as well as his present one.

The investor should think through, with his attorney, what happens to the business in which he is considering an investment if there is a contentious divorce proceeding during the period of his locked-in investment. At this time, consideration should also be given to the disposition of the entrepreneur's shares, and votes, in the event of his death. Does the investor want to be in the position of dealing with the widow's attorney or next husband? Similarly, from the entrepreneur's point of view, does he want to be dealing with the ex-wife or widow of the investor? These contingencies can, and should, be discussed openly between the entrepreneur and investor and can be provided for in much the same way as for a partnership. In covering the possibility of a change in principals, a buy/sell option and/or a voting trust arrangement can be helpful.

TIMING AND DEGREE OF INVESTOR INVOLVEMENT

The investor must determine his own timing and degree of involvement in a private company, since the entrepreneur will have the natural reaction of wanting to be left alone and "let me run my business" without the "assistance" of the investor. It is true that simply having the money available for investment and the courage and/or greed to make the investment do not mean that the individual has the ability to assist in the management of the enterprise. And down deep, the entrepreneur frequently has contempt for the individual with resources to invest. Sometimes that contempt is well deserved. Nevertheless, the investor must have the ability to gain as much information as he wishes about the company, its problems, and its prospects. The investor must be in a position to increase his influence and control, and, therefore, involvement, as his investment becomes increasingly jeopardized. The entrepreneur will usually not welcome the involvement of the investor, and this may become a friction point between the two.

The involvement of the investor may take the form of requiring the company to hire a management consultant or an officer, perhaps even a new chief executive officer. His involvement does not mean that the investor is going to step in and physically manage the company's affairs on a day-to-day basis. Time is money for the investor also, and although he has the right to be increasingly involved in the company, he should view the investment of his hours in the same way he viewed the investment of his money. He may be better off putting the same five or eight hours on a weekend into studying new investment opportunities than in working with one already made. As with money, one should not throw good hours after bad.

The investor makes money with his mind (using his memory and his intuition) and his time; skills can equally well be focused on new opportunities as on one in which he has a present involvement. He must consciously decide how to expend his energies. Years ago, Maurice R. "Hank" Greenberg, chairman of the American International Group, who I think of as one of the most outstanding executives I have known, told me that the most important thing for an executive to do is to determine how he is going to use his own time and not give up control of it to others—right down to which telephone calls are returned, which letters are answered, and which meetings are attended.

The effective investor, like the effective executive, cannot be in a position of simply responding to the needs of others. He must dictate his own areas of focus, based on his own objectives.

The following short article from *Private Placements* reviews how active the professional venture capital investor's role really is.[1]

"Our venture capital investors do not run the company," say five CEOs of venture-backed private firms which were recently profiled in PRIVATE PLACEMENTS. The CEOs discussed the advisory roles played by their venture capitalist board members.

"We have a working board of three that meets once a month for one hour. In addition to myself, board members are Dag Tellefsen of Glenwood Ventures and Bay Partner's Chuck Hazel," says Donald Pedrotti, founder and president of Adaptive Intelligence Corp. (AIC). AIC, a startup manufacturer of light-load computer-controlled robots, raised $2 million in seed capital in an April private placement. Two weeks before each board meeting Pedrotti sends an agenda to the board members.

"Brentwood's Kip Hagopian is on our board of six, which meets every other month. But, I see Kip about every three weeks," says Tim Martin, president of CENSTOR. "Kip monitors our activities, assists in the financial area and keeps us informed about what other, similar companies are doing." CENSTOR, a disc drive maker, raised $6.5 million in a March deal. Five venture capital firms invested in that round: Brentwood Associates, First Capital of Chicago, Norwest Growth Fund, Morgenthaler Management Corp. and the venture capital arm of Allstate Insurance.

Applix, a startup maker of office automation software, raised over $2 million in an April financing. Investors were New Enterprise Associates, Matrix Partners and Chatham Venture. "We have a five-member board which meets every 2½ months. Paul Ferri from Matrix and Chatham's Stephen Gaal hold seats and they act in an advisory capacity. Of late, they have assisted me in recruiting personnel," says Jitendra Saxena, president of Applix.

"Steve Banks [The Hillman Company], who has been on our board since our firm's founding in 1980, and Gene Miller [Montgomery Ventures] are operating directors, coming in every month," says Axonics president Mike Beigler. "Generally, they watch trends in markets and products and pay particular attention to finance and personnel. In addition, Steve Banks is on the West Coast every other month and he stops in. I rely on both men for their judgment," Beigler adds.

"We have an 11 member board, with three venture capital firms represented," says Conrad Schmidt, Parkview Centers' president. In February, the operator of alcohol and drug treatment centers raised $2.5 million from Norwest Growth Fund, Matrix Partners, North Star Ventures and Montgomery Ventures. Norwest's Len Brandt, Montgomery's Frank LaHaye and Mike Humphreys of Matrix Partners hold board seats and attend monthly executive committee meetings. "Their financial and organizational expertise is helpful and they are involved in policy decisions. They have also helped me locate personnel," adds Schmidt.

Formal reporting requirements are pretty uniform among the five companies. Each month, Conrad Schmidt of Parkview sends a financial report, including a cash flow

---

[1] Copyright © 1983 by Howard & Company, 1528 Walnut St., Suite 2020, Philadelphia, PA 19102. All rights reserved. Reprinted by permission from *Private Placements*, vol. 1, no. 15, July 26, 1983.

analysis to his venture capital backers. AIC's Donald Pedrotti gives monthly financial statements to all his investors. CENSTOR's Tim Martin says, "Our private stock purchase agreements require monthly financial documentation to stockholders holding a certain portion of equity."

Mike Beigler of Axonics says that all his firm's venture capital investors receive monthly reports. "That was a requirement in our last round." In April, Axonics completed a $9 million bridge financing. And an IPO may follow the bridge financing soon. "We're hoping to go public early next year," Beigler adds.

CONSULTANTS AS OVERSEERS

It is perfectly reasonable for a consultant to be retained to review, on a periodic basis, the progress of a company. An accountant hired to review the monthly financials is likely to see things in them that the investor would have missed. Technical and marketing consultants are regularly employed by companies to oversee developments periodically. While the investor's perspective is usually different from that of the management, he too can benefit from these consultants' findings. Periodic management reviews by a consulting firm can be of particular benefit to investors.

The investor must really view himself at times as part of management and at times as one company investing in another company. He must in fact try to act as his own financial consultant, viewing himself as if he were accountable to the owners of the money invested, even though of course it is his own. This will force him to be more decisive and to make provisions for unpredictable events, just as professionals do; if they didn't, they would be criticized for their omission. All too frequently, an investor, when dealing with his own money, acts as if he does not understand that dollars lost have to be recreated. Frequently, the dollars were earned at a time when they were easier to make than at the time when they were lost. Money made in a bull market and lost in a bear market must often be replaced by money made in that same bear market, which may not be an easy feat to accomplish. When the investor loses his money, it is likely to be at a time when it is most difficult to reearn it.

ENTREPRENEUR EXTRAVAGANCE

Investors are frequently bothered by what they regard as the personal extravagances of entrepreneurs. While unauthorized loans to officers and similar transgressions should require the instant dismissal and perhaps prosecution of the entrepreneur, many other expenditures amount to gray areas. Did the entrepreneur's office have to be redecorated in such lavish style? Perhaps, it will impress customers and pay for itself many times over in higher orders. If the investor feels that the entrepreneur tends toward extravagance, it should be an easy matter to draw up an agreement giving the investor the right to cosign every check for over $1,000 or at least see a record of them.

By agreement, the investor can also review a synopsis of every new contract entered into by the company, including a description of the relationship with the other company, the financial condition of the other company, how the contract came about, who is responsible for it, whether there are friends or relations of the entrepreneur in the other company, the profit margin at which the sales contract was figured, and how it compares with the profit margins of other sales contracts.

By and large, I have found entrepreneurs to be honest to a much greater degree than employees. I know of very few instances of entrepreneurs being con men—they may fool themselves but, typically, they are not crooks. They do not start out with the purpose of taking advantage of the investor. A number of them have bad habits left over from their days as employees, so it is important the investor lay down the guidelines as to what is expected. A policy memo approved by the investor regarding entertainment, first class travel, and so forth may be necessary if there is not to be future unhappiness.

Although the investor cannot police the entrepreneur, he can let him know what is expected of him and let him know the probable results of a breach of their agreement.

One of the reasons I like to use the revenue-participation certificate method of investing in private companies is that matters of management perks are then of no concern to me. The entrepreneur should be free to live well "on the company" and spend as he feels justified without fear of shareholder or profit-interest holder criticism. That's fine as long as every week, month, or quarter I receive the agreed upon share of revenues. I fly economy class, and I expect others spending my money to do so also if my interest (and reason for my assuming financial risk) in their activities is profit related. The RPC works wonderfully well in lots of deals.

ENFORCEMENT OF AGREEMENT BETWEEN INVESTOR AND ENTREPRENEUR

One of the facts of commercial life is that people agree to almost anything suggested or required by a source of funding prior to obtaining the money. The most troubling problems likely to confront the investor are those relating to the entrepreneur not adhering to agreements made prior to a period of problems. The entrepreneur under stress frequently feels cornered and trapped by circumstances beyond his control and sees his agreement with the investor as being the part of the closing circle that is the weakest. After all, the entrepreneur may reason, the investor is really either his partner or someone who is trying to take advantage of him anyway, and, therefore, his obligations to the investor are of lesser concern than those to others. Although it may be easy to understand how the entrepreneur may reach such an erroneous conclusion, it behooves the investor to protect himself by having the means already at hand with which to enforce his agreement with the entrepreneur.

Perhaps the most common means of ensuring compliance is for the investor to hold as security, and have the right to vote, the shares of the company owned by the entrepreneur. Although this sounds onerous, it really is not inasmuch as all the entrepreneur has to do is that which he promised to do and on which premise the investor risked his capital. A less direct method would be for the shares of the entrepreneur to be held, and voted under certain circumstances, by a third party acceptable to both the entrepreneur and investor.

Another technique of assuring the cooperation and compliance of the entrepreneur is to have a money obligation, perhaps secured or collateralized with property or third-party guarantees, which becomes effective only in the event of the entrepreneur breaching his agreement with the investor. Such an agreement could call for the entrepreneur, in the event of certain previously stipulated developments, to purchase nonvoting shares or to lend an agreed upon amount of money to the company on a noninterest-bearing subordinated (to the investor) basis.

Developments warranting either a forced provision of funds to the company or a surrender of complete control to the investor might include threatened bankruptcy, asserted by creditors or demonstrated by the investor and confirmed by the auditors; loss of an agreed percentage of the company's sales; the denial of patents; or entering into contractual relationships or borrowings unauthorized by the board of directors or the investor. The entrepreneur may agree that these would be important eventualities but point out that the chances of their happening are remote. The investor can reply that since the chances of their happening are so remote and since the agreement is important to the investor and costs the entrepreneur nothing, there can be little risk for him to accept the agreement.

LETTERS OF INTENT

See Appendixes M, N, and O for specimen letters of intent from underwriters to privately held companies for proposed initial public offerings.

SHAREHOLDERS' AGREEMENT AS MANAGEMENT TOOL

Martin Solomon, in his interview with me, summed up this technique:

I use the shareholders' agreement to define the terms and conditions and day-to-day running of the business. The agreement specifies that the investor is to be financially reimbursed before the entrepreneur/manager. Rights of first refusal are given to both sides. The investor may or may not have a man on the board but always maintains a way of exerting influence on the day-to-day management of the company.

THE INVESTOR AS CORPORATE ENTITY 12

The serious private company investor should give consideration to whether he as a person should be doing the investing. Circumstances may make it more advantageous for him to invest as a corporate entity. Here, he is faced with another question: Mirror, mirror, on the wall, which is the fairest entity of all?

Corporations, trusts, and partnerships—foreign and domestic—are all worth study. The investor may wish to keep relatively small investments on a personal level. There is liability to almost anything an investor does in business, and tax consequences too, for both winning and losing situations. The use of well designed entities can reduce potential loss and maximize retention of benefits.

The tax situation, marital status (and the likelihood of its remaining unchanged), and other activities of the investor all will affect his decision as to the best and most appropriate investment vehicle to use.

One of the most attractive investment vehicles is certainly the S corporation. S corporation shareholders can deduct corporate losses from their personal income for tax purposes and, once profits exceed losses, still have the ability to elect to be taxed as a corporation. Besides this, the shares of the S corporation can be held in the names of various individuals, directly or through certain trusts.

For further material on S corporations, see Appendixes P and R.

I believe it better to invest in private companies as an active investor through the medium of a corporation. There are clear advantages to owning a corporation when it comes to estate planning, taxes, insurance, business expense allocations, and permissible tax deductions. There are even real advantages in the employee-benefit-plan area which can be of major significance. In most cases, the majority owner will also be an employee of the corporation. However, it is possible for the investor's children or spouse to be the founding shareholders, directly or through trusts, and for the investor (who may also lend to the business on either a secured or unsecured basis) to be the paid employee. Of course, the manager of the investing corporation can have a profit-sharing arrangement with the corporation. In establishing such a corporate entity, care must be taken not to create a personal holding company and to preserve S corporation status. In most cases, it is wise to make the Section 1244 election in order for the original shareholders to "benefit" in the event of disaster through ordinary income tax credits.

Persuasive as all these reasons are, it is not primarily because of them that I recommend the use of a corporation to the investor. Successful investing in private companies is a serious business and will be accomplished with a higher level of success if it is conducted as such. The following are some of the functions the investor representing a corporation (which he owns totally or nearly so) will find easier to perform than the individual investor: considering and researching an investment opportunity; structuring a deal; and negotiating contracts, in which, of course, the investor's decision must be ratified by his board of directors, providing a chance to change a position previously adopted or decide not to proceed.

The investor representing a corporation finds these functions easier to perform because (1) he is acting as a fiduciary, which is in itself an advantage, since it is always easier to represent the interests of others than one's own; and (2) those with whom he deals take him more seriously and cooperate with him to a greater extent in his investigations, monitoring, and, perhaps, collection efforts.

The investor finds that financial institutions will take him more seriously, in most cases, as a corporate representative than as an individual, as will entrepreneurs and company employees. This will be the case even when it is recognized that the investor owns the corporation and that there is not much more capital in it than that invested in the entrepreneur's company.

In instances where the investor uses borrowed funds or guarantees, a corporate vehicle is desirable even when the lender to the corporation requires the personal guarantee of the shareholder of the corporation.

The ability to be flexible and imaginative in the disposition of the shares of the investor-owned corporation is an advantage in tax and estate matters. In addition, in the case of a pending or possible marital dispute, arrangements can be made to specifically exclude the shares of the investing corporation from that which may be later claimed as marital property. The corporation can have shareholder agreements which can be useful in estate planning.

There are too many considerations to go into detail here, and the investor should only consider these matters in conjunction with his attorney. All wealthy investors should consider ownership or control of foreign corporations and/or ownership of their domestic corporations by friendly foreign entities. "If it is not illegal, it is legal" is a doctrine appropriate for those intent on maximizing returns and retentions at all levels. For many, however, the possible savings will be offset by the concern that they are doing "something wrong." So be it. I am not advocating or advising on tax minimization or avoidance techniques. No doubt the reader is already aware that many very rich people do not seem to pay a lot of taxes and that there must be reasons why this is possible. The intelligent use of U.S. and foreign corporations and trusts is one of the ways to achieve a minimization of tax burden for the wealthy and well advised.

An important benefit was pointed out by Dan Lufkin. "The investor who invests as a corporate entity will have less of an ego problem in reviewing troubled ventures than one who has invested in his own name, and he will be less likely to feed things that should be let die."

STRUCTURING AND PRICING THE FINANCING FOR THE INVESTOR'S ADVANTAGE

13

My friend Stanley Golder originally gave me permission to edit his excellent article in Stanley Pratt's *Guide to Venture Capital Sources* from the standpoint of the investor, changing it from that of the entrepreneur/seeker of investment funds. Instead, I decided to reproduce his article as it was written and add my own observations—set off by brackets and italics—to his text. Incidentally, *Guide to Venture Capital Sources,* in which this article and others appear, contains a listing of venture capital organizations which entrepreneurs may find helpful.

STRUCTURING AND PRICING THE FINANCING[1]

Stanley C. Golder

Stanley C. Golder *is a general partner of Golder, Thoma & Co., Chicago, Illinois, a $60 million venture capital fund founded in 1980. For the prior nine years, he was president of the Equity Group of First Chicago Corp., one of the largest and most successful bank holding company business development investment affiliates, with assets over $100 million. He is a past president of both the National Association of Small Business Invest-*

[1] Copyright © 1983 by Capital Publishing Corporation. Reprinted by permission from Stanley E. Pratt (ed.), *Guide to Venture Capital Sources.*

ment Companies and the National Venture Capital Association. Golder, Thoma & Co. is an active investor with a diversified investment philosophy.

STRUCTURING

It is the experience of the author that the structure of the financing can have a material effect on the eventual result of an investment and, therefore, the structure is an important element in setting the price. [*I can propose a deal which will be satisfactory to me if the seeker of funding will provide just one element which will be satisfactory to him. If he sets price, I will set payment terms and performance criterion. If he sets maturity, I will set rate. If he sets maturity and rate (five-year loan and two over prime), I will set security requirements to make that an attractive arrangement. By attractive, I mean that which yields more than a comparable security having the same investor attractions. A good deal can be defined simply as one which you can sell immediately at a profit to an investor of equivalent sophistication to yourself. If the original investor cannot turn around on the day of the closing and remarket the securities purchased from the entrepreneur AT A PROFIT to another investor who shares the same acceptance of predicted future events on which the original investor premised the investment, then the deal was not well priced and/or structured. Packaging deals for investors is clearly a business in itself, and such activity is the essence of investment banking. However, I stipulated that the buyer be "of equivalent sophistication" to the seller, which is more difficult than selling securities to the public at a markup.*] At times, there are differences of opinion within the venture capital industry as to whether to purchase preference issues (such as convertible preferred stock, subordinated debentures, and notes with warrants) or to buy common stock. [*There is never any doubt in my mind. The investor should have a preference in liquidation and dividends.*] It is clear that new companies cannot afford to pay interest or dividends, and if the venture capitalist structures an instrument that calls for their payment, he is merely taking back his own money. [*I do not necessarily agree. Money is a commodity to be rented. I believe it better to have a "return on investment" structured into the deal, even if payment is deferred until profits reach a certain level, until the net worth of the company is at a particular level, or prior to any executive compensation changes. Money has to earn in order to multiply. The investor can always trade away the interest owed for something at a later date. That something can be an equity increment or another member on the board of directors or just a greater ability to influence and/or control the company. Interest due is an obligation, even if it is only interest which is contingently paid, and as such has a value.*] In addition, consideration should be given to the fact that the balance sheet will be more appealing to other creditors and suppliers if the investment is in the form of common stock rather than debt instruments. [*I agree, and a class A common for the investor can be used instead of a preferred, although I prefer to have the proper label on things.*]

Although these are truisms, they do not address themselves to several key questions, one of which is the possibility that a company might move sideways, rather than up or down. If a company does not go public or sell out to a large company, but remains on a modest plateau, it is difficult for the private investor to recover an investment held in straight common stock. [*Unless there is an agreement among the shareholders that the company or other shareholders will either purchase the shares of the investor or, better yet, agree to purchase on demand (a put) after a certain date. The price of the contracted sale, which can be conditional upon the achievement of agreed upon objectives, can be either a set amount or a function of earnings or revenues.*] Even if the company goes public, the market will not accept a large amount of stock unless the company makes major progress. The only way out for the venture capitalist would be the sale of the company. The company managers do not have the problem to the same extent for, after all, they can receive high salaries and fringe benefits. They may be strongly opposed to the sale of the company. [*Of course, if there is a buy/sell agreement in place, there need not be an impasse, since those who wish to maintain the status quo can acquire the shares of those who wish to exit or can themselves be bought out at the price they offered.*]

To avoid this kind of stalemate, it has been the preference of many not to make an outright purchase of stock in a case in which management has the controlling interest in the business or can block the sale or merger of the business with a larger company. Before taking a common equity position, there should be some waiting period to see if the company performs as expected and to see if management has objectives similar to those of the venture capitalist and, therefore, will protect his interests as a minority shareholder.

The question of ultimate liquidity for the investment is also very significant. To deal with both liquidity and capital protection, the best financial structure entails a limited amount of money invested in common stock, with the rest employed in debentures, notes, or preferred stock. These instruments will provide some income and protection in case the business starts to decline. By having less dollars invested in common stock, the pressure to liquidate is reduced, allowing the venture capitalist time to find less painful ways to dispose of his holdings.

The third major problem is that of control. Most businessmen want to control their own businesses. The difficulty is that small-company management often consists of technical or sales people and there usually is not a well-rounded management team with depth of experience. The loan agreement or preferred stock indenture should give the management sufficient flexibility to run the business as long as things go reasonably well. On the other hand, such an instrument should give the investor an opportunity to exert pressures in case problems develop. Many people misunderstand the purpose of the terms of a loan agreement or preferred stock indenture. They presume that simply because a default exists, which could justify exercising the right to take control, the venture capitalist will immediately exercise such right. In fact, the record shows that this is rare.

There are major differences between investors. Not all money is the same in the venture industry, and nearly every group has different operating philosophies. While there may be a few waiting for a default in loan agreements so that they can take over a company, decrease their equity costs, or increase their percentage of ownership, the majority of venture capitalists do not have this attitude. This does not mean, however, that any of us are "patsies" or that we will not use appropriate remedies when necessary to protect an investment.

It is important for entrepreneurs to understand the general philosophies under which most venture capitalists operate. Loan agreement covenants are not the key aspect of pricing, but they do bear on the issue. Reasonable loan and preferred stock covenants are nothing more than a reflection of a good business plan. They often act as a disciplinary measure for management. This discipline is particularly important for young, growing companies, in which management often has a tendency toward exuberance.

Venture Capitalist versus Entrepreneur

Naturally, there are some basic differences between the entrepreneur and the venture capitalist. The businessman is by nature an optimist and is enthusiastic about his ability to succeed. While the venture capitalist is not a pessimist (if he were, he would not be in this business), he can appropriately be described as a skeptic.

The businessman feels his company is worth more than does the potential investor. His projections show excellent growth over the next two-to-four years, and he believes that the investor should be willing to pay a high price to buy into this "bonanza." The venture capitalist, on the other hand, is skeptical because the young business simply has not proved whether it concepts and ideas will work. The business may be profitable, barely profitable, or, more likely, in a loss position at the time of investment. Competition can suddenly become much more disagreeable, or any number of other problems can arise to prevent a company from achieving its targets.

These major differences can raise major obstacles between entrepreneur and venture capitalist when they discuss structure and pricing, and the differences often prevent their getting together. Yet the problem can be resolved, and techniques for structuring the investment have been developed to help bridge this gap. The following examples have been developed to illustrate the use of structuring for three types of situations.

As will become apparent, these methods are somewhat complicated which fact can have a negative impact both on the future prospects of the company and on the relationship between the entrepreneur and the investor. *It is better not to have such a formula but rather to keep the arrangements as simple as possible.* However, in certain circumstances the techniques described below can be very helpful and the examples serve to outline approaches.

Resolving the Differences

Example 1 is a new company, so both entrepreneur and venture capitalist had a free rein in structuring the financing from the inception of the deal. After the entrepreneur's projections were modified by our analysis, it was decided that the company would need $1 million. The projections indicated that profits would be generated within the first year, an unusual expectation for a startup investment. Management, although capable and experienced, had nominal funds that could be invested; thus the venture capitalists initially would have voting control. [*The investor should decide whether or not it is in his best interest to require the entrepreneur to "invest" through the incurrance of obligation when the entrepreneur does not have funds available for investment. I think it better to have the entrepreneur put at risk, since he himself then has something to lose if his decisions do not work out as he anticipated. The investor should not be in a position of having all the downside risk, while the entrepreneur has only upside potential.*]

As the investors did have control, we were willing to invest in common stock. However, even if the projections were realized and a public market developed rather quickly, it would be impossible for the investors to sell all of their shares except over a long period of time. [*I do not understand the reason for being concerned because of an inability to sell all of a holding right away in a company which is doing well. The whole point of investing—when not reflecting the special needs of the venture capital general partner (which are different from the needs of the individual investor) to register a gain for profit calculation and profit sharing purposes—is to hold shares of companies which are doing well. There seems almost to be an unspoken statement that the name of the game is to invest only in companies before they go public and to sell out as soon as possible once they do go public. In my view, this approach is not necessarily in the investor's best longer-term interest. My own practice is to borrow on the shares of companies in which I have invested that have gone public and to use these borrowed funds to invest in new private situations. In doing this, of course, an investor has to be careful not to become too highly leveraged.*]

This arrangement, by which the management can receive a maximum equity position through reaching its projections, is called an earn-out. Critical aspects of this transaction were the considerations under which the earn-out numbers were determined. Originally, the proposal was that the earn-out be based on an earnings formula for the first three years of operation, but this approach created problems for us as the venturers. Although there was no disagreement with the principle and although the formula was considered fair in practice, even if the company could meet its projections for three years, we would not have a value to show on the books or a gain that could be realized. In addition, it was important to focus the company management's attention on providing the investors with ultimate liquidity.

For these reasons, it was decided to use a market value formula to avoid an argument about the value of the company. The higher the earnings multiple placed on the shares by the market, the easier it would be for management to get its maximum percentage under the formula. While none of us wanted to create a premature public offering, it was generally agreed that sometime in the three-year period, market conditions would be such that the company could go public. A three-year period was chosen to give management flexibility in deciding when to go public.

If a public market has not been created at the end of that period (because of inadequate earnings growth or some other management-related problem), we considered that a multiple of five times net after tax earnings was appropriate for pricing the shares purchased. [*I prefer to use a relative price/earnings ratio to setting an absolute one. After all, in certain markets five-times after-tax earnings may or may not be attractive. Is it not easier to establish that the multiple will be a percentage of the multiple of the S&P 500 or some stock which is in an industry comparable to that of the company or an index of stocks in the same industry?*] You will note that the valuation formula included a 30 percent discount from the public market price of the shares. This represented an estimate of the average discount appropriate for the nonregistered stock. Since the investors would own about 50 percent of the company, the shares could not be easily sold in the public market without a long holding period or considerable registration expense. The discount was considered appropriate to take these problems into account. (Actually, if such shares were sold in a private transaction, the discount could range from 25 percent-to-50 percent of the price in the public market.)

Management's projections seemed reasonable to us, and in turn the managers agreed to a formula for pricing the equity that would be tied to the future profit performance of the business. In many cases this suggestion results in a severe downward revision of projections of profits by the entrepreneur.

A preferred stock issue backed by a sinking fund was created to provide liquidity for the investment. Because of the early expectation of profits, it was felt that this company could afford the sinking fund payments in years four through six without jeopardizing its equity position. If things worked out badly, we could have 82 percent of the equity. On the other hand, if projections are met, and the company were to go public within three years at a multiple of 10 times earnings or better, the investors would be cut down to 51 percent and management would receive 49 percent of the equity with only a nominal investment. We wanted management to have every possible incentive to bring the company to an optimum growth rate. However, the longer it takes the company to go public, the lower will be management's equity. [*Note the concept of the "rental" cost of money for the period of illiquidity and assumption that the invester automatically sells out to the public.*] We reasoned, too, that this move would protect our interests until the "earn-out" arrangement becomes effective.

The above situation was made somewhat easier because we were dealing with a brand new company without a previous capital structure. But imaginative structuring and pricing is also possible with existing businesses.

Beginning capital structure

6 percent sinking fund preferred	$ 900,000
(sinking fund reduction in years 4–6)	
Class A common	102,500
Class B common	22,500
Total capital	$1,025,000

Class A shares initially represent 82 percent of the company ownership and can be diluted down to 51.25 percent if the earn-out formula is achieved. Class A shares are owned by the investor group. [*In this case, the assumption is that the shares are given to the entrepreneur(s). It is also possible to have the entrepreneurs purchase their shareholdings through the issuance of notes. The notes can be for a variable amount, depending on the achievement of earnings. In other words, the shares could be "given" through the variable amount being very low in the event that the earnings objectives were achieved or exceeded; conversely, if earnings were disappointing, the variable amount could be at least that of the per-share cost to the investor.*]

Class B shares initially represent 18 percent of the company ownership, which votes on a share-for-share basis with Class A ownership and is subordinate to Class A in liquidation. Class B shares are convertible into Class A shares at the resolution of the earn-out and are owned by management.

Earn-Out Arrangement

The earn-out is based on the first public market price of the company, provided a public market is established in the third to fifth years. [A public market is defined as either (1) an offering in which at least 20 percent of the company is sold to the public or (2) a merger in which control is sold to a listed company.] Management will receive no more than 18 percent of the company until the value of the original Class A position meets the following values.

Time of First Public Offering	Class A Value
Year 3	$5,000,000
Year 4	6,000,000
Year 5	7,000,000

If a public market is not established by the end of the fifth year, then for earn-out purposes an "internal" value will be calculated which is five times the lower of (1) average earnings in the third to fifth years or (2) fifth-year earnings.

Because of the restricted nature of the original Class A position, a 30 percent discount will be applied to the public market value for calculating the company value used for the earn-out formula. Assuming a public market is established in the third year, placing a value on the company of $12 million (or $8.4 million), and the management group would increase its position from 18 percent to 40.5 percent through conversion of Class B into Class A stock.

The company's projected after-tax earnings for the third through fifth years are as follows:

Year	Net profit
3	$1,525,000
4	1,892,000
5	2,303,000

Assuming the company went public in year four, the following chart shows the net profit that would be required in year four to enable management to earn its full 48.8 percent ownership participation at different price-earnings multiples:

Multiple	Net Profit Required ($000)
8 times	$2,091
9	1,858
10	1,672
12	1,394
15	1,115

Under this arrangement, management would receive its full percentage earn-out if it achieved its fourth-year projections and the stock sold at an 8.8 multiple. Looking at the earn-out a little differently, if the company's stock sold at a multiple of 12 times earnings in the fourth year, management would have to earn approximately 74 percent of its projections to earn the full percentage.

Example 2 involves a company that was in existence, had a capital structure, was already publicly-held, but was not profitable when the investment was completed. Its prospects appeared good, though. A reasonable deal was worked out, but not until a number of problems had been resolved.

The market price of the stock was about $8 at the time of negotiations. The problems were whether or not the company would make the profits it projected over the next two years and whether or not the marketplace would recognize these profits in terms of a healthy price-earnings multiple. The company wanted to convert subordinated debt into common stock as soon as possible to improve the balance sheet. The solutions were evolved through the use of a sliding scale in the exercise price of warrants. At the same time, though, investors gained the protection of a market price provision that must be met if the sliding scale prices are to be effective. This was further modified by establishing minimum earnings levels between those anticipated by management and those anticipated by management and those anticipated by the investors.

While this situation required a simpler capital structure than the case in Example 1, the needs of both management and venturer had been resolved satisfactorily.

1. *Investment.*
   $3,700,000 (8½ percent subordinated note payable in years four through seven).

2. *Warrant.*
   To purchase 518,260 shares of the company's common stock; the warrant exercise price per share is calculated as follows:
   a. Basic exercise price.
      1) Years 1–3. $6.50 per share.
      2) Years 4–5. $7.75 per share.
      3) Years 6–7. $9.00 per share.
   b. Effectiveness of basic exercise price.
      1) Years 4–5: common stock must be valued at least at $15.50 per share at the end of the third year; otherwise, the exercise price is $6.50 per share.
      2) Years 6–7: common stock must be valued at least at $18.00 per share at the end of the fifth year, otherwise, the exercise price is $7.75 per share.
   c. Exercise price modification for earnings.
      1) If earnings are less than $.20 per share for the first year, the exercise price shall be $4.00 per share.
      2) If earnings are less than $.40 per share for the second year, the exercise price shall be $4.00 per share.
      3) If earnings are less than $.20 per share for the first year but more than

$.40 per share for the second year, the exercise price shall be $5.25 per share.

Example 3 created particular problems for the venture capitalist. This situation represents third-round financing for a profitable company that needed significant money for additional expansion, beyond amounts that would be available from senior sources. A majority of this company's equity is controlled by one individual. The entrepreneur thought he might want to go public, and he was willing to give up some share of the business to develop a partner-like relationship with the venture capitalist in order to obtain the needed funds. However, he could have changed his mind for any number of reasons.

Since the company is controlled by the entrepreneur, our firm did not want to be a common stockholder under any circumstances short of holding liquid, nonrestricted securities. The structure adopted was a subordinated loan with warrants to purchase a convertible preferred stock. The loan was fully subordinated and carried an 8 percent interest rate.

We agreed that the investment called for a 10 percent equity participation. We also agreed that if the company went public in the next five years, our warrant would be exercisable only into common stock. [*Note that even though the warrant conversion was into a convertible preferred, the conversion was to be into common if the shares were publicly traded within five years. I might have tried to scale the conversion privilege to provide an incentive to the entrepreneur to go public sooner, and have the 10 percent equity be the low figure in the early years. I also assume that the agreement called for the shares either to be registered or to have full registration rights, not just piggyback-registration rights.*] However, if the company had not provided a public market at the end of five years, we could convert the balance of the subordinated note into preferred stock, which carries a high dividend rate (10 percent in nondeductible expense). Even though 10 percent is a high rate for a nondeductible expense, the actual $20,000 in dividends was small in relation to the anticipated profits. There was a specific reason for setting the dividend rate high: If the company had not provided the expected public market it was felt that the investor was entitled to a high current return to compensate for the long holding period of the investment and the risks incurred. In this example the investor was a corporation, which meant that dividends were subject to the 85 percent dividend received credit (100 percent credit for an SBIC).

1. *Investment.*
   $400,000 (8 percent subordinated note payable in years four through seven).

2. *Warrant.*
   To buy a 10 percent cumulative, convertible preferred stock:
   a. Exercise price: $200,000.
   b. Not exercisable into convertible preferred stock before the end of the fifth year.
   c. If a public market is established prior to the warrant's being exercised into preferred stock, the warrant is exercisable *only* into common stock.
   d. Expiration date: 10 years. [*I prefer warrant expiration dates to be for a number of years after the repayment of debt rather than for a fixed number of years; in this case, it would be for three years after full repayment of debt, including all accrued interest. From the standpoint of the entrepreneur, it will make no difference if he does what he has promised to do.*]

3. *Terms of convertible preferred.*
   a. Convertible at par at any time, into 10 percent of the company's common stock.
   b. The holder is required to convert into common stock if a public market is established. [*I might have established the premise that the initial public offering price*

had to be at a minimum price of either a fixed dollar amount per share or a percentage over the exercise price of the warrant. Also, there should be a definition of "public." How many shares trade in an average trading day? What percentage of the company shares are in the hands of nonaffiliated public investors? Clearly, the investor does not want the entrepreneur to be able to acquit his responsibility by buying a "shell" company, such as an old mining company for a couple of thousand dollars, and merging in the company for which the investor had an obligation to convert into common shares.]

c. Put: the holder can put the convertible preferred to the company any time after the seventh year at a price of $400,000, as long as net worth is at least four times the put price just before the exercise of the put.

d. Call: the company can call the convertible preferred on 30 days' notice after the seventh year at the following prices:

Year	Call price
8	$1,000,000
9	900,000
10	800,000
11	700,000
12	600,000
13 and thereafter	500,000

[*One of America's most successful investors advised his son always to get and not give options. I agree. Why should the investor give away the right to maintain a position except to improve the position? The entrepreneur has had the investor's money to work with all these years at only a very low rate of rent. Call provisions only work against the investor. Entrepreneurs and investors can at any time negotiate a transaction. Investors should retain and acquire options and not grant them, without adequate compensation or inducement.*]

Liquidity

This still leaves the liquidity question: How do we get our money out of the situation if management changes its plan? A put-and-call arrangement was the solution. If the company built net worth of $1.6 million, the stock could be put to the company for $400,000 (cost basis was $200,000). At the same time, the investors provide management with a call at a high price in the eighth to thirteenth years of business. This protects us, the venture capitalists, from being bought out just before a public offering, in the event the company is successful. The call price declines with each passing year.

You might note that we were willing to accept a lower rate of return on the investment (smaller percentage of equity for a given amount invested) in Example 3, as compared to Examples 1 and 2. Our assessment indicated that the downside risk is less in this case than it is in new ventures or in companies running in the red.

Each situation in these three examples has its own peculiarities, each carries different assessments of risks and rewards, and there are any number of structuring and pricing possibilities that can be applied to take these differences into consideration. The needs of both the entrepreneur and the investor must be coordinated if a successful financing arrangement is to be negotiated. Generally, there is always some reasonable way to meet the needs of both in an attractive project. [*While this is true, the investor must remember that he does not "have to do" any deal and that the deal must be to his advantage for it to be a good deal. The investor loses control after the documents are executed, unless he has structured in his protections. The investor can always be a "nice guy" and modify or amend terms once into the deal. But he should be able to do so from a position of strength. Therefore, he has to have strong deal points originally. Unlike the case for the venture capital partnership general partner or SBIC manager, the money being invested here is the investor's own and, thus, (1) he is not under pressure to invest since this is not what he is being paid to do, and (2) money lost (or not made) will have to be made up by his own hard work and the incurrence of risk not otherwise necessary.]*

PRICING

Pricing refers to the total return expected to be received over the life of the investment and includes both current income (interest and dividends) and the capital gains. The common denominator used is the valuation of the business—a $500,000 investment that receives 25 percent of the equity of the business values the company at $2 million (20 percent × $2 million = $500,000).

Arriving at a price for any investment is a matter of negotiation between the parties. This section will examine some of the considerations involved in setting a price, and methods for reducing some of the subjectivity of pricing from the perspective of the venture capitalist.

How Venture Capitalists Think about Pricing

The variable ingredients that go into price determinations are covered in the following questions.

1. How much money is the entrepreneur putting up relative to the total funds initially required? [*This raises the question of whether the entrepreneur's money has a greater value than that of the investors. I am not sure it does. Perhaps the entrepreneur should invest on the same terms as the investors and be paid bonus shares for performance.*]

2. What is the total in equity financing needed to launch the business? Or, conversely, how much additional dilution over the years will be necessary to keep the business moving forward at the desired pace? [*This is a most difficult question to answer, and the one which most often causes problems because of the investors' inability to understand that, in most cases, the entrepreneur will, intentionally or otherwise, understate the ultimate capital requirement of the business.*]

3. How attractive will the company and industry be in the stock market, and what kind of price-earnings multiple will it be able to command in the marketplace now and in the years when the investors become interested in liquidating? [*The concept that the investor will be interested only in liquidating his position when the company goes public is overstated by many venture capitalists. This is a function of their situation as managers of a money pool which is, they usually hope, ever-increasing. The investor should focus on additional profit possibilities, such as negotiating an additional tranche of warrants to be issued at the public issue price at the time of the offering. Most entrepreneurs will not fight this suggestion, and it can be a very important source of future profit for the investor.*]

4. What is the upside potential of the investment; that is, how much in profits can be generated and in what period of time? What are the odds that the earnings and time projections can be met? [*Certainly, the evaluation must be made. However, the shortfall between achieved and projected results should be paid for by those making the projections.*]

5. What is the downside potential; that is, what percentage of the total investment is likely to be lost if the project does not progress as anticipated? What are the odds that a loss will occur? [*To whatever extent possible, the investor should structure the deal in such a way as to benefit personally through the use of the losses. This can be done most readily through the use of partnerships and S corporations. However, the individual investor can also provide (pay for) services to the entrepreneur and, if not reimbursed, may be able to claim a deduction against his taxes. Marketing tax shelters, as opposed to R&D tax shelters, sometimes can be used by investors. In this case, the investor pays for, say, advertising for the company in return for a royalty on sales. Such a royalty can be structured in conjunction with other elements of the investment and favor the investor.*]

These considerations are directly related to many of the key issues discussed in other parts of this text concerning the cash flow of the business; how much lead time is needed before new products are accepted by the marketplace or by key customers; what it takes to educate a new market; how much has to be invested to carry losses while the operation is building up; what equity investments will be required to carry receivables, inventories, build new plants, and so forth; and how much the business can expect to borrow from conventional lenders and whether such financing will entail equity rights. [*And remember that Murphy's law is fully operative. It is almost axiomatic that revenue production items take longer and production costs are higher than was anticipated.*]

Profit Targets Set by Venture Firms

It is also important to keep in mind that venture capitalists have different profit targets. In fact, different investors could and do have different ideas of the appropriate expected rate of return for the same investment. For example, if a venture capitalist wants a return of four times his money in four years, the compound annual rate of return would be 41 percent. To illustrate rates of return, the following table has been prepared.

Profit Targets of Venture Capitalist	*Compounded Annual Rates of Return (pre-tax)*
Triple their money in three years	44 percent
Triple their money in five years	25
Four times their money in four years	41
Five times their money in three years	71
Five times their money in five years	38
Seven times their money in three years	91
Seven times their money in five years	48
10 times their money in three years	115
10 times their money in five years	58

These are internal rates of return. As a general rule, if venture capitalists are financing startups or first-stage projects, they are looking for expected returns at the high end of the scale. Thus, these investors would be looking for 40 percent, 50 percent, or more compounded return on their investment. On the other hand, investors in second-stage financings tend to be looking for a 30 percent-to-40 percent return per year and those making third-stage deals generally seek 25 percent-to-30 percent per year. [*All of these calculations are on a cash on cash basis. In other words, the implicit assumption is that all of the cash was invested on day one. This does not have to be the case, and the rate of return calculations would be different for a staged investment (and so would the risk assumption if there were achievement requirements which had to be met prior to the funding committment becoming effective). Further, the return on investment tables assume a cash investment rather than a leveraged one. It is frequently better either (1) to invest in a more secure venture on a leveraged basis, rather than in one having higher potential but greater risk on a cash basis, or (2) to structure a senior (and possibly secured) instrument, with a lesser equity-related play, using borrowed funds in part. I reject the idea that the act of borrowing funds for private company investment is by definition more speculative than investing all cash. It depends on how the money, borrowed or otherwise obtained, is put to use.*]

In reviewing venture capitalists' pricing attitudes it is important also to keep in mind certain other things that have been repeated often throughout this text.

1. Nothing progresses along the originally projected pathway. (Murphy's Law stated another way: if things can go wrong, they will.) This is one of the world's more unpredictable activities, thus venture capitalists leave a great deal of room for such errors in arriving at valuations.

2. It is likely to take more money to accomplish objectives than indicated in projections by both management and venture analysts. Thus, venture capitalists like to leave room in the pricing for more dilution than might otherwise be expected. [*The two preceding paragraphs of this excellent article are worth committing to memory.*]

3. It is difficult to realize profits on venture investments. Shares received are not readily tradable as marketable securities. Instead, they must be sold under special rules established by SEC (Rule 144 stock sales), or they must be sold pursuant to the expensive and somewhat unpredictable action of obtaining a registration statement. [*Or, shares must be sold by prior arrangement to the company or its other shareholders. A buy/sell agreement would be very applicable here. Also, the pension and profit-sharing plans of the company can, and perhaps should, own either preferred or common shares of the company.*] The complications and obstacles involved in both of these alternatives are described by others in this text. The third alternative is to sell the entire business to a large listed company. This is also a complicated procedure and requires cooperation by all parties involved.

Obviously, it is erroneous to assume that venture capitalists can use yardsticks like those used by regular security analysts in arriving at a fair valuation for their investment in the company.

Calculations Used by Venture Firms in Setting Price On the other hand, some of the security analyst's tools are used in setting guidelines for valuation. The venture capitalist is likely to make a list of the various companies that are in the same industry as the firm requesting financing. Such a list will include industry leaders, medium-sized companies, and small firms. Key operating statistics for each company are likely to be compared; these include sales, operating costs, profits and margins, overhead and administrative expense, and net profit and its ratio to sales. [*This comparative analysis should be prepared and presented by the entrepreneur in his business plan. Firstly, if the entrepreneur does not do this work and use the experience of others engaged in the same areas, his projections, upon which the business and to a degree the structure of the deal are premised, will be weakened. Secondly, if the entrepreneur does not know well the industry operating statistics, and particularly those of the direct competition (certainly, if publicly available), then the investor should be skeptical of the entrepreneur's having sufficient sophistication for the running of a business.*] Net worth and return on equity will also be calculated, together with long-term debt and current ratios. Price-earnings ratios in the current market are likely to be compared with an average worked out for the different classes of companies. If stocks of the leading firms are selling at 25 times earnings, medium companies at 15 times, and small companies eight times, there will certainly be a hesitancy to consider a price-earnings ratio of more than 10-to-12 in estimating what the venture equity could be worth at the time of sale. [*Ratio analysis is of much greater utility in comparing publicly traded securities than in valuing private companies. The focus should be on those elements of information regarding other companies which can be used to validate projected operating results. Using market-place ratios as a means of determining private company values is, I believe, overly simplistic and possibly misleading. Certainly, the investor must have an awareness of current market valuations and also, perhaps more importantly, of current valuations being placed upon initial public offerings and subsequent market performance. However, the major focus must be on that which is being projected by and for the company in which investment is being considered. No one can predict with certainty the stock market for any length of time, and certainly not for the three to five years a private company investment is likely to be illiquid.*

I believe that in the present market and economic environment, the ranges of return suggested in this article, as being expected by venture capitalists, are fair and realistic for the individual investor also. Therefore, the investor should select his target expectation (hopefully, the natural greed of the investor will not prod him to heights of expectation which are unnatural and, therefore, exceedingly dangerous) and structure the deal so that the earnings yield of the company provides the desired return over the period of the investment. An earnings yield is the reciprocal of a price-earnings ratio. It is calculated the same way a dividend yield is calculated. Stated another way, the cumulative projected earnings yield (investor's prorata share of a company's earnings divided by the cost of the investment) should be substantially greater than that of publicly traded shares of companies having similar prospects. Private company investors would, I believe, make better investment decisions if they forgot about price/earnings ratios and assumed that the companies in which they are involved will not go public. The lure of a public offering (which is frequently an act of taking advantage of those who are less sophisticated) often confuses the investor's decision-making process.]

To further illustrate this thinking, let's assume that the financing situation will be as follows. A company makes a medical instrument that has major potential for treatment of a serious disease. An analysis shows that the stocks of leading medical instrument companies are selling at 30 times earnings, medium firms at 20 times earnings, and small companies at 12 times earnings. Assume that the company seeking financing has current sales of $750,000 and is losing money, but evaluated projections by a venture capitalist indicate that in five years, sales will be $7.5 million and earnings $600,000 after taxes. (The entrepreneur's projections might have been $12 million in sales and $1 million in after-tax earnings.) Key questions about management, marketing, finance, etc. have been satisfactorily answered. [*It is important in this process also to have an idea as to the earnings increases being projected for the publicly traded companies being used in the comparative analysis.*

The figure charts on pages 98 and 102 display the discount ranges necessary to equalize the accumulated earnings yield of companies if one accepts the basic premise that the acceptance of illiquidity entitles the owner of the money to a premium return of: 5–10 times for seed capital financings, 3–6 times for startups, 2–4 times for development stage, and 1.5–3 times for investment in an already profitable company.]

The venture capitalist might assume that in five years he will be able to liquidate his holdings on the basis of the company's being valued in the marketplace at $7.8

million (13 times earnings). He feels that this investment should produce a 44 percent compounded return on capital. Analysis indicates that it will take an initial investment of $500,000 to accomplish the five-year plan of the company. (The venture capitalist might also have to calculate a dilution factor if additional capital will be required.) Calculating the present value of the $500,000 investment for the five years using a 44 percent annual compounded growth rate factor, the $500,000 investment must have a value of $3,205,000 at the end of the fifth year. Assuming that the company will have a value of $7.8 million by that date (earnings of $600,000 times a multiple of 13), he would then require an initial 41.09 percent equity interest for his investment.

There are many variables. Will the venture capitalist really use a price-earnings multiple of 13 to calculate his value at the end of five years? [*I prefer the approach of thinking in terms of a percentage of the multiple of the Dow Jones Industrial Average or an industry index that relates to the business of the company rather than in absolutes. A multiple of 13 can be either high or low depending on the timing of market cycles.*] This factor often depends on the state of the stock market. In good times, the venture capitalist might well use such a calculation, but during down markets, a price-earnings multiple of 10 or less is more likely. The difference has a major bearing on the equity percentage he will want for his $500,000. How accurate will the projections be? Will the company really be able to get by with only $500,000 in equity, despite the fact that it will grow from $750,000 to $7.8 million in five years, an average growth per year of 58 percent compounded?

These are only a few of the questions that the venture capitalist would ask himself in pondering the return he wants on his investment and the price to pay for the equity position.

The Pricing of Startups

In the case of startups, the pricing question becomes considerably more obscure. While the venture capitalist may go through a similar calculation, the returns expected are likely to be much higher than they are in the above illustration; thus, the investment will require a greater percentage of equity. Naturally the factors of unpredictability are much greater.

As a rough rule of thumb, if the venture capitalists are putting up all of the capital in a startup venture, they will probably want voting control of the venture. [*As should the individual investor in some form, in case the venture should fail to achieve projected results.*] As described above, they might also include an earn-out program in the investment so that if certain prescribed targets are met, the entrepreneurs will be able to "earn" increasing amounts of equity. On the other hand, over the years some notable investments have been made where venture capitalists receive only 33 percent to 45 percent of equity after putting up all the capital. However, such transactions were generally worked out during strong stock markets with companies whose management represented some of the nation's leading executives in a "hot" industry.

Naturally, the greater the amount that the entrepreneur can invest, the less equity will be requested by the venture capitalist. For example, if the entrepreneur is putting up 30 percent of the capital, the venture firm might require only a 40 percent equity interest. Obviously these questions relate directly to key factors such as potential, quality, and risk. It should be noted that venture capitalists generally want the entrepreneur and his team to retain sufficient equity interests to ensure that they will be properly motivated. At the same time, if initial members of the management team are found to be inadequate or if they decide to leave, many venture capitalists will want to provide for a practical way to retire a portion of their initial stock interests. [*The issue here is the price at which the entrepreneur or members of the management team invest. I suggest it be on the same terms as the other investors. The entrepreneur and members of the management group can and should be given options and bonus shares in some form. They have to be motivated, but rewards and capital risk assumption are different consider-ations and should be treated differently.*]

How the Stock Market Affects Pricing

There is a direct relationship between venture pricing and the overall condition of the securities market. When the stock market is high and speculative stocks are quite popular, pricing will be quite different than it is during a down period when venture capital is more difficult to obtain and prices of small, speculative securities are quite low. While such conditions don't affect the pricing of startups as much as ongoing busi-nesses, obviously the best time to raise money is when the stock market is strong and speculative fever is high.

The most astute entrepreneurs and managers will attempt to time thier money-raising forays during these periods and then use debt during the down periods to implement the cash flow of the business, but these are highly unpredictable periods, and luck is as important as brains in raising capital during such periods.

During good times, venture capitalists generally feel that public offerings are the best way out of their investments. They are more generous with assumptions about price-earnings multiples than they are during a period like the 1973 liquidity crisis in the over-the-counter market, when it was virtually impossible to float a new issue and prices of small OTC stocks were exceedingly depressed.

Double-Check Values with the Venture Firms

There are ways to double-check pricing and valuation questions. Since most entrepre-neurs will talk to various capital sources, they should compare the investors' suggestions on reasonable valuation. If three or four venture firms tend to agree on the equity percent-age for a given investment, the entrepreneur should have more than adequate proof. Counsel with such intermediaries as accountants, lawyers, special consultants, investment bankers, and others can also help the entrepreneur decide what is the reasonable value of his company. [*A large part of the investor's "valuation" of a project is going to depend on his instinctive reaction to the entrepreneur. In my case, it is almost instantaneous. I either like and want to do a deal with the individual or not. "Like" is perhaps not the best word—"respect of his ability and presumed integrity" is a better description of the feeling. The drive and need to succeed of the individual is also a key factor in the initial instinctive reaction.*]

To transfer some of the qualitative assumptions about an investment into quantitative terms, the following model was developed while the author was at First Chicago Corpora-tion. It can be a useful tool, but it is only a tool. None of the methods discussed is necessarily right or wrong generally or in a given situation.

XYZ Corporation is placing $300,000 in 7 percent convertible debentures. The com-pany has been in existence for several years. The current year's operations will result in breaking even at $1,800,000 in sales. The product involves a high degree of technology. Four-year projections of sales and earnings are as follows (Figures are in thousands).

Year	1	2	3	4
Sales	$2,800	$4,300	$6,300	$9,200
Net earnings				
Before tax	420	890	1,300	1,900
After tax	210	445	650	950

The problem is to determine what percent of equity would be fair compensation for investing $300,000 in XYZ Corporation. [*"Fair" is a matter of perspective and perception. Frequently, the investor is more financially sophisticated than the entrepreneur. The investor may propose a deal—I think it better for the entrepreneur to propose the deal and the investor to make counterproposals—which is truly fair, yet the entrepreneur is not sophisticated enough to realize it. After all, to gauge fairness one has to have a reasonably good idea of current marketplace values for comparable properties.*] It should be pointed out that there are three pricing methods compared in this illustration, described as traditional method, fundamental method, and The First Chicago Model.

Traditional Pricing Approach

Assumptions:

1. Basic profit criterion is five times invested funds in four years, for example, 50 percent compounded return on investment.

2. No explicit adjustment for risk.

3. Price earnings ratio of 15 in Year 4. [*A price-earnings ratio (p/e) of 15 is very conservative for a company which has enjoyed a 50 percent annual average compound growth in earnings. The P/E multiple and profit criterion are not the same, but clearly, save for a "greater fool" theory, there is a correlation between the earnings growth and investment gain.*]

Calculation:

1. Year 4 net after-tax earnings are $950,000; therefore, total value of XYZ Corporation in Year 4 is $950,000 × 15 = $14,250,000.

2. Desired value of investor's position in Year 4 is $300,000 × 5 = $1,500,000 + $300,000 = $1,800,000.

3. Percentage of equity required is $1,800,000 ÷ $14,250,000 = 12.6 percent. [*This is a perfectly standard approach to pricing a deal. However, it fails to take into consideration market cycles and presumes that a 15 P/E is valid. Would it not be better to use the average or mean p/e of a group of preselected stocks as the basis for equity participation calculation? I am assuming that the investor has accepted some of the views reflected in this book and is initially holding an instrument which will ultimately relate to equity but, in the initial instances, is senior thereto. Why should the investor be the only party to have a risk of general market in determining his ultimate profit or participation? The matter can also be addressed on a dollar amount basis where the investor at X point in time and under Y conditions has the right to the greater of agreed upon percentages of the then outstanding shares or an amount of shares which have a minimum market value of an agreed upon amount.*]

Fundamental Pricing Method

The basic premise is that a venture investor ought to receive 20 percent or more, compounded annually, on all invested funds; [*I prefer the concept of relativity to long-term fixed-income rates or the performance of an index to a fixed-percentage return figure. Today, a 20 percent compound return from speculative investments is not that attractive, and certainly was much less so in 1982 when interest rates were hovering around that level.*] therefore, the percentage of the company's equity accruing to the venture investor should equal the sum of the compounded earnings on the new investment divided by the total pre-tax projected earnings for the company over an equivalent period of time.

The earnings on $300,000 at various compounded rates over four years are as follows (figures are in thousands).

Rate	Year 1	2	3	4	Total
20 %	60	72	86	104	322
30	90	117	152	198	557
40	120	168	235	329	852

Dividing each of the totals (less interest received) by XYZ Corporation's four-year cumulative pre-tax projected profits of $4,510,000 produces the following percentages of equity required.

$$(322 - 81) \div 4{,}510 = 5.3 \text{ percent}$$
$$(557 - 81) \div 4{,}510 = 10.6 \text{ percent}$$
$$(852 - 81) \div 4{,}510 = 17.1 \text{ percent}$$

[All of this assumes that the investor can sell the equity for something close to the then current quotation to realize a profit. This is most often not the case and should, therefore, be factored into the basis for establishing the means of profit potential. It is not unfair for the investor to say to the entrepreneur: "To justify the investment you want me to make, I have to earn a minimum of three times the yield which I would receive from a money market fund, and, therefore, such a return, paid in stock of the company, is the least I will consider. Now, let's work together to see if we can structure an arrangement which will insure that result."]

First Chicago Pricing Model

There are three basic directions a venture situation can take:

1. Successful: profitable to the point of being a solid public company. *[Or, it should just continue to provide returns to the owners. The individual investor has the advantage of being able to profit in ways the professional venture capital investment manager cannot. The individual can draw income in fees. He can enter into joint ventures with the company. He can borrow money from the company or have the company buy preferred stock in, or lend money to, other companies in which he may have or can create an interest. All this assumes, of course, that the other owners of the business agree. The point being made here is that going public is not the only answer, nor in some cases even the best answer, to the issue of how to profit from the success of a venture.]*

2. Sideways: marginally profitable with limited growth—not a viable public company but able to service debt over a period of years.

3. Failure: bankruptcy or reorganization

Cash Flow for the Successful Investment The cash flow to the investor if the company is quite successful might look like this (assume capital gains are realized in Year 4; figures are in thousands).

Year	1	2	3	4	5	6	7
Principal	0	0	0	0	0	0	0
Interest	21	21	21	18	0	0	0
Capital gain	0	0	0	X	0	0	0

Cash Flow for the Sideways Investment The cash flow to the investor would be different, however, if the company became a limited growth situation (figures are in thousands).

Year	1	2	3	4	5	6	7
Principal	0	0	0	75	75	75	75
Interest	21	21	21	18	13	8	3
Capital gain	0	0	0	0	0	0	0

Cash Flow for the Failure Investment If, unfortunately, the investment turned out to be a disaster, the cash flow might follow this pattern (assume a 10 percent recovery in Year 2; figures are in thousands).

Year	1	2	3	4	5	6	7
Principal	0	30	0	0	0	0	0
Interest	21	0	0	0	0	0	0
Capital gain	0	0	0	0	0	0	0

Compared Cash Flows Comparing the cash flows for each of the three directions a venture investment might take produces the following (figures are in thousands).

Year		1	2	3	4	5	6	7
Successful	↑	21	21	21	18+X	0	0	0
Sideways	→	21	21	21	93	88	83	78
Failure	↓	21	30	0	0	0	0	0

Probability Selection The next step in this method involves assigning probabilities (P) to each of the three possible directions. The sum of these probabilities must, of course, equal 1.0. For the purposes of this example, we have chosen the following probabilities, but each type of project might well receive different weighting for probabilities of success and failure.

$$P \uparrow = .3 \text{ (3 chances in 10)}$$
$$P \rightarrow = .5 \text{ (5 chances in 10)}$$
$$P \downarrow = \underline{.2} \text{ (2 chances in 10)}$$
$$1.0$$

Total Pricing Layout After having selected an appropriate discount factor (for the entire portfolio), the overall layout is as follows (we have assumed an annual 20 percent compounded target portfolio return; figures are in thousands).

Discounted value of dollar	.83	.69	.58	.48	.40	.33	.28
Year	1	2	3	4	5	6	7
P ↑ .3	21	21	21	18+X	0	0	0
P → .5	21	21	21	93	88	83	78
P ↓ .2	21	30	0	0	0	0	0

Reduction to Present Value Equivalents The next step is to reduce these numbers to their present value equivalents by multiplying them by the discount factor at the head of the column.

Year	1	2	3	4	5	6	7
P ↑ .3	17	15	12	9 + .48X	0	0	0
P → .5	17	15	12	45	35	27	22
P ↓ .2	17	21	0	0	0	0	0

Pricing Equation We now total each row and then construct the basic equation that will provide the desired output.

Probability	Row Total
P ↑ .3	53 + .48X
P → .5	173
P ↓ .2	38

$$300 = P (\uparrow)(53 + .48X) + P (\rightarrow) 173 + P (\downarrow) 38$$

Using the probabilities shown above,

$$300 = (.3)(53 + .48X) + (.5)(173) + (.2)(38)$$

Decision Matrix

P1	P2	P3	X	Percentage of Firm Needed at		
				P/E10	P/E15	P/E30
0.8	0.0	0.2	648.0	6.8	4.5	2.3
0.7	0.1	0.2	704.7	7.4	4.9	2.5
0.6	0.2	0.2	780.3	8.2	5.5	2.7
0.5	0.3	0.2	886.1	9.3	6.2	3.1
0.4	0.4	0.2	1,044.9	11.0	7.3	3.7
→ **0.3**	**0.5**	**0.2** ←	**1,309.5**	**13.8**	**9.2**	**4.6**
0.2	0.6	0.2	1,838.7	19.4	12.9	6.5
0.1	0.7	0.2	3,426.2	36.1	24.0	12.0

The row set in bold type shows the present value of $300,000 if a 20 percent compound growth rate is to be achieved, based on different probability assumptions shown on each line. The line marked ← → shows the assumptions given in this problem about success, failure, or sideways movement of the investment.

Thus, if a price-earnings multiple of 15 is to be used to calculate the value of the company, a 9.2 percent equity will be required to achieve the compound growth rate of 20 percent, given the probability requirements in the example. The columns headed P/E 10 and P/E 30 show the percentage of equity needed under those price-earnings multiples.

Comparison of Three Pricing Methods The percentage of equity required under the three pricing methods is as follows: traditional, 12.9 percent, fundamental, 5.3 percent, First Chicago, 9.2 percent.

Effect of Varying the Interest Rate What happens if the interest rate on the debenture is doubled, from 7 percent to 14 percent, for example?

P1	P2	P3	X	Percentage of Firm Needed at		
				P/E10	P/E15	P/E30
0.8	0.0	0.2	529.2	5.6	3.7	1.9
0.7	0.1	0.2	566.3	6.0	4.0	2.0
0.6	0.2	0.2	615.9	6.5	4.3	2.2
0.5	0.3	0.2	685.2	7.2	4.8	2.4
0.4	0.4	0.2	789.2	8.3	5.5	2.8
0.3	**0.5**	**0.2**	**982.5**	**10.1**	**6.8**	**3.4**
0.2	0.6	0.2	1,369.1	13.8	9.2	4.6
0.1	0.7	0.2	2,348.9	24.7	16.5	8.2

This table shows that the equity percentage required on the investment will drop from 9.2 percent to 6.8 percent and still produce the same return to First Chicago if the interest rate on the debenture doubles, from 7 percent to 14 percent.

Effect of Varying the Time Horizon What is the effect of pushing out the realization of capital gains to Year 7?

P1	P2	P3	X	Percentage of Firm Needed at		
				P/E10	P/E15	P/E30
0.8	0.0	0.2	1,119.7	11.8	7.9	3.9
0.7	0.1	0.2	1,217.7	12.8	8.5	4.3
0.6	0.2	0.2	1,348.4	14.2	9.5	4.7
0.5	0.3	0.2	1,531.2	16.1	10.7	5.4
0.4	0.4	0.2	1,805.6	19.0	12.7	6.3
0.3	**0.5**	**0.2**	**2,262.8**	**23.8**	**15.9**	**7.9**
0.2	0.6	0.2	3,177.2	33.4	22.3	11.1
0.1	0.7	0.2	5,920.5	62.3	41.5	20.8

This table shows the effects of moving the realization of capital gains from the fourth to the seventh year, keeping all other assumptions the same. The investment now will require a 15.9 percent equity interest rather than 9.2 percent.

BENEFITS OTHER THAN FINANCIAL OF INVESTING IN PRIVATE COMPANIES

14

What I have said so far in this book has not been a full and honest reflection of my true feelings about investing in private companies because I have emphasized mostly the negative aspects, leaning heavily to the side of caution. I have felt it my duty to do this in order not to encourage the reader to make investments that inherently have high probability of loss. Now, I must counter this and come out of the closet by saying I know of no more exciting and fulfilling role in the commercial world than that of playing a part in the creation of successful enterprises.

Exciting, frustrating, fulfilling, frightening, rewarding . . . along with the possibility of making a fortune in both relative and absolute terms, when it works out well. When it works out poorly, investing in private companies can result in financial ruin and the destruction of personal and family relationships. My greatest hope is that this book will be helpful in providing readers with ideas which will enhance their gains and minimize their losses.

Most of the good things, and some of the bad, result only from the investor's active participation in the business in which there is financial involvement. There is no doubt in my mind that the active role is preferable to the passive. The rewards of success for the active investor are much more than money alone, and the passive investor is denied these most of the time.

The major risk of the investor's active involvement in a company is that it will encourage him to make follow-on investments that may not be warranted in terms of the availability of comparable investment opportunities or justified in terms of his own resources. The reason for this is obvious. The investor becomes a full or quasi-entrepreneur, sharing the hopes and, worse, the beliefs of the managers of the business. As he becomes "one of them," he cultivates friendships with the managers and, still more inadvisedly, perhaps even with their families. He then does a terrible job of negotiating or renegotiating adequate return or security for his follow-on investments.

The actively involved investor is much more likely to fall prey to "hostage" or "ransom" investments than the passive investor. These are investments made by investors in attempting to recoup by making further investments in the belief that the company will succeed "if only we could keep at it a little longer." When a private company is significantly behind business-plan-projected levels, most follow-on investments do not work out well for the investor. Nevertheless, and unfortunately most of the time, the active investor is indeed likely to play angel up to the point where he can no longer do so.

The real and potentially tragic problems come from the use of leverage by the investor to fund ventures. For follow-on investing, the original investor is, in all probability, initially going to use personal guarantees rather than cash. I strongly urge the original investor to invest follow-on funds in a company *only* after the deal has been negotiated by another noninvolved, and, therefore, more dispassionate, investor. If no other investor can be found, there must be a reason. The investor must never place himself in jeopardy simply to be a nice guy or team player. The investor must remember who he is. He is the investor and not the entrepreneur. Switching roles seldom benefits the investor.

The destruction of the entrepreneur, in both financial and personal terms, is an unfortunate and occasional by-product of the current high levels of corporate formation and entrepreneurial activity. There is a lesser need for the investor to share the same fate. He must remember that his investment is a business opportunity and not a cause. Although he may have to suffer the embarrassment and remorse of a failed venture, he can come back to finance a new idea or company so long as he has not permitted himself to lose all his money. *The psychological need to vindicate the initial judgment, by breaking even, is the single greatest cause for all investor losses.* How often one hears an amateur investor say that he is going to sell "as soon as he can get even," which makes total nonsense as a plan. The question the investor must ask himself is if he were not already holding a position would he recreate it. If not, why consider any follow on investment? It is possible, and perhaps probable, that the investor would be better served by assuming a comparable level of risk in a different situation than the one in which he is presently embroiled.

On balance, the risk-accepting (or relishing) investor is best off sprinkling money on patches of talent in seed-capital investments. Doing this, he will get greater play for his dollar in terms of percentage interest, even after all the subsequent dilutions that occur as the company acquires the funding necessary for its development. The nearer in development a private company approaches profitability and the probability of going public, the lesser its discount in value from comparable public securities. This is shown in the figure on page 98. Therefore, in spite of their greater risk, very early-stage speculations are frequently the most appealing.

Most venture capitalists seek second stage investment opportunities rather than startups or, certainly, seed investments. The risk involved is one reason for this, and another is the amount of time required of an investor in monitoring and assisting the entrepreneur. Thus, this is one of the few areas where the individual investor has some sort of advantage over the professional investor.

Another possible advantage the individual investor has over the professional is that his livelihood is not going to be threatened by admission of a venture failure. Some venture capitalists are likely to keep throwing money at a problem company for no better reason than to keep it and their reputations afloat. One of the true luxuries associated with being wealthy is that the individual investor does not have to apologize for his financial mistakes to anyone—except perhaps his wife.

Traders in commodities and securities say "The trend is your friend" and "Don't fight the tape." The same can be said for private company investment. If the company in which you are invested is going well, then invest more in it. If the company's performance is disappointing, try to extricate yourself—or at least do not become more heavily involved. If you have properly structured your investment, your interest will be protected. Let someone else be the hero.

When a successful enterprise results in a cash bonanza for me, my wife asks me what I will do now with all this new money. She already knows the answer. I am like the Australian pastoral property owner who was asked the same question when he won a big lottery and answered, "I guess I'll just put it into my property until it's all gone."

Starting and financing young companies is the activity of which I am a willing captive. And I believe there is no more constructive and rewarding way to live a business life. I wish well those involved in entrepreneurial investing in private companies, our country needs you. To those who have not had the experience, I suggest that it can be a wonderful adventure.

APPENDIX

A

INFORMAL INVESTORS—WHEN AND WHERE TO LOOK[1]

William E. Wetzel, Jr.

No one has studied the phenomenon of the informal investor more than the author of this article. Owing to his constructively understanding attitude and experience, he typifies the academic that investors should attract to the board of directors of private companies. [A. L. III]

William E. Wetzel, Jr., is Professor of Finance at the Whittemore School of Business and Economics at the University of New Hampshire in Durham. With sponsorship from the Office of Advocacy of the U.S. Small Business Administration he directed a study of the cost and availability of informal risk capital in New England. The emphasis of the study was upon firms without access to traditional venture capital sources or the public equity markets.

Entrepreneurs seeking risk capital should be aware that risk capital is not a homogeneous commodity and that the risk capital markets are both diverse and dispersed. Risk capital sources range from the public new issues market, through professional venture capital funds and wealthy individuals, to local investors with a few dollars to back an

[1] Copyright © 1981 by Capital Publishing Corporation. Reprinted by permission from Stanley E. Pratt (ed.), *Guide to Venture Capital Sources,* Capital Publishing Corp., Box 348, Wellesley Hills, MA 02181.

acquaintance or relative. Investment objectives are equally broad. For example, risk capital investors vary dramatically in their taste for risk, ranging from investors willing to back inventors with unproven ideas to those preferring second or third round financing for established firms. Investors differ as well in the size of the investment they will consider, their exit horizons or level of patience for cash flow, their degree of personal involvement with a venture, their geographic and industrial preferences, their rate of return requirements, and in the substitutability of non-financial for financial rewards.

For many entrepreneurs seeking risk capital, informal investors represent the most appropriate source of funds, if not the only source. The term *informal investors* includes sources of risk capital other than professionally managed venture capital funds, equity-oriented Small Business Investment Companies (SBICs), other institutional investors, and the public equity markets. Informal investors tend to be financially sophisticated individuals of means, e.g. net worth in excess of $250,000 and annual income in excess of $50,000, often with previous investment or management experience in new or rapidly growing ventures.

Assuming that a venture proposal is economically sound in terms of market potential, competitive advantages, production capability, etc., and that competent management is available or can be acquired, then there are definable circumstances under which a search for risk capital from informal investors would be appropriate.

FINANCING TECHNOLOGY-BASED INVENTORS

Informal investors, in particular individuals with past experience in the formation of ventures in related fields of technology, are often the most likely source of risk capital for technology-based inventors prior to the startup of a business enterprise. Venture capital firms typically have little interest in inventors. The odds of picking a winner are slim, downside risks are close to 100 percent, relatively small amounts of money are involved, the costs of investment supervision and guidance are high, and the length of time between investment and potential cash recapture generally exceeds the exit horizons of venture capital firms. Informal investors may accept these risks in view of perceived non-financial benefits, such as the satisfaction of business creation or the stimulation of involvement, but professional venture capitalists consider the financial risk/reward relationship to be paramount.

The successful commercialization of new technology typically depends more upon "demand-pull" than upon "technology push." An individual investor with technical and managerial experience in the commercialization of related technology can bring a "sense of the market" to the work of a technology-based inventor. Personal satisfaction derived from a fresh involvement with emerging technology may also convert what would be a cost to a professional investor into a significant non-financial benefit for the right individual investor. Technology-based inventors should be aware, however, that despite the potential attractiveness of participation in new technology, the financial risks are extreme. Capital gains potential on the order of 50 to 100 times or more within 5 to 10 years is not unreasonable and may require sale of a major share of equity to attract funds. By reducing the risk and the waiting period for investors, the longer an inventor/entrepreneur can survive on personal funds and "sweat equity," the lower will be the cost of external capital.

Increasingly, technology-based inventors and small firms can turn to public and quasi-public organizations for risk financing. These relatively recent programs have been created in recognition of the contribution of young, technology-based firms to the generation of new jobs and to the pace of technological innovation, and in recognition of the difficulty these ventures encounter in raising small amounts of very high risk seed financing. At the national level, the National Science Foundation's Small Business Innovation Research

Program (SBIR) is perhaps the best known and most successful. The SBIR program was initiated in 1979 to fund high-quality research proposals on scientific or technical opportunities that could have significant public benefit if the research is successful. A second goal of the SBIR program is the conversion of funded research into technological innovation by private firms. The SBIR program is designed to increase the incentive and opportunity for small firms to undertake high-risk research that has a high-potential payoff and can effectively lower the risk for follow-on investors. Other national programs with similar objectives include the Department of Energy's Appropriate Technology Program and Energy-related Inventions Program and the new (1981) Department of Defense Small Business Advanced Technology Program.

Several New England states have created their own programs to stimulate economic growth by providing risk capital for firms with promising ideas and innovations. Examples include the Connecticut Product Development Corp., Maine Capital Corp., and the Massachusetts Technology Development Corp.

FINANCING BUSINESS STARTUPS

Since the late 1960s, most professional venture capital firms have adopted a policy of avoiding startups and have put their available capital into safer, more liquid investments. The National Venture Capital Association found that in the mid-1970s 143 venture capital firms were investing at the rate of about $150 million annually with less than 10 percent of these funds, under $15 million, going to startup situations. Fifteen million dollars will finance perhaps 20 new ventures, equivalent to one corporation out of every 10,000 that are formed annually.

While the 1978 reduction in capital gains tax rates and a modest revival in the public new issues market have attracted several hundred million dollars into professional venture capital portfolios, less than 15 percent of these funds appear to be available for startups and then only for firms with the prospect of a public share offering or merger with a larger, established firm within 5 to 10 years. Individual investors and groups of individuals are frequently the most likely sources of startup financing.

Providing seed capital or startup financing to an inexperienced management team can be enormously time consuming. Many of the management decisions involved in creating a new venture are unique to the startup process and will set the course of the venture through its perilous early years. Investors experienced with seed capital and startup situations can provide invaluable guidance to entrepreneurs who typically are engaged in the process for the first time. Ideally, investors in new enterprises would also be experienced in related fields of business or technology. In other words, a search for the "right" investors is part of the search for funds. The right informal investors will also be individuals who are fully aware of the risks involved and who are emotionally, as well as financially, able to bear those risks; who recognize the inevitably of unforeseen delays and other problems; who are prepared to invest additional funds if the venture succeeds and/or are realistic about the cost of additional outside risk capital; whose exit expectations are consistent with those of the founder and with the cash flow requirements of the venture; and, finally, whose role in the management of the venture is compatible with the needs of the venture and the founder.

Financially sophisticated individuals and groups of individuals are an appropriate source of startup funds under some or all of the following conditions:

a. *When the total financing required is over $50,000 but under $500,000.* The lower boundary represents the approximate limit of funds often available from an entrepreneur's personal savings and other friendly sources and is the bare minimum required to start anything but a "Mom & Pop" operation. The upper boundary represents the minimum investment typically required to interest a professional venture capital firm or equity-oriented SBIC, though they will occasionally entertain proposals involving less than $250,000

b. *When the sales potential of the venture is between $2 million and $20 million per year within five to 10 years.* Ventures with a potential volume of $20 million and up are generally necessary to provide the prospect of cash recovery through a public share offering or merger with a larger firm within the typical 5 to 10 year investment cycle of a professional venture fund. Informal investors tend to exhibit longer exit horizons and can accommodate firms with slower growth rates. Young, privately held firms with sales under $20 million generate the majority of new job opportunities and are a major source of technological innovation. These "foundation" firms are often initially financed by informal investors. Entrepreneurs seeking risk capital from informal investors for new foundation firms should identify the cash recapture expectations of these investors early in their negotiations and be prepared to offer appropriate buy-back arrangements or other liquidation options as an alternative to traditional exit mechanisms.

c. *When the proposed new venture is expected to generate "psychic income" for an investor in addition to adequate financial rewards.* More than impersonal financial incentives usually influence the investment decisions of informal investors. For example, a sense of civic or social responsibility often motivates individuals of means. A wealthy citizen in a community suffering from chronic unemployment may have more than a pecuniary interest in backing a venture expected to create 50 to 100 new jobs over a period of 5 to 10 years. Other individuals may derive "psychic income" from financing an inventor/entrepreneur involved in the commercial development of a new technology with significant social benefit, e.g. medical technology or energy-related technology. Other informal investors, in particular previously successful entrepreneurs, are often interested in investing both their funds and their experience in assisting promising new ventures get started. The rewards are partly financial and partly the satisfaction and stimulation of playing a role in the entrepreneurial process.

FINANCING GROWING ESTABLISHED BUSINESSES

Retained earnings are the primary source of equity capital to finance the growth of both public and privately held established corporations. General Electric's retained earnings are 5 times its paid-in capital, Kodak's 7 times, and General Motors' 10 times. For privately held corporations, retained earnings are generally the only source of new equity capital. For example, there are over two million incorporated businesses in the United States, but only about 12,000 (approximately one half of 1 percent) enjoy sufficiently wide ownership to be considered publicly owned. The shares of about 4,000 firms are traded on an organized stock exchange. In other words, the public equity markets are not a source of capital for most corporations. In testimony before the House Sub-Committee on Capital Investment and Business Opportunities during 1977 hearings into small business access to equity and venture capital, M. William Benedetto, Vice President of E. F. Hutton & Co., was quoted as follows:

> Speaking directly as an investment banker, I can tell this Committee that we are unable to provide startup capital for new enterprises. The marketplace has caused us to substantially increase our criteria for providing capital to existing businesses. In short, capital in meaningful terms is available only for medium-sized companies those with annual after-tax earnings in excess of $2.8 million.

In a 1977 position paper, the National Association of Small Business Investment Companies cited similar criteria:

> Smaller underwriters are currently insisting that a company have a minimum of $500,000 to $1 million of after-tax earnings to undertake a public offering while the larger underwriters generally look for a minimum of $2 million.

After-tax profits of $1 million to $2 million imply sales of $20 million or more, given typical profit margins of 5 percent to 10 percent.

Only the exceptional expanding foundation firms with sales between $2 million and $20 million, can generally raise funds in the public equity markets. Professional venture capital firms concentrate on businesses with prospective growth rates high enough to propel a venture into public offering status within 5 to 10 years or to attract major corporate acquisition.

In the absence of alternative external equity sources, growth rates for foundation firms are constrained by the growth in internally generated equity. A firm earning a 15 percent return on equity and paying no dividends can grow no faster than 15 percent per year without distorting the debt/equity proportions of its balance sheet. Growth rates in excess of 30 percent per year typically are necessary to attract the interest of institutional venture investors. The troublesome firm to finance is the established foundation firm growing faster than retained earnings can support but not fast enough to attract venture capital. These troublesome but attractive growth rates tend to fall between 10 percent and 30 percent per year. Passage of the Small Business Investment Incentive Act of 1980 and a series of new SEC Rules that simplify the raising of relatively small amounts of long-term capital are indicative of an emerging awareness of the financing problems of smaller established firms.

For foundation firms growing at a rate too slow to attract venture capital, private individuals are the most likely financing source. A great deal of time can be wasted talking with institutional venture capital sources about deals which they are very unlikely to do.

PROFILE OF INFORMAL INVESTORS

Any attempt to describe a "typical" informal investor is bound to result in a profile with as many exceptions as examples. In the first place, these individuals exhibit a natural tendency toward anonymity when it comes to their investment activity. The Commerce Technical Advisory Board, in its 1976 report on The Role of New Technical Enterprises in the U.S. Economy, stated: "There are no data regarding the individual and truly private sources of seed money." In the second place, the personal backgrounds and investment objectives of informal investors are so diverse that generalizations about these characteristics are, at best, only suggestive.

The importance of informal investors to the vitality of foundation firms prompted the Whittemore School of Business and Economics at the University of New Hampshire to undertake a systematic examination of the volume and characteristics of informal risk capital financing in New England. The research was sponsored by the Office of Advocacy of the U.S. Small Business Administration, and focused on the role of informal investors as a source of funds for three types of investment situations:

1. Financing technology-based investors.

2. Startup and early stage financing for emerging firms.

3. Equity financing for small established firms growing faster than retained earnings can support.

A comprehensive investment history and interest questionnaire was employed in the research. To reach informal investors a variety of experimental techniques were employed, including assistance from the Smaller Business Association of New England (SBANE), the Vermont Bankers Association, and the National Association of Securities Dealers (NASD). Responses were received from 133 informal investors.

Research results confirm and document generally held impressions that informal investors are a significant and appropriate source of risk capital for technology-based inventors and for both emerging and established firms without access to traditional venture capital sources or the public equity markets. Informal investors are difficult to reach. Useful generalizations about the characteristics of informal investors can be drawn from the sample data. Of equal significance, however, is the degree of variation in characteristics represented by individual investors. They are a characteristically diverse as well as geographically dispersed group and therefore difficult to identify.

The total population of informal investors in New England is unknown, The 133 investors in the research sample represent approximately 10 investors per million population, or about 1 percent of the 1,000 per million incidence of millionaires, based on 1972 IRS personal wealth data. The comparison suggests that the total informal investor population in New England is substantially greater than the research sample, perhaps by a factor of 10 or more.

Respondents reported risk capital investments totalling over $16 million in 320 ventures during the five years from 1976 through 1980, an average investment rate of about $3 million per year in 64 ventures per year. The average size of past investments was in the neighborhood of $50,000, while the median investment size was about $20,000. Investment goals of respondents for 1981 and 1982 represent an expected investment rate of about $5 million in over 100 ventures per year. If the research sample represents one informal investor in 5 or 10, total informal risk capital financing in New England is in the neighborhood of $15 million to $30 million per year for 300 to 500 ventures.

Small Business Investment Companies (SBICs) invested about $8 million in equity securities and $7 million in debt-with-equity securities of approximately 75 New England firms in 1979. Based on national statistics, the monthly median SBIC debt-with-equity investment averaged $167,000 during 1979, and the monthly median equity investment averaged $306,000. The data suggest that total risk capital financing by informal investors is at least equal in dollar volume to the equity-type funds provided by SBICs and that, by investing in smaller amounts, informal investors finance perhaps five times as many ventures.

The data support the conclusion that informal investors are an appropriate source of relatively small amounts (under $100,000) of very early, very high-risk financing. One third of the sample expressed a "strong interest" in financing technology-based inventors and 78 percent expressed "strong interest" in startup and early stage financing for emerging firms. Investors interested in inventors tend to limit their interest to fields with which they are familiar and typically consider investing approximately $35,000 in any one situation. Investors interested in startup and emerging firms typically consider investments in the neighborhood of $40,000 to $60,000. In both cases, investors tend to have postgraduate college training, prior startup management experience, and expect to maintain an active relationship with ventures in which they invest, typically a consulting role or service on a board of directors.

Approximately one respondent in five expressed a "strong interest" in growth financing for established small firms. Investors interested in established firms typically consider investments in the neighborhood of $75,000 in any one firm. The incidence of advanced technical training and startup management experience was lower among investors interested in established firms than among investors interested in either technology-based inventors or in early-stage financing for emerging firms.

The investment size and venture age preferences of informal investors combined with a high frequency of post graduate college training (51 percent, frequently technical, and prior startup management experience (75 percent fill a need for risk capital financing typically not met by professional venture capital firms or the public equity markets. In addition, the tendency of informal investors to participate with other financially sophisticated individuals adds flexibility to the total financing available for any given venture and permits venture financing approaching the typical $250,000 to $500,000 interest thresholds of venture capital firms and equity-oriented SBICs.

Informal investors generally learn of investment opportunities through friends and business associates. During the course of this research, it was not uncommon to discover that finding one informal investor led to contacts with several others. A network of friends and associates appear to link these individuals. However, the majority of respondents were less than satisfied with the effectiveness of existing channels of communication between bonafide entrepreneurs seeking risk capital and investors like themselves. Over 80 percent expressed an interest in a regional refereal service that would permit them to examine a broader range of investment opportunities. These widely held opinions suggest that an appropriately designed regional network linking investors with opportunities could materially improve the efficiency of the informal risk capital market. Confidentiality and timeliness appear to be two essential characteristics of such a network. In cooperation with Massachusetts Technology Development Corporation, the Whittemore School of Business and Economics is developing plans for an experimental program designed to link risk capital investors with bonafide investment opportunities. The program is expected to be in place by mid-1982 and, initially, will be limited to the risk capital financing of technology-based ventures.

Generalizations about a group as diverse as the informal investor population are hazardous. Nevertheless, the data reveal a number of interesting characteristics of informal investors. Despite the pitfalls, and as a starting point for discussion and further research, the following profile of the mythical, "typical" informal investor is offered:

INFORMAL INVESTOR PROFILE

1. Age 47.
2. Education: Post-graduate degree, often technical.
3. Previous management experience with startup ventures.
4. Typically invests approximately $25,000 in any one venture.
5. Invests at a rate of approximately once a year.
6. Typically participates with other financially sophisticated individuals.
7. Prefers to invest in startup and early-stage situations.
8. Willing to finance technology-based inventors when technology and markets are familiar.
9. Limited interest in financing established, moderate growth, small firms.
10. Strong preference for manufacturing ventures, high technology in particular.
11. Invests close to home—within 300 miles and usually within 50 miles.
12. Maintains an active professional relationship with portfolio ventures, typically a consulting role or service on a board of directors.
13. Diversification and tax sheltered income are not important objectives.
14. Expects to liquidate investment in five to seven years.
15. Looks for compound annual rates of return on individuals investments ranging from 50+ percent from inventors to 20 percent to 25 percent from established firms.

16. Looks for minimum portfolio returns of about 20 percent.

17. Often will accept limitations on financial returns in exchange for non-financial rewards.

18. Learns of investment opportunities primarily from friends and business associates.

19. Would like to look at more investment opportunities than present informal system permits.

Having enumerated the above characteristics, it must be said that exceptions to all of the above abound and there appear to be few bonafide opportunities for which an appropriate informal investor cannot be found. Copies of the complete research report; *Informal Risk Capital in New England,* can be obtained from the National Technical Information Service (NTIS), U.S. Department of Commerce, 5285 Port Royal Road, Springfield, Virginia 22161. NTIS accession number is PB81-196149.

Informal investors, essentially individuals of means and successful entrepreneurs, are a diverse and dispersed group with a preference for anonymity. Creative techniques are required to identify and research them. Currently, inventors and entrepreneurs must find their own way through the maze of channels leading to informal risk capital. Private market makers are unable, by and large, to reap the substantially public benefits of improving the efficiency of the informal capital market. Therefore, entrepreneurs can expect to find little guidance in preparing sound investment proposals and in identifying potential individual investors, and investors themselves will continue to rely largely on random events to bring investment opportunities to their attention. Among the major objectives of the current SBA sponsored research is an assessment of the feasibility of creating an experimental mechanism to improve the efficiency of the informal risk capital markets.

SUMMARY

Wealthy individuals, successful entrepreneurs in particular, are a significant source of risk capital for certain types of situations. These informal investors are a diverse and dispersed group about which very little is known. Situations suggesting a search for risk capital from an appropriate individual, or group of individuals, include the following:

1. Financing technology-based inventors prior to commercialization of an invention or innovation.

2. Financing business startups, especially for firms with 5-to-10-year sales potential between $2 million and $20 million and requiring between $50,000 and $500,000 of risk capital.

3. Financing business startups with the prospect of providing psychic income in addition to adequate financial rewards. Examples of non-financial incentives for informal investors include the creation of jobs in a community experiencing chronic unemployment, participating in the commercialization of a socially useful new technology or innovation, and the satisfaction of playing an active role in the entrepreneurial process.

4. Financing privately held, established businesses growing too fast to finance from retained earnings but not fast enough to attract institutional venture investors. Attractive, but troublesome growth rates, tend to fall between 10 percent and 30 percent per year.

The search for informal risk capital under the best of circumstances can be tedious and time consuming. Entrepreneurs with sound ideas, strong management skills, and well-documented proposals may find the search productive. Financially sophisticated individuals will often undertake investments that are similar, riskier, and less liquid than those that interest professional venture investors. Appropriate incentives are necessary to offset the costs, risks, and limited liquidity of these investments and entrepreneurs seeking informal risk capital will find it essential to carefully match their objectives with those of their financial partners.

APPENDIX   B

CHARACTERISTICS OF AN ENTREPRENEUR

John L. Hines

The author, president of both Continental Illinois Venture Corporation and Continental Illinois Equity Corporation, is an extremely successful venture capital investor and has been most helpful in the preparation of this book. [A. L. III]

It is difficult to enumerate in order of priority the most important characteristics of an entrepreneur. There are two reasons why this task is formidable. First, there are several characteristics which seem both inherent and essential to all successful entrepreneurs; a deficiency in any of these essentials usually portends failure. Second, most venture capitalists tend to be quite subjective when weighing other characteristics which may not be so universal or prominent. I believe that it is best to dispense quickly with the essential traits and then elaborate on the more subjective ones. These may be considerably more subtle and controversial. It is these more elusive qualities that seem to distinguish one entrepreneur from another, define individual style.

ESSENTIAL CHARACTERISTICS DEFINED

Every venture capitalist concurs that successful entrepreneurs must be honest, intelligent, skillful, and well educated in their chosen fields (not necessarily as a result of a formal education). There have been relatively few, if any, long-lived, successful venture companies led by people deficient in any one of these four essential qualities. Knowledgeable investors would decline participation opportunities in such ventures.

There are at least nine other characteristics which I value highly. Some of my priorities may be questioned by more experienced and knowledgeable venture capitalists. The values which I list are not meant to be all inclusive. I look for the following traits in all venture candidates in whom we have an interest (in no particular order of priority): energy level, ego, courage, enthusiasm, desire to make money, creativity, resourcefulness, tenacity, and leadership qualities. Unless an entrepreneur has an abundance of all these qualities, one might pause and be more careful when considering becoming his or her partner. The weighing of each of these characteristics must by necessity be purely subjective.

ENERGY LEVEL: STAYING AHEAD OF THE PACK

Energy level is very important because all businesses, particularly new ones, need a person at the top to set a brisk pace. One who expects others to work and think more than eight hours a day must be able to consistently demonstrate an ability to stay ahead of the pack. If one's own energy wanes, one may excuse subordinates of the same pleasure.

Young businesses do not frequently possess the many and varied skills of larger and more successful enterprises. The entrepreneur, by necessity, must participate directly in a wide variety of challenging tasks. Raising venture capital is in itself an extremely demanding chore, especially if one is concurrently trying to expand sales and manufacturing capabilities and hire and train personnel.

CONFIDENCE IN ABILITY TO EXCEL

Ego is related to self-appraisal of one's own capabilities and pride in achieving. Unless the entrepreneur holds himself in high esteem (is even a bit egocentric), it may be difficult to inspire confidence in others important to him—investors, creditors, and subordinates alike. Ego, if unmantled or uncontrolled, may be a glaring negative. It appears that many of the more successful entrepreneurs really believe that they possess most of the abilities necessary to succeed in their chosen fields. Generally, if they consider themselves lacking in particular skills, they tend to compensate by hiring and encouraging others who may possess them. Successful entrepreneurs tend to rate themselves at the top of their chosen fields. If they do not honestly believe this, they will be risking more than their financial backers—reputation, future, time, and capital.

COURAGE TO KEEP FORGING AHEAD

Courage is rare and elusive. It is extremely hard to appraise. Every growing business requires this quality of its leader, because they all encounter serious difficulties periodically. Among other qualities, it takes courage, and plenty of it, to cope with money woes, fuel shortages, labor difficulties, patent infringements, veiled threats of competitors and customers, regulatory agencies, and obsolescence of products and services. Most executives who are relatively secure in their jobs occasionally dream about owning and running their own "show"; few have the courage to start or buy a business. The best entrepreneurs are generally cognizant of many negatives inherent in their ventures but generally believe in their own solutions. These successful types possess the courage to keep forging ahead.

PEOPLE BACK AND FOLLOW A WINNER

It is difficult to distinguish between enthusiasm and a positive spirit. Entrepreneurs who have these qualities generally have a better chance of engendering such spirits in their followers—money, people, customers, and employees. People like to back and follow a "winner."

If a young entrepreneur is truly enthusiastic about his or her product, the long-term business outlook for it, and the chance to build an enterprise to purvey it, he usually has a better chance for success. If he radiates optimism and enthusiasm, no matter how difficult times may be, he should have an easier time attracting those elements which may be necessary for his company's success. It is difficult to sell any goods or services unless the seller portrays that he would be a buyer, and an enthusiastic one. One might interject the adjective "charismatic" here to help describe an entrepreneur who is able to affably reflect enthusiasm about his company and its prospects.

THE DESIRE TO WIN TRANSLATES INTO DESIRE TO MAKE MONEY

Many confuse the desire to make money with greed. I, on the other hand, confuse this money desire with the will to win, to be successful, and to be able to demonstrate business accomplishments. Capitalism's score card seems to be money, return on invested capital. Unless the entrepreneur wants to win, respects the value of earning high returns on invested capital, and has a desire to acquire wealth, he may end up with just another start-up situation. Without this important quality, he will have little opportunity to earn returns on invested capital, much less make important social contributions. Either one of these ambitions should promote a desire to win or make money.

CREATIVE APPROACH TO INVENTION, MANAGEMENT, FINANCE, AND MERCHANDISING

Creativity is one of the most unique qualities. The ability to be able to add a new "twist" to an existing product or service and merchandise, it well is indeed unusual. McDonald's was a late starter in the hamburger business; Revlon in cosmetics; Polaroid in photography; H. R. Block in accounting; Intel in electronics; Syntex in drugs; and Hyatt in motels. Despite their tardy entries, the founders of these companies had one thing in common—they were all creative. They all improved upon, invented, and delivered newly packaged products or services to consumers at attractive prices. Creativity for our purposes should not merely be confined to inventive genius. It should be coupled with management, financial, and merchandising skills. Creative entrepreneurs usually are able to adroitly package products and services and select growing market areas which they might penetrate.

RESOURCEFULNESS: MAKING USE OF TALENT, DEFINING COURSE OF ACTION

Resourcefulness is a quality that entrepreneurs must possess if their companies are to be viable, much less be successful. Entrepreneurs must be able to deal effectively with a multitude of problems quickly, to act and react with dispatch. Their actions do not have to be correct all of the time; however, they should be able to recognize their own mistakes and alter their positions frequently—as would a field general.

Part of resourcefulness is making use of all the talent at hand; the ability to listen well is the key here. Resourceful entrepreneurs have the ability to assimilate conflicting views and varied inputs regarding complex problems and then to define skillfully their priorities and courses of action. Handling venture capitalists' negatives is a fine test of this quality, but only one small measure.

TENACITY SEPARATES THE DOER FROM THE QUITTER

Tenacity is also very difficult to judge, because it is often confused with stubbornness or inflexibility. It is important to place proper value on tenacity because most young, growing enterprises are plagued with problems that would cause average people to quit or compromise their ethics, standards, or objectives to the detriment of shareholders and others. I believe that tenacity for our purposes should include a toughness which causes an individual to hang on when circumstances are most difficult. Appraising tenacity is very much like appraising honesty; the task is difficult to perform unless the entrepreneur is tested under adverse circumstances.

SENSITIVITY TO PEOPLE'S NEEDS

Leadership qualities embody all of the important characteristics already considered, and more. A key addition here is the ability of the entrepreneur to stimulate, relate to, and empathize with his employees, officers, directors, and shareholders. To lead effectively, one must be able to recognize and encourage the best qualities in one's people. This is one of the most difficult assignments, because the entrepreneur must be sensitive to people's needs, personal as well as economic.

The exercise of listing and actually making value judgments with reference to each one of these essential and/or subjective characteristics can be a most instructive exercise for any investment analyst, especially those dealing with venture situations. The fact that individual priorities will differ for each appraiser is of little consequence. The prime advantage to this exercise (formally listing one's priorities) is to sharpen one's own appraisal techniques and standards. The most important consideration in evaluating any venture company is the manager, founder, or entrepreneur. It is both necessary and natural to alter and refine one's standards and methods for making these value judgments.

APPENDIX

C

WHEN INVESTORS ASSEMBLE THEIR OWN COMPANIES

Harrison L. Moore

*Entrepreneurial investing can sometimes be institutionalized, such as when professional venture capital investors start, rather than solely finance, their own companies. This article appeared in **Venture** in October 1982. [A. L. III]*

Edwin Snape journeyed to Chicago on a mission. Snape, a venture capitalist with Whitehead Associates in Greenwich, Conn., was hunting for someone to run the new biotechnology company he had planned. In the ballroom of the Americana Congress Hotel, Snape settled down to listen to a discussion of liposomes, or fat particles, presented by Mark Ostrow, a young University of Chicago associate professor. Snape was impressed. Ostrow, he thought, might be the right guy.

Two thousand miles to the west, Bill Chandler, head of Bay Ventures, a San Francisco venture capital partnership, tipped back in his chair, put his feet on the desk, and gazed out of his office window. In his lap rested a blue-vinyl, three-ring notebook with articles covering genetic engineering. Chandler wanted an investment opportunity. A knock on the door interrupted his thoughts. In stepped Wayne Harvey, looking for a job in venture capital. It turned out that Harvey had an MBA and a master's degree in marine biology.

The gears in Bill Chandler's head started spinning. "Wayne Harvey," he thought, "would make a good entrepreneur. Now, we need a product for him."

Snape and Chandler represent a new direction in venture capital. Because of competition, venture capitalists are increasingly concocting their own deals rather than waiting for inventors in search of funds to knock. They're acting as both entrepreneur and financier.

Phil McCarthy, head of INCO's New York-based venture capital arm and the man who conceived the idea for Immunogen, a Boston-based venture capital startup in monoclonal antibodies, explains the current phenomenon this way: "Venture capitalists sniff around in promising fields and see deals too expensive with talent too shallow. So they say, 'We can organize a new venture as well as anybody. So why not start our own?' "

McCarthy is an investor with Edwin Snape in the project that ferreted out Dr. Mark Ostrow at the conference on emerging medical technologies in November, 1980. The idea for the venture was Snape's. It emanated from some articles he'd read in science magazines about liposomes, which are naturally occurring, microscopic biomembranes, shaped like balloons, made up of lipids, or fat particles. They can transport drugs or other substances to diseased cells without triggering the body's rejection mechanism.

Although the articles were scientific, the undiscussed commercial potential of liposomes is what intrigued Snape. With a couple of other like-minded venture capitalists, he put together a scientific advisory group which concluded that commercial potential existed. The next step was to pick a man to head the endeavor. After approaching and being rejected by several prominent members of the scientific and academic community, Snape turned to Ostrow.

"Others wouldn't take the risk," says Ostrow. "But I wasn't tenured, and they don't pay beans in academics. I didn't see the venture as that much of a risk. And I'd get a share of the company. But what clinched it was this thought: 'If I don't do it and somebody else does, and it works, I'll never forgive myself.' "

They agreed to join forces. The venture capitalists, INCO and Whitehead, each put in $650,000 in return for a third of the equity, and management took the remaining third. They chose to locate the company in the Forrestal Center in Princeton, N.J., a commercial development in which high-technology firms nesting there enjoy a symbiotic relationship with the University. On July 1, 1981, Mark Ostrow motored into Princeton to launch Liposome Co. He had to start from scratch—finding lab space, designing it, stocking it, and recruiting employees. His title was director of research while Snape served as chairman. Snape spent a day a week in Princeton providing business and managerial advice.

Ostrow's lab started percolating in October, 1981. In six months, he boasts, it achieved "miraculous" results—three patents, including a cure for *brucella abortus,* a bacteria that causes livestock to abort. Affected animals have traditionally been slaughtered, yet after injecting over 100 animals with massive doses of the bacteria, Ostrow claims a 100 percent cure rate. He sees a world-wide market for the serum easily exceeding $100 million

The business of Liposome is coupling drugs or a radioactive tracer element with liposomes. Ordinarily, these foreign substances would be attacked by the body's rejection mechanism, but when encapsulated in a fat particle, they survive for a predetermined length of time. Yet, these liposomes by themselves can't be targeted to diseased cells. So Liposome is working on splicing them to monoclonal antibodies which seek out affected cells like heat-seeking missiles.

To Ostrow, the group's success is due in no small measure to its structure—no bureaucracy to debate new proposals. Decisions come quickly. Says Ostrow, "We've got to keep ideas moving quickly from research to production to market. Or we'll go broke." So far, Liposome has not brought to market any product—they're still in the testing stage. The company employs a team of 12 scientists. Yet, the company's planning a number of different routes in product manufacturing and marketing, which include licensing and joint ventures.

As Liposome has matured over the past 18 months, its demands on Snape's time have lessened. In his role as chairman of the board, he spends only about 10 percent of his time on the company's marketing and financial affairs.

Carl Thoma is another venture capitalist who hopes to reduce his role in a company he started from a couple of days a week to half a day. Golder, Thoma & Co., Chicago, is heavily committed to Pagenet, the new radio-common-carrier paging company that general partner Thoma has created. His experience in telecommunication traces back to his days with the venture capital arm of First Chicago Corp. Since acquiring cable television systems for First Chicago, Thoma's kept on top of the evolving telecommunications industry.

"Paging and mobile telephone systems have proven themselves over the past five years and indicate potential of continuing growth," says Thoma. "We looked for some companies to invest in, but found no good deals. Since the industry is young and highly fragmented, it's penetrable. So we decided to start our own company."

Thoma hired a headhunter to approach George Perrin, a man with 10 years of management and regulatory experience in the business. Perrin was itching for a change. When he met Carl Thoma in June, 1981, the proposition enticed him. At their second meeting eight days later, Thoma and Perrin made a deal. Golder, Thoma committed $6 million and took 80 percent of the equity, allotting 15 percent to Perrin and reserving 5 percent for additional management. Thoma took the role of chairman and handled the financial affairs of the company. Perrin became chief executive officer and administered the daily operations. Their strategy was to build the company primarily through new frequency applications and, to a lesser degree, through acquisitions. But since no new frequency applications have cleared the FCC, Pagenet has grown only by acquisitions—one each in New York, San Francisco, Tulsa, and Houston. For the next 12 months, Thoma expects revenues for Pagenet to run around $12.5 million.

"But what you're buying is cash flow," says Thoma. "Cash flow from existing operations hits 35 percent to 40 percent of revenues. However, for incremental paging services—for new growth on existing systems—it jumps to 60 percent of revenues."

Luring financing is the hardest part of any startup, and the venture capitalist who plays entrepreneur sometimes finds himself in the awkward position of selling his deal to other venture capital firms. Bill Chandler, the San Francisco venture capitalist hasn't yet had to do that, and his Bay Ventures partnership, therefore, usually underwrites the germination of an operation alone. Ocean Genetics, the company he founded with Wayne Harvey, is still germinating. The pair formed a limited partnership in October, 1981, with Bay Ventures committing $200,000. More recently seven research scientists from various universities have joined the venture, taking 40 percent of the company with Harvey and Chandler's group holding 30 percent each.

Ocean Genetics intends to apply genetic biotechnology to marine organisms. It's now focused on the artificial production of red marine algae. The algae contains agar, the solidifying agent for bacterial culture and in a costly, purified form, the main component of an electrophoresis gel in which strands of DNA are separated by an electrical current.

The Japanese, the leading farmers of this algae, dive to the sea bottom, tear it off rocks and stuff it in bags. Ocean Genetics is screening various species of the red algae for qualities of growth and adaptability. If a suitable species can be found, the company will cultivate it in large inland ponds, allowing for easy harvest and processing. At present, a dozen people on the project are using the research facilities of a pair of West Coast universities.

Some venture capitalists have had a good deal of success starting and then financing their own companies. Take Kleiner, Perkins, Caufield & Byers, the San Francisco venture capital firm, which ranks as the leader in internally generating startups. Tandem Computers Inc., which former KPCB associate James Treybig founded for the firm, has more than earned its keep, and the firm has high hopes for a couple of more recent genetic engineering startups, Genentech and Hybritech, both public companies.

In companies started by venture capitalists, the chemistry between founder and manager is usually strong. At Pagenet, for example, Perrin is impressed with Thoma's grasp of the industry. "They've always kicked in when we needed more work on an acquisition or preparation for a filing," says Perrin.

Similarly, most of the other scientists and managers feel more positively about the venture capitalists they're dealing with than do most entrepreneurs. In the startup instance where they've shared the risks and toils, a together-in-the-trenches camaraderie develops. "Bill Chandler has helped a lot in identifying product, markets, and resources," says Harvey of Ocean Genetics. Liposome's Ostrow adds: "The venture capital backers haven't vetoed a single one of my lab purchases. They give latitude and stand behind the guy they hired."

These concept startups seem to indicate that most venture capitalists are closet entrepreneurs. Is this true?

"By no means," says Bill Egan of the Boston firm of Burr, Egan & Deleage, "is the nature of venture capitalists entrepreneurial. We don't initiate things. And before we move on a venture, we research the situation methodically. We're very conservative."

But competition in the venture capital business has created this ostensible paradox of conservative men engaged in the risky business of entrepreneurship. Some, no doubt, will prosper through the 1980s. "The others," according to Egan, "will be out of business, tearing tickets in the movie theater."

APPENDIX

D

PRESTARTUP SEED CAPITAL[1]

William R. Chandler

This article is one of the few writings by a recognized venture capitalist which indicate any real interest in the sort of investment opportunity the informal investor most likely will find available to him. The author concludes that investing in startups can be a good business and one that is getting better due to the higher skill levels of venture investment managers in dealing with and assisting early developing situations. [A. L. III]

William R. Chandler is a co-founder and general partner of the Bay Venture Group, San Francisco, a company specializing in startup and seed capital investment for new venture development. Before organizing Bay Venture in 1976, Mr. Chandler had been active as a venture capitalist and in operating management responsibilities for the prior 15 years.

GENERAL OBSERVATIONS

Most new venture financings occur, at least conceptually, in three stages: seed, startup, and early growth. Seed financing is a relatively small amount of capital provided to an

---

[1] Copyright © 1981 by Capital Publishing Corporation. Reprinted by permission from Stanley E. Pratt (ed.), *Guide to Venture Capital Sources*, Capital Publishing Corp., Box 348, Wellesley Hills, MA 02181.

inventor or an entrepreneur to investigate a business concept. It may involve product development but rarely involves initial marketing. As the term *seed* denotes, this capital is used to "germinate" the entrepreneur's vision of his business and to transform it into the tangible reality required to attract additional capital for continued product development and initial marketing (the startup stage).

Although the new venture management team may expect to raise startup or growth-stage capital from professional venture capital sources, any seed financing is likely to be from private investors since there are few seed financing specialists within the venture capital community. Ninety percent of the active professional venture capital groups seldom, if ever, make seed-stage investments. Typically, entrepreneurs at the seed and very earliest startup stages tap private investors to combine with whatever personal capital they and their families have. I would guess that at least 95 percent of the successful seed financings, and a significant percentage of startup financings, come from such nonprofessional sources. Family and friends may invest based on their knowledge of the individual, but the private investor must, like the professional venture capital manager, make his personal assessment of the business venture. If the proposed venture will need professional venture capital later in its startup or growth stages in order to succeed, an important part of that assessment must include an estimate of the business' future appeal to the venture capital managers.

In considering a seed-stage investment, the venture capitalists recognizes the likelihood that they may have to wait 8, 10, or 12 years to liquidate the investment. Most venture capitalists are working with an objective of securing liquidity within 5 to 7 years. Seed capital often has to be invested 2 or 3 years before startup venture capital—perhaps longer. Therefore, seed capital has to be the most patient of the venture investments. If a venture capitalist is willing to expend the time and resources to develop a business from its seed stage, he must perceive a minimal risk and an outstanding opportunity for return.

Raising seed capital is the first and most important selling effort of a business' life. During the seed stage, the entrepreneur will typically assemble the key management, prepare a business plan, and make extensive market studies—all three of which are the basic tools needed to sell his company to the venture capital community for future financing. The new venture team should look at the startup financing as their first $250,000, $500,000, or $1 million sale—and I am sure in their past employment they didn't close many sales of that magnitude without a carefully prepared, first-class sales program. Such a program starts with an effort to learn what the customer has been buying in the past, why, and what his needs are in today's market. If the management team hasn't had experience with the venture capital industry they should try to build up a very clear picture of what the venture capitalist will be looking for in their financing presentation.

I recommend that a team identify those sources of startup capital they expect to approach before they raise any significant seed capital or prepare a business plan. The management team should study the existing investments of these sources, from a picture of the original state of the sources' early-stage investments, and try to develop a business plan incorporating the special characteristics of their industry.

The new venture team should then turn back to their own business and try to make a cold-blooded appraisal of the management résumés, the market characteristics, and the product features they are attempting to sell. Comparing that picture to the model they have to match reveals the holes that have to be filled during the seed development stage of their venture. These needs may take the form of adding more staff, reassigning people, gathering additional market information, or establishing hardware credibility. The seed-stage business plan is a critical tool to convince a venture capitalist that the business is feasible, and the plan may take as long as 9 to 15 months to prepare. It should be well structured and thought out, yet it must be adaptable and flexible to not only adjust to changes in the developing business but also to take into account its initial presentation to various venture capitalists whose strategies and priorities may differ. The seed-stage plan should also include a realistic estimate of the amount of capital required for seed and startup financings.

If the venture team at this point decides they have the credentials to solicit a combination seed/startup financing package from one of the top venture capitalists, they should prepare their business plan and go. If they can measure up, I think they will be tapping the best source of startup capital on earth. Venture capitalists will add talents the new venture team probably does not possess, and they will drag in behind them a lot of financial credibility when the enterprise needs it most.

A few new sources of seed financing have appeared recently which should represent important new sources of funding over the next few years. The National Science Foundation's Small Business Innovation Research program's successes with expenditures of only $2 million to $3 million per year spawned the 1982 enacted Small Business Innovation Research Act, to implement small business R&D in 10 key federal research agencies. This program should be very helpful to ventures trying to demonstrate commercial value with new technologies in areas of national need. Research and Development Partnerships, with the tax benefits flowing out to the investors as incurred, are also being used more each year to fund product development programs. However, the R&D Partnerships leave the entrepreneurs with the problem of finding seed capital to finance all items that cannot be expensed in the development partnership.

THE EXPERIENCE OF BAY VENTURE GROUP

Bay Venture was organized as a pre-venture capital seed investor. I thought I saw an opportunity for front-end, venture capital investment financings in the range of $100,000 to $150,000, with early-stage oriented venture capitalists providing subsequent financing. I was also convinced that the American financial community was, collectively, leaving a lot of technical market opportunities lying stillborn. I knew of a number of potentially attractive growth markets and other venture capitalists were seeing few good, startup offerings. In those potentially attractive markets, I wanted Bay Venture to take the initiative in organizing, staffing, and financing startup ventures.

In 1976, I sold this investment development strategy to 14 individual investors and organized Bay Venture Management, Inc. We found out after investing an average of $100,000 in each seed venture that our projects fell far short of the quality standards needed to raise startup financing from professional venture capitalists.

The venture capitalists were investing in raw startups, but they were truly skimming the cream—in 1976 and 1977 perhaps a total of 40 to 50 such proposals were being funded a year, nationwide. Not surprisingly, I found I could not put together one of the 40 or 50 best startup ventures with an expenditure of $100,000. My seed financing strategy had run into a stone wall. The basic problem was that we were taking competent, entrepreneurially inclined people and giving them seed capital when only a market had been defined, and they were identifying all kinds of potentially attractive but unproven product concepts. Locating these product opportunities and developing functioning hardware demonstrated our venture team's competency, but we were reaching the startup stage with a business plan based on a lot of assumptions, a few bits and pieces of hardware, and a lot of blue sky stretched over it with regard to what we were going to do someday. I had worked with these people for 14 to 16 months and had confidence in them. However, they weren't attractive to disinterested venture capitalists and, as a result, Bay Venture rather quickly evolved from a seed specialist into a supplier of both seed and startup capital.

In our investment program, to date, we have been operating on the assumption that each venture must produce marketable products with a cumulative investment of $200,000 to $500,000. In out initial years we asked that our startup venture teams not embark on projects requiring the development of new technologies, or even that they push the state-of-the-art in an advanced technology. In fact, most of the ventures we backed in those years were based upon instrumentation or electromechanical products where we could gain a performance edge through the incorporation of the control and information processing skills of the microcomputer.

In early 1981, we reorganized our seed capital into a limited partnership small business investment company. This structure enables us to work a three-stage financing plan: $100,000 to plan and launch the enterprise; $200,000 to develop products and begin manufacturing and marketing operations; and a later $250,000 or so to bring the venture to economic viability. Even with this kind of financing we find our venture projects very tightly constrained with little margin for error. We must run with too thin a startup management team, and depend too much on outside contractors. We have difficulty recruiting skilled people even when we think we can afford them because of the modest capital base.

We have experienced delays, performance shortfalls, and technical problems in every venture we have participated in thus far. We are often far under our sales forecasts during the first year or two. People who haven't been through it cannot believe how hard it is to sell unique, new products offered by an unknown, new company. But thus far we have not suffered an outright product failure and we have had one of the startups continue for two years after first delivery of products without reaching a sales level sufficient to support profitable operations.

However, as we have enlarged our capital available for investment we have also raised our sights. During the last two years we have started to mix in three or four new ventures, trying to bring significant new technologies into the marketplace—technologies such as fiberoptic biomedical sensors, flat panel computer displays and microacoustic electronic test instruments. In these situations we are working with teams incorporating both scientific and business skills. Our overhead and manufacturing startup expenses are typically in excess of Bay Venture's means and we must seek R&D Partnerships or venture capital investment partners before the venture can offer its first product in the marketplace. Clearly this type of investing is going to increase our risk of outright failure, but we believe the potential rewards more than justify the risks.

People often ask me why our investors have been willing to participate in this kind of risky, long-term investment. I usually hear something like this: "Well, I admire your investors' courage, but I can't understand taking those kind of risks. After all, only 1 out of every 10 or 15 of those kind of deals ever works out." Even a few venture capitalists seem to believe this line. It is not true.

I don't believe the risks are unacceptably high when investing in startup ventures that are based on marketing product concepts from experienced people who have a good grounding in applications engineering. If one follows our practice of only investing at the inception of the business at founders' share prices, and, as with our ventures to date, the company goes on to reach profitable operations within three or four years, that going business is probably worth several times per share what we initially paid.

After allowing for some dilution of ownership to acquire added equity to fund growth, the founders' share in such ventures will appreciate at an average rate of 35 percent to 40 percent per annum over a 5- to 10-year period—even if one never manages to invest in that ubiquitous "next Xerox." The big successes, if any, will do better, and the failures may only yield a tax writeoff, but an investor can make a very acceptable return in this business even if he is writing off one out of every three or four ventures he invests in. And I don't think any of the early-stage-oriented, California-based venture capitalists are losing 25 percent of their investments, nor do I expect Bay Venture to suffer losses exceeding 25 percent, even though we are investing entirely at the startup stage.

We have been telling our investor group that they should expect to see their position in each venture held 8 to 10 years. A little less than 7 years into the investment program, we are still working primarily for growth—though we expect to be seeking liquidity on our oldest investments within the next 2 years.

CONCLUSION

Throughout the 1970s, seed and startup capital were extremely difficult to locate. Since the reduction in the capital gains tax rate and changes in pension fund regulations at the end of the decade, venture capital has become a strong growth industry, with more and more dollars becoming receptive to earlier-stage investing. An increasing number of venture capitalists have learned to evaluate, finance, and assist in the new venture development process. There is every indication that these skills can be learned and taught; and when they are assimilated they are yielding venture investment managers who are beating down the historic fear of loss on early-stage investments. The knowledgeable individual investor who is prepared to learn and apply the professional venture investment management techniques can participate very successfully in the new venture development process. Particularly if he is willing to accept a somewhat longer investment window than the professional venture capital managers. For time can be a problem, but seed- and startup-stage investing can be the most profitable segment of the venture capital marketplace.

APPENDIX

E

LEGAL DOCUMENTS OF VENTURE FINANCING[1]

Robert R. MacDonald
Updated by Richard J. Testa

This article has been added to and changed slightly from the original by the author to make it more relevant to individual investors. [A. L. III]

Robert R. MacDonald is presently pursuing entrepreneurial rewards as president of Lifeline Systems Inc., Waltham, Massachusetts, a venture-backed company which markets home-based medical electronics to hospitals and social service agencies. He was formerly a general partner of Idanta Partners, La Jolla, California, a leading private venture capital firm.

Richard J. Testa is a partner in the Boston law firm of Testa, Hurwitz & Thibeault. He and his firm have served as counsel for several professional venture capital companies as well as for a large number of businesses that have been financed by venture capital sources.

The purpose of this article is to summarize the legal documents the venture capital investor and the entrepreneur are likely to encounter in the closing of a venture financing. These documents are typically long and complex, but all deserve close scrutiny, because they establish the ongoing rights and responsibilities of the parties to the financing.

---

[1] Copyright © 1981 by Capital Publishing Corporation. Reprinted by permission from Stanley E. Pratt (ed.), *Guide to Venture Capital Sources,* Capital Publishing Corp., Box 348, Wellesley Hills, MA 02181.

After an informal agreement is reached on the principal terms of the financing, it is the investor's prerogative to have his lawyer prepare the legal documents. Although the bulk of the documents will cover relatively conventional ground, there will be areas for negotiation. These areas can be ferreted out by counsel experienced in the private placement area. Counsel inexperienced in venture financings may find fault with points that are standard practice in venture financings.

Although it is unlikely that an aggressive negotiating approach by the entrepreneur will "sour" the deal, it should be noted that these initial negotiations do establish the tone for ongoing, working relationships. The entreprepreneur should use his lawyer's advice and his own judgement to determine a negotiating posture.

Various documents and provisions that may be used for a venture financing are discussed below. Any particular financing would require deletions and additions; therefore, the parties should work closely with their respective attorneys to make sure the documents are applicable and complete for the financing.

PURCHASE AGREEMENT

The basic document of venture capital financing is the purchase agreement. Other agreements are usually mentioned in the purchase agreement and are then either appended to it or circulated as separate documents. The purchase agreement usually includes the sections discussed below, but the venture capitalist will tailor the agreement from the provisions listed in the sections.

The purchase agreement is structured to accomplish three main objectives:

1. To serve as a disclosure document to give the investor a detailed view of various legal, business, and financial aspects of the company he is investing in.

2. To set forth various conditions with respect to which the investor must be satisfied before he makes the investment.

3. To set forth various agreements between the investor and the entrepreneur/company relating to the ongoing operation of the company and the ongoing relationship between the investor and the entrepreneur/company. This is necessary because typically no single investor assumes control over the company. SBICs are prohibited from initially assuming control.

The disclosure objective is accomplished through the "representations and warranties" section of the purchase agreement. The conditions to closing are contained in a separate section of the purchase agreement. The ongoing relationships are spelled out in a section or sections relating to "covenants" of the company and other ancillary agreements such as a stock restriction agreement. The typical sections of a purchase agreement are discussed in more detail below.

Section I. Description of the Financing

1. *Authorization* The company states that the securities to be issued have been properly authorized. The securities are described briefly, and, if the investor is acquiring a note (whether or not convertible) or a stock purchase warrant, reference will be made to the form of the security, which will be attached as an exhibit to the purchase agreement. If the investor is acquiring preferred stock, the terms of the preferred stock (which must ultimately be reflected in an amendment to the corporate charter) will also be attached to the purchase agreement as an exhibit.

2. *Sale and Purchase of Securities* The company agrees to sell the securities, and the purchaser agrees to buy them at the specified price. The time and place of the closing are specified, and various procedural terms of the purchase are enumerated.

3. *Other Participants*   Other participants in the financing may be listed or referenced, and the point may be made that identical purchase agreements are being executed simultaneously with the other participants. A condition of the investor's obligation to purchase may be that all other agreements have not been amended and are in full force on the closing date.

4. *Use of Proceeds*   Restrictions on the use of the proceeds can be enumerated, or reference may be made to a specific investment schedule.

Section II. Representations and Warranties of the Company

The lengthy documentation of venture financings performs a vital function in obtaining detailed disclosure of material financial, business, and legal information about the venture company. This function is as important as that of establishing rights and remedies in the event of default or misrepresentation. Included in the list of representations and warranties are those items that the purchaser has relied on in making his investment decision and whose accuracy the company is in a position to verify. The company must review these representations and warranties extremely carefully because any misrepresentation or breach of warranty may give the investor rights to damages or even to rescind the entire transaction.

As noted above, the section on representations and warranties, like the other sections, will be drafted with the investor's viewpoint in mind. The lawyer doing the drafting who will be largely unfamiliar with the company, will make the *assumption* that the company is totally "clean" and may draft page after page of detailed representations and warranties to this effect. Although the investor will expect that major legal and financial problems have already been disclosed to him at this point, he will also expect that there are some minor "skeletons in the closet." The fact that a representation in the first draft is not true does not mean the investor will want to back out of the deal. What the investor is looking for and what the entrepreneur is expected to provide is a detailed disclosure of what the business is like at a given point in time—a balance sheet approach. If any representation is not correct the investor and his lawyer should be informed so the document can be revised. The entrepreneur is expected to represent only what he should know about his company, and the principal points of negotiation in the representations and warranties section are to limit the representations to non-trivial areas and to areas reasonably within the knowledge of the entrepreneur.

A list of typical venture financing representations and warranties follows:

1. *Organization and Corporate Power*   Statement that the company is duly organized, is in good standing, and is qualified to do business in all appropriate jurisdictions.

2. *Subsidiaries*   Description of any subsidiaries and any investments in the securities of any other firm.

3. *Business*   Description of the business in which the company is engaged and/or intends to engage.

4. *Authorization*   Statement that the company will be bound by the agreement and that execution of the agreement has been duly authorized by all necessary actions of the company.

5. *Capitalization*   Description of the company's authorized capitalization and status of the company's outstanding securities, including warrants, options, and convertible securities. In addition, any transfer restrictions, repurchase rights, and preemptive rights will be described.

6. *Financial Statements*   Statement that audited and interim financial statements are accurate and complete and have been prepared in accordance with generally accepted accounting principles. Specifics, such as method of inventory valuation and status of accounts receivable, may be included.

7. *Absence of Undisclosed Liabilities*   Statement that, except as disclosed or reserved against on the balance sheet, there are no material undisclosed claims, encumbrances, or liabilities.

8. *Absence of Certain Developments* Affirmation that there have been no material adverse changes since the date of the last balance sheet. A detailed listing could include such items as no dividends or other distributions, no loss of property, no labor trouble, no change in assets, and no condition that constitutes an event of default (as defined elsewhere).

9. *Offering Circular* Statement that the offering circular or business plan used by the company in seeking the financing was accurate and complete.

10. *Title to Properties* Affirmation that the company has good and marketable title to all of its properties and assets. An exhibit will normally list any real property owned or leased by the company and any liens, restrictions, or encumbrances on such property. Assurance that the company has necessary property and assets to conduct its business as presently conducted and that they are in good condition and adequately insured.

11. *Applicable Laws* Statement that the company is in compliance with applicable statutes, regulations, and rules necessary to do business.

12. *Tax Matters* Statement that all tax returns have been duly filed and that taxes have been paid or provision has been made on the latest balance sheet.

13. *Contracts and Commitments* All material contracts and commitments will ordinarily be listed in an exhibit to the purchase agreement. These may include employment contracts, stock agreements, financing agreements, licenses, leases, pension plans, or stock-option plans. Statement that the company is not in default under any contract and that no contract will have a material adverse effect on the business.

14. *Patents* Statement that the company holds the necessary patents, trademarks, and copyrights to conduct its business, and that to the best of its knowledge it does not infringe patents, trademarks, or copyrights of others. Patents and similar proprietary rights may be specifically identified in an exhibit to the purchase agreement.

15. *Effect of Transactions* Statement that the execution, delivery, and performance of the purchase agreement and the issuance and delivery of the securities being acquired by the investor will not conflict with or result in any violation or breach or any default under any other obligations of the company; that transactions do not violate any statutes or regulations or the corporate charter of the company.

16. *Litigation* Declaration that there is no litigation, suit, claim, or governmental investigation pending or, to the company's knowledge, threatened against the company.

17. *Other Agreements With Principals* Declaration that there are no material undisclosed agreements with, or obligations to, principals.

18. *Insider Agreements* Disclosure of material contracts and commitments between company and stockholders or officers.

19. *Registration of Securities* Statement that the issuance of the securities will not require registration under the Securities Act of 1933 or the state securities ("blue sky") laws of any jurisdiction. If blue sky registration or qualification is required, there will be a statement that all such necessary registrations or qualifications have been obtained.

20. *Corporate Charter and Bylaws* Statement that the investor has been furnished with copies of the corporate charter and bylaws, as amended to date. If such amendments have been made, the documents may be appended to the purchase agreement.

21. *Brokerage* Description of any finder's fee or broker's fee or commission payable in connection with the financing.

22. *Disclosure* Declaration that no document, certificate, or statement furnished by the company in connection with this financing contains any untrue statement of a material fact or omits to state a material fact necessary in order to make the statement not misleading and that all facts have been disclosed that would materially adversely affect the business.

Section III. Representations of Purchaser

This section is short and usually has only two purposes. The first is to represent that the purchaser has full power and authority to perform the agreement in accordance with its terms. The second is to establish that the transaction qualifies as a private placement. For this purpose, the purchaser represents that he is purchasing the securities for investment and not with an intent to sell or distribute them. He also represents that he considers himself to be a sophisticated investor, that he has made detailed inquiry concerning the company, and that the officers have made available all information requested by the purchaser. If exemption from registration under the Securities Act pursuant to Regulation D is being relied upon, the purchaser may represent that he is an "accredited investor," as defined in Regulation D.

Section IV. Conditions Precedent to Closing

The purchase agreement normally specifies certain conditions to the purchaser's obligation; occasionally, there is, in addition, a separate section detailing conditions to the seller's obligation.

Unless the purchase agreement is signed before the closing takes place, there is technically no need for a condition section—the purchase agreement is simply not signed until the deal is ready to close. Generally, deferred closings do not take place in venture financing situations, but the agreement may be signed up if some future event (such as delivery of audited year-end financials) must take place before the closing, and the parties wish to "lock up" the deal. In either case, for convenience, the purchase agreement is drafted *as if* there will be a deferred closing and specifies the following typical conditions which must be satisfied before the investor will close the deal.

1. *Opinion of Counsel for the Company* A favorable opinion from counsel for the company covering the proper execution and the binding nature of the various agreements, the good standing of the company, the capitalization of the company, the absence of litigation, the absence of violations in contracts or in the company's charter, the conformance with applicable state blue sky and federal securities laws, and other requested items. The purpose of this requirement is to give the investor the "comfort" of knowing that an independent party familiar with the company has reviewed all important legal matters.

2. *Opinion of Counsel for the Purchasers* Counsel for the investor supplies a favorable written opinion dated the closing date and covering the same basic points as those received from the company's counsel. He may rely on certain opinions provided to him by counsel for the company.

3. *Representations and Warranties* Certification that the representations and warranties made by the company are true and correct on the closing date.

4. *Performance* Assurance that the company shall have conformed and complied with all of the agreements and conditions prior to closing.

5. *No Event of Default* Assurance that, if there are any default provisions in the agreements, there shall exist at the closing date no event or act that constitutes default or will lead to default. This provision would be included only in deals in which debt was issued.

6. *Other Agreements* Statement that any important credit or loan or other agreements have been effected.

7. *Other Purchase Agreements* Statement that the agreements of all other participants in the financing have been signed and payment tendered for a specified minimum number of shares or amount of money. This provision is important when there is more than one investor, so that if any investor backs out, the others can restructure the deal.

8. *Compliance Certificate* Statement that the purchasers will receive at the closing a certificate signed by the president and treasurer certifying that the conditions specified in the preceding paragraphs have been fulfilled.

9. *Other Provisions*   Provision for execution of employment contracts and stock restriction agreements, receipt of revised financial statements, resignation of specific directors or officers, payment of all amounts owed to the company by officers and directors, or anything else peculiar to the particular deal which must be effected before the investor purchases the securities.

Section V. Covenants of the Company

The covenants describe the continuing obligations of the company to the purchaser with respect to future actions of the company. This section often is presented under two headings to separate affirmative and negative covenants. Affirmative covenants are those positive actions the company promises to make, and negative covenants are actions or results that the company promises to avoid. The previous sections of the purchase agreement are in many respects standard—or boilerplate. This section is more often tailored to the individual deal.

In an equity-oriented venture capital investment, where the purchaser will control the board of directors, the covenants are often kept to a minimum. In such situations, the affirmative covenants might merely provide that the purchaser will receive periodic financial information and will be represented on the board. The negative covenants might limit only the company's ability to amend its corporate charter or merge or sell its assets without the purchaser's consent. A venture capital firm with board control will generally rely upon this to influence the direction of a company. Accordingly, it will not, as a rule, find it necessary to impose in advance extensive restrictions on the conduct of the business by insisting on strict affirmative and negative covenants. (Where the venture capital firm is acquiring securities which are debt-oriented and where there is no board control more extensive covenants are appropriate). Among the covenants which are found in venture capital purchase agreements are the following:

Affirmative Covenants

1. *Maintenance of Corporate Existence*   The company will maintain its corporate existence and all rights, licenses, patents, copyrights, trademarks, etc. useful in its business, and will engage only in the type of business described in the representations and warranties.

2. *Payment of Taxes and Claims*   The company will pay all lawful taxes, assessments, and levies upon the company or its income or property before they become in default. A separate covenant sometimes provides that principal and interest on any debt securities acquired by the purchaser will be paid when due.

3. *Legal Compliance*   The company will comply with all applicable laws and regulations in the conduct of its business.

4. *Repair and Maintenance*   The company will keep all necessary equipment and property in good repair and condition, as necessary to permit the business to be properly conducted.

5. *Property and Liability Insurance*   The company will maintain insurance against hazards and risks and liability to persons and property to the extent customary for corporations engaged in the same or a similar business.

6. *Life Insurance*   The purchaser will often require the company to maintain insurance on the lives of key officers and employees. The face amount in some cases may be as much as the purchase amount of the securities, and the insurance proceeds are often payable directly to the purchaser, particularly if the purchaser holds debt securities.

7. *Employment Contracts*   The company may covenant to enter into employment contracts with all key employees covering salary, nondisclosure of information during and after the term of employment, assignment of patents, and noncompetition for a specified period (often several years) after termination of employment.

8. *Accounts and Reports*   The company may be asked by the purchaser to agree to maintain a standard system of accounting in accordance with generally accepted

accounting principles consistently applied, and to keep full and complete financial records.

9. *Financial and Operating Statements*   The company will generally agree to provide the investors with detailed financial and operating information. The information to be provided may include annual, quarterly, and sometimes monthly reports of sales, production, shipments, estimated profits, cash balances, receivables, payables, and backlog; all statements filed with the SEC or other agencies; and, any other information that the investor may need for his own voluntary or involuntary filing requirements. The right to receive certain financial information is often terminated when the company goes public to avoid dissemination of "inside" information. A covenant may also establish preparation and approval procedures for budgets.

10. *Adverse Change*   The company will advise the purchaser of any event—financial, legal, or otherwise—that represents a material adverse change in the condition of the business.

11. *Current Ratio, Working Capital, or Net Worth*   These covenants normally are included only in debt financings and are ageeements to maintain the current ratio, working capital, or net worth, either at a minimum amount or as specified for various time periods. They may be keyed to projections made by the company.

12. *Board of Directors*   Venture capital firms will generally seek assurances that they will be represented on the company's board of directors. The right to be represented on the board may be backed up by stock voting agreements with the principal stockholders. If the investors are not to be represented on the board, the company may be required to notify the investor of the time and place of board meetings and to permit the investor or his representative to attend such meetings.

13. *Access to Premises*   The investor of his representative will generally be permitted to make inspections of the company's property and books and records.

14. *Future Financings*   The investor may be given the right of first refusal or preemptive rights on any future financings.

15. *Use of Proceeds*   The use of funds may be broadly stated in terms of the business of the company, or it may be narrowly defined to comply with a financing plan.

16. *Dealings With Related Parties*   The company covenants that all transactions between the company and stockholders of the company shall be conducted on an arm's length basis and shall be on terms no less favorable to the company than could be obtained from nonrelated persons.

Negative Covenants

1. *Nature of Business*   The company agrees not to change the nature of the business from that described in the representation and warranties.

2. *Business Entity*   The purchaser may, under certain circumstances, be able to compel the company to agree not to amend the corporate charter or bylaws without the consent of the purchaser. More narrowly drawn covenants might prohibit only certain specified actions (e.g. change of fiscal year or a change in the capital structure) without the purchaser's consent.

3. *Issurance of Stock or Convertible Securities*   The investor may require the company not to issue any securities that would result in dilution of the purchaser's position. This includes restrictions on issuance of securities of the type issued to the purchaser and any securities convertible into such securities at a price less than that paid by the purchaser.

4. *Redemption of Securities*   The company may covenant not to repurchase or redeem any of its securities except in accordance with the terms of the particular securities, stock option plans, and agreements with the holders.

5. *Sale or Purchase of Assets, Mergers, and Consolidation*   Consolidations, mergers,

acquisitions, and the like without the investor's advance approval are often prohibited. Liquidation and dissolution of the company and the sale, lease, or other disposition of substantial assets without consent may also be barred. Restrictions may also be placed on the company's purchase of capital assets.

6. *Liabilities Assumed*   The purchase agreement may provide for restrictions on liens, pledges, and other encumbrances, with exceptions for such liabilities as real estate mortgages. Separate restrictions can be placed on leases of real property or equipment.

7. *Indebtedness*   The company may agree to restrictions on future indebtedness, with exceptions for institutional senior borrowings, indebtedness on personal property purchase money obligations, and trade indebtedness, up to certain limits in the ordinary course of business.

8. *Investments*   Restrictions against making investments in any other companies may be imposed by the purchaser.

9. *Distributions*   The company frequently agrees not to make any dividend distributions to stockholders. Dividends may be eliminated until a given date or may be limited to a fixed percentage of profits above a set amount.

10. *Employee Compensation*   The company may agree to limit employment and other personal service contracts to a maximum term and a maximum amount of annual compensation.

11. *Loans and Advances*   Loans to stockholders and employees may be barred unless approved by the board of directors.

12. *Aging of Payables*   The company may covenant not to allow accounts payable to exceed certain aging. Limitations can also be placed on assets or other liabilities. These covenants are normally seen only in debt-oriented investments.

13. *Default on Agreements*   The company may expressly covenant not to default on this purchase agreement or any other agreement.

Section VI. Covenants of the Purchaser

Occasionally, the purchaser may agree at the time of the initial investment to participate in a second round of financing. The terms of such second-round financing, including the timing of the financing, the amount and type of securities to be acquired, and any conditions to the purchaser's obligation to participate in such financing, will be set forth in a separate section of the original purchase agreement.

Section VII. Registration Rights and Related Provisions Regarding Resale of Securities by the Purchaser

The securities acquired by a venture capital firm are not registered under the Securities Act of 1933 at the time of issuance; instead, they are issued by the company pursuant to one of the several "private placement" exemptions from the registration requirements of that Act. As privately issued, "restricted" securities, they can be resold only if they are subsequently registered under the Act or an exemption from registration is available for the proposed resale. To maximize his ability to resell the securities, the purchaser typically negotiates with the company for the right to require the company to register the securities under certain circumstances. These registration rights will generally give the holder the unilateral right to "demand" registration of its securities as well as the right to "piggy-back" its securities on any other registration of securities by the company. The following is a brief summary of typical provisions relating to registration rights:

1. *Demand Registrations*   If permitted at all, the purchaser's right to demand registration will generally be limited in number and/or in time. Usually, a holder or holders of only a stated percentage of the securities must request the registration.

2. *"Piggy-Back" Rights*   Because piggy-back registrations are less burdensome finan-

cially, the provisions regarding piggy-back registrations are generally more liberal than the demand registration provisions and will not, as a rule, be limited as to time or number. Piggy-back rights are, however, often subject to cut back rights of the managing underwriter of the offering.

3. *Registrations on Form S-3*   If the company's stock is publicly traded and if certain other conditions are met, the company may be able to register the purchaser's stock on Form S-3, an inexpensive, abbreviated registration form. The company will often be asked to agree to register the purchaser's securities on Form S-3, if that form is available, without significant limits as to time or number.

4. *Allocation of Expenses*   The purchase agreement may provide that the company will pay all expenses of future registration or that the expenses will be allocated among the sellers. Often, the company will agree to pay the expenses of one, or perhaps two, demand registrations, with the expenses of any subsequent demand registrations being borne by the sellers.

5. *Indemnification*   The company will generally agree to indemnify and hold harmless the seller against any losses, claims, or damages that result from an untrue statement or a material omission by the company in any registration statement. The seller will also agree to indemnify the company if claims result from similar actions or omissions by the selling security holder.

As noted above, the purchaser's securities may be resold without registration if an exemption from registration is available. Rule 144, promulgated under the Securities Act of 1933, establishes ground rules for qualifying for an exemption. In order for the purchaser to be able to resell under Rule 144, the company's securities must be registered with the Securities and Exchange Commission under the Securities Exchange Act of 1934 (which should not be confused with the Securities Act of 1933), and the company must have filed certain reports required by that Act. Alternatively, certain information must be publicly available concerning the company. The purchaser may request the company, in the purchase agreement, to agree to register under the Securities Exchange Act of 1934 upon the demand of the purchaser. At a minimum, the purchaser will request that, should the company become subject to the reporting requirements of the 1934 Act, the company will take all action necessary to make Rule 144 available.

Section VIII. Miscellaneous

The following provisions are generally noncontroversial, boilerplate items.

1. *Survival of representations and warranties*   Statement that the representations and warranties made in connection with the transaction shall be binding after the date of closing.

2. *Successors and Assigns*   Assurance that the agreement shall bind and inure to the benefit of successors and assigns of the parties of the agreement, including any assignee of the purchaser who purchases any of the securities from the purchaser in a transition exempt from registration.

3. *Notices*   List of addresses for communication among parties to the agreement.

4. *Expenses*   The company generally agrees to pay all out-of-pocket expenses arising in connection with the transaction, including reasonable counsel fees, incurred by the purchaser. The purchaser may represent that he has not dealt with any broker or finder, or, if brokerage or finders fees are to be paid, such fees will be specified.

5. *Entire Agreement*   Statement that the purchase agreement embodies the entire agreement and understanding between the purchaser and the company and supersedes all prior agreements and understandings relating to the subject matter of the agreement.

6. *Amendments and Waivers*   Statement that terms and provisions of the purchase agreement cannot be modified except in a writing executed by the company and holders of a certain percentage of the securities, and a statement that a waiver by the investor of his rights under one provision shall not be considered a waiver of other rights.

7. *Counterparts* Statement that the purchase agreement may be executed simultaneously in two or more counterparts, each of which is deemed an original, but all of which together constitute one and the same instrument.

8. *Governing Law* Designation of the state under whose laws the agreement is to be governed.

DESCRIPTION OF SECURITIES

A venture capital deal may involve any combination of debt, warrants, preferred stock, and common stock. The purchase agreement, as discussed above, usually presents the general terms of the agreement and is supplemented with the forms of the debentures or warrants, or a description of the terms of the preferred stock. It is possible for these forms to be only several pages in length if such items as restrictive covenants, events of default, and conversion privileges are covered in the purchase agreement.

If there are separate descriptions for common or preferred stock, the agreements would detail the specific class of stock and any dividend, voting, and conversion privileges of those shares.

In recent years, the most common form of investment made by venture capital firms in the early-stage companies has been the purchase of a class of preferred stock which is convertible into common stock or the purchase of debentures or notes, also typically convertible into common stock. Some of the more conventional terms of these securities are described below.

Preferred stock

Preferred stock offers the investor and the issuer a great deal of flexibility in tailoring important investment terms relating to management control and return on investment. These issues are addressed by the following terms:

1. *Dividends* Convertible preferred stock involved in venture capital financings generally does not carry dividend rights, although the preferred will typically participate with the common stock to the extent dividends are declared. If desired, dividends may be on a cumulative or noncumulative basis and at a fixed rate or based upon a formula.

2. *Liquidation* Holders of preferred stock will have a priority claim over the common stockholders to the assets of the corporation upon liquidation. The liquidation preference will be equal to the original purchase price plus accrued dividends, if any.

3. *Voting Rights* Convertible preferred stock will typically vote together with the common stock as a single class. In addition, the preferred stockholders, voting as a separate class, will often have the right to approve certain matters affecting their rights (such as the issuance of senior securities, mergers, and change in stock terms). Other preferential voting rights may include (1) class vote for election of directors and (2) extraordinary voting rights to elect a majority of directors in the event of a breach of the terms of the preferred stock, such as the failure to pay dividends.

4. *Conversion* Holders of convertible preferred may convert their shares into common stock at their discretion (except as limited by automatic conversion obligations). Conversion provisions should address the following matters:

Automatic conversion upon the occurrence of certain events, principally the completion of a public offering or the attainment of specified financial goals.

Mechanics of conversion.

Conversion ratio, usually expressed by a formula based on original purchase price, which initially yields a one-for-one conversion factor.

Adjustment of conversion ratio to take into account (1) stock splits, stock dividends, consolidations, etc., and (2) "dilutive" common stock issuances, that is, sales of common stock at prices lower than those paid by the investors.

Certification of adjusted conversion ratios by independent accountants.

The nature of the anti-dilution adjustments can have a dramatic effect on the number of common shares issuable upon conversion. "Rachet-down" anti-dilution provisions apply the lowest sale price for any shares of common stock (or equivalents) as the adjusted conversion value. "Formula" anti-dilution provisions adjust the conversion value by application of a weighted formula based on both sale price and number of common shares sold.

5. *Redemption*   Redemption offers the investor a means of recovering his initial investment and the issuer an opportunity to eliminate the preferential rights held by the holders of the senior security. Issue addressed include:

Optional and/or mandatory redemption.

Stepped-up redemption price or redemption premium designed to provide investors a certain appreciated return on the investment.

Desirability of a sinking fund.

Redemption call by issuer.

DEBENTURES

The following are typical provisions found in debentures or notes:

1. *Description of the Note*   This will include such items as the interest rate, the aggregate principal amount, and the date of maturity. If the notes are convertible, a section will be added covering the items discussed above under preferred stock.

2. *Conditions of Prepayment*   The notes may be prepaid according to a schedule that results in reduced prepayment penalties as the notes mature. Sometimes, they can be prepaid without penalty as long as the prepayments are in specified minimum amounts and are made on specified payment dates.

3. *Collateral*   The note may be secured with assets of the company.

4. *Subordination*   If the note is subordinated, the agreement will acknowledge subordination to certain forms of senior debt, including bank borrowings. Normally, debts to officers of the company will be subordinated to this debt.

5. *Covenants of the Company*   This section may refer to the covenants in the purchase agreement or may elaborate on those covenants. When debt is a part of the purchase, the covenants are normally more strict and include restrictions on the current ratio and net worth. These stricter covenants give the venture capitalist more bargaining power if the company develops problems.

6. *Default*   The events of default and the remedies upon default are enumerated. Possible events of default are:

Default in payment of interest or principal.

Default in payments on any other loans.

Default in any covenants.

False information in the agreement.

Institution of bankruptcy proceedings.

Nonpayment of court judgments.

The section on remedies upon default will state that the holders of more than a given percentage of the outstanding principal amount of notes can declare the principal and accrued interest due and payable. The holder of any note may proceed to protect and enforce his rights by legal action, and the company will reimburse the holder for all reasonable costs associated with enforcement of his rights.

7. *Waiver and Amendment*   This provision states how many noteholders are required to amend the agreement, with the stipulation that payments due to an individual noteholder cannot be changed without his consent

ANCILLARY AGREEMENTS

Mention was made in the discussion of the purchase agreement of supplemental information that would be appended to the purchase agreement. Some of this additional information is factually oriented, such as a current stockholder list, a list of the participants in the financing, additional information about the business of the company, and the purpose of the financing. Other agreements appended as exhibits to the purchase agreement may include employment contracts, personal guarantees, and a restatement of certain key representations and warranties for which the investors want to hold the officers personally liable. The age and form of the venture dictate the type and form of ancillary agreements. The following agreements are examples.

Employment Agreements

These will stipulate that key employees agree to work for the company for a specified period of time, that they will not compete with the company for a specified period of time after leaving the company, and that they will not reveal confidential company information while employed by or after leaving the company. Such an agreement may also stipulate that the company is given the right to all discoveries, inventions, processes, etc., discovered or created while an employee is under employment, whether or not he is actually "on the job," so long as the inventions relate to areas of his work.

Previous Employment

In a startup venture, the investors want to make sure that the entrepreneurs are free from restraints imposed by previous employment agreements and that prior employers do not intend and do not have grounds to take legal action against the entrepreneurs. Toward this end, there may be copies of prior employment agreements, statements from prior employers concerning the status of the entrepreneurs, and representations by the entrepreneurs that they have not revealed or transferred trade secrets or confidential information of previous employers and are not bound by any agreements with former employers, or otherwise restricted from participating full time in the company's business.

Stock Restriction Agreements

Investors may require that they be given a right of first refusal on all stock transitions by any officer, director, or key employee. As previously mentioned, the investors may also require that the principal stockholders agree to vote for the investors' nominees to the board of directors. The form of the stock restriction agreement will generally be attached to the purchase agreement as an exhibit.

DOCUMENTS THAT FORM A BASIS FOR INVESTMENT

Key documents that were used in evaluating the company will often be listed and described on an exhibit attached to the purchase agreement. These can include leases, title documents to patents or processes, development grants, purchase orders issued and received, licenses from regulatory bodies, and business plans. These documents will be made available to the investors and their counsel for inspection.

CONSULTING CONTRACT

Some investors may require the company to contract with the investor for financial and management consulting services. This type of consulting contract will usually be a brief document reciting a simple description of the services engaged and the terms and amount of payment to be made. Venture capitalists who play an active role in the management of their investments usually intend to provide these services without charge as a means of protecting their investment.

THE CLOSING PROCESS

After the parties have reached agreement on the terms of purchase agreement and the other documents which set forth the fundamental terms of the transaction, the parties may, as previously noted, elect to "lock up" the deal by executing the purchase agreement. In any event, counsel for both parties will at this stage review the proposed transaction and the records and proceedings of the company and will prepare opinions for delivery to the purchasers at the closing. Ancillary agreements will be finalized. Also, good standing certificates and tax status certificates will be obtained from appropriate government agencies. Other closing documents may include: the compliance certificate, signed by the company's president and treasurer indicating that all representations and warranties set forth in the purchase agreement are true and correct as of the closing date and that all conditions to closing have been satisfied; a "cold comfort" letter from the auditors stating that there are no material adverse changes; an incumbency and signature certificate listing the officers of the company and showing their signatures; the investment, or nondistribution, letters of the investors; and, cross receipts acknowledging the transfer of securities and money.

Representatives of the investor, officers of the company, and counsel for both parties will generally be present at the closing. At the closing, the parties will deliver executed originals of the closing instruments and documents required by the purchase agreement. The sale is consummated when the company delivers the certificates or other instruments representing the securities sold and receives from the purchaser the full purchase price of the securities.

APPENDIX

F

ARTHUR LIPPER CORPORATION'S STATEMENT OF POLICY AND PROCEDURE FOR THOSE SEEKING FUNDING

We seek to earn an extraordinarily high return on our investments through intelligently assuming higher than normal risks. We are prepared to make our own judgments as to certain future events, including the likely reaction of other investors to predicted events. Our judgments are based, in part, upon both statements of fact and opinion as offered by those seeking funding. However, we require that the entrepreneur who hopes to benefit through our placing our financial resources at risk make a clear distinction as between fact and opinion.

In order that there be no future misunderstandings, we will require those making statements of fact to so warrant and represent in the investment contract. Clearly, any statement made which is subsequently found to be other than factual will give rise to possible liability for the parties having made the statement.

Almost all investments involve the making of projections as to future events. We know that very few projections are ever achieved within the predicted time period. We also believe that those seeking funding for their business based upon the assumption of future events (as opposed to being based on current assets) are in a better position than ourselves to make such projections. As we will base our valuation of the business opportunity on projections provided, by those expecting to receive the benefit of our funding and risk incurrence, we will hold the providers of the projections responsible. The form of penalty for nonachievement of projected results will be that of participation reduction. Similarly, we will usually permit entrepreneur/managers increased participation in the event projections are exceeded. Therefore, those preparing and submitting projections, which we, of course, require, are urged to only provide their "worst case" projections or those which the entrepreneur believes he is certain of achieving. If there is a projection shortfall we expect to be insulated to the extent possible. Please be conservative. It will work out much better for you if you are.

You are in a position to be aware of both the positive factors affecting your business project as well as possible adverse elements. If you are aware of adverse elements we expect that you will advise us. In the investment agreement you will be required to affirmatively state that you have advised us of any adverse factors which may negatively affect the investment under consideration, which are known to you at the time.

Frequently, entrepreneurs and businessmen seek funding from more than one source at a time. We value our time and effort highly and, therefore, require that we be informed of both the identity of those other funding sources already contacted and those with which there are negotiations currently in progress. It is possible that we will request either an exclusivity period, during which you agree not to have any contact with other sources of finance, or that you agree to compensate us for our time and out-of-pocket expenses in the event you reject a proposal we offer in good faith based upon the facts which you have presented.

We are professional providers of finance and, as such, probably have a level of experience and financial sophistication greater than your own. Therefore, we urge you to consult your attorney and other advisors prior to making or accepting any proposal. As it is not our intention to take unfair advantage of anyone, we do not wish to be in a position of doing so inadvertantly.

Finally, we believe that entrepreneurs should "rent" money from financers, such as ourselves, rather than initially be given it in the form of equity. Therefore, our favorite medium of funding is through the provision of commercial bank guarantees. Such guarantees require the recipient of the loan to ultimately repay the loan as well as to pay interest on a current basis. Our inducement to provide guarantees frequently takes the form of revenue participation in the guaranteed entity. We may also require other forms of guarantee fee payment, all dependent upon our assessment of the individual situation. We are not inflexible as to format but do believe strongly that the investor's funds should, at least initially, enjoy a preference to the interests of those not at the same level of financial risk.

We try to be fair and to respect (and reward) the entrepreneur. We require, however, that our capital be respected. We have worked long and hard to earn it.

Arthur Lipper III
President

APPENDIX

G

REQUEST FOR PROSPECTUS USED BY CONTINENTAL
ILLINOIS VENTURE CORPORATION AND CONTINENTAL
ILLINOIS EQUITY CORPORATION

John L. Hines

For investment consideration by CIEC or CIVC, please prepare a prospectus providing the following information.

1. *The Company*   Name, nature of business, stage of development, history, mergers, acquisitions, divestitures, affiliates.

2. *Funding History*   Details of prior financings, amount currently sought, proposed use of funds.

3. *Product Lines*   Description, pricing, proprietary and patented features, lead times on competition, licenses.

4. *Research, Development, Engineering, and Design*   Development timetable, long-term product development strategy.

5. Manufacturing   Production methods, operations cycle, capacity, level of integration, subcontractors, significant sources of supply, shipping, status of raw materials availability.

6. *Service*

7. *Management, Directors, and Organization*   Resumes and compensation of key executives, organizational chart, union affiliations, training requirements, availability of labor, number of employees, incentives, stock ownership by executives.

8. *The Market and Competition*   Segments, product substitutes, size and growth, seasonal or cyclical market, share of market, rate of technological change, lease to sale ratios.

9. *Marketing Strategy*   Product literature, promotion, advertising, sales cycle (prospect to installation), pricing, credit, sales organization, leasing and rental options, dominant customers, sales and distribution of product.

10. *Financial Summary and Projections*   Audited financial statements for last three years (if available), latest monthly financial statements, five-year projections of P & L, balance sheet and cash flow, together with all supporting assumptions pertaining to pricing, share of market, margins, volumes, inventory, receivable and payable turnovers, capital expenditures.

11. *Financial Information*   Capitalization, credit lines, leasing agreements, major stockholders, banking relationships, details of prior equity financings, purchase agreements from prior financing.

12. *Legal Considerations*   Contingent liabilities, legal counsel retained, litigation pending.

APPENDIX

H

WHAT'S MY BUSINESS WORTH?[1]

Stephen Blum and Cynthia Morrison

    Stephen Blum is a partner in Peat Marwick's Executive Office, where he directs analytical work for the Acquisition Advisory Service.
    Cynthia Morrison is a consultant in Peat Marwick's Acquisition Advisory Service.
[A. L. III]

The question asked by the title of this article can be pivotal in the managing of any company, especially if it is privately held. Several factors may compel the owner or investor to measure what may be his or her only important source of income. The following list gives some of the reasons for business valuations.

Reasons for a Business Valuation:

Purchase or sale of a business or business segment.

Estate planning.

Strategic planning: resource allocation between business segments.

Employee stock ownership plan.

Tax calculation support (gifts, contributions, etc.)

Recapitalization or new financing.

Required distributions by private foundations.

Management incentive plans.

Shareholder buy-sell agreements.

Litigation.

Gauging the worth of a business is often easier in theory than in practice. Take the apparently straightforward concept of fair market value, the price at which property would change hands between two willing and knowledgeable parties both aware of the relevant facts and circumstances. Although economists and financial experts bandy about the term with utter confidence, until a transaction actually occurs, fair market value must be estimated indirectly, through hypothesis and comparison. The challenge is even greater if the property is a closely held business: there is no daily trading in its shares to provide an analytical starting point. Indeed, it is hard to value even publicly traded businesses, as shown by the wildly varying premiums offered by acquirers in order to gain control of such businesses.

Still, more complications are likely to cloud the valuation of a privately held business. It may occupy a unique market position. Financial planning may have been aimed at reducing taxes rather than maximizing profits. The business may depend on an energetic and charismatic owner-manager. Formal projections or even budgets may not exist. Transactions with affiliated businesses may distort the financial picture.

THE "RIGHT" ANSWER IS HYPOTHETICAL

Where does this leave the private business owner who doesn't know what the investment of a lifetime is worth? Fortunately, there are several common methods of business valuation. Sometimes, a single method will be best suited; at other times, a number of perspectives can be combined to develop an estimated range of fair market value. At all times, numerous assumptions and adjustments are needed. There can be no "right" answer without an actual sale of the business.

One should investigate several analytical valuation methods in order to ensure that the estimate of value is (1) objective, (2) relevant, and (3) adequately documented. Objectivity is needed to remove the impact of personal involvement, or "gut" feelings. Relevance is crucial if the analysis is to provide real guidance to whoever uses it. Documentation reinforces the overall credibility of the analysis.

These four generally accepted business valuation methods have received wide attention:

Discounted cash flow analysis.

Asset appraisal.

Acquisition analysis.

Comparison to similar publicly traded companies.

Consider the advantage and drawbacks of each of these approaches. This will reveal which methods are better suited to various valuation needs.

DCF RELATES THE PRESENT TO THE FUTURE

Discounted cash flow (DCF), or net present value, analysis has been highly publicized as a method of assessing business value. The method consists of relating future cash flow to fair market value. The theoretical foundation of DCF analysis is constructed from at least three hypotheses:

1. Cash now is worth more than an equal amount of cash in the future.

2. Future cash flows (e.g., from business operations) are reasonably predictable.

3. The marginal cost of capital available to the business, and its alternative returns on invested capital, are similar and are subject to estimation.

DCF analysis is an elegant theoretical method for translating cash-generating capacity into value at present. Few business owners would question the first of the three underlying hypotheses. The other two, however, do not always hold when DCF analysis is applied to an operating business.

Cash flows may be difficult to predict in businesses facing rapid change, heavy capital requirements, regulatory shifts, volatile product price swings, or similar uncertainties. A time frame must be assumed. Proceeds from disposing of the business at some future date must be estimated. Many privately held businesses do not regularly prepare projections.

In any case, the cost of capital and the return from alternative investments are functions of the desired risk level and are unclear in times of fluctuating interest rates. Also, the true cost of equity capital is hard to quantify.

In certain business activities, such as real estate or insurance, DCF analysis is extensively relied on because cash flow in these activities has been historically more predictable.

How does DCF measure up in terms of objectivity, relevance, and documentation? Since many investments are evaluated by the cash returns they yield to investors, DCF analysis of a business can be highly *relevant*. When projections are available and research has been performed on capital costs and investment returns, DCF analysis can be *documented*. In terms of being *objective*, however, a DCF approach is often vulnerable to attack because of the likelihood that a number of key assumptions are highly subjective and will greatly affect the resulting value on a DCF basis.

IF THE WHOLE IS THE SUM OF THE PARTS . . .

A second frequently used business valuation method is the appraisal of corporate assets, net of liabilities. From an accounting standpoint, the method consists first of analyzing the balance sheet, isolating categories of assets and liabilities and identifying any unstated assets and liabilities. Fair market values are assigned to each category and then to intangible and unstated items, based on professional appraisals, reliable market data, and estimates. The resulting amount, often referred to as the net asset value, may provide an asset-oriented perspective on the fair market value of a business.

The asset appraisal approach is particularly well suited to businesses which derive value from underlying assets rather than from the prospect of an earnings stream. This may be true when there is substantial investment in real estate, a large proportion of marketable securities, or the intention to liquidate part or all of the company. Most other businesses derive value from their ability to generate future earnings, rather than intrinsically from their net assets. Valuing these businesses requires the use of other methods instead of, or in conjunction with, asset appraisals.

The asset appraisal approach often necessitates the participation of several appraisers, each with a specialized knowledge of a category of assets or liabilities. For example, real estate could be handled by one appraiser, machinery by a second, inventory by a third, pension accruals by a fourth (probably actuaries), and intangibles by a fifth (possibly with expertise in evaluating research efforts, patents, or the like). Each appraisal can be done on several bases, such as, in the case of buildings and machinery, liquidation value, replacement cost, or depreciated replacement cost. The valuation of a business as a going concern is usually incompatible with liquidation-basis asset appraisals. Rather, assets must be appraised under the assumption that they will continue to be used in the normal course of business.

Can the asset appraisal method of business valuation be objective, relevant, and documented? If the various asset and liability categories are fairly ordinary and subject to analysis by outsiders, then *objectivity* is possible. Many, if not most, going business concerns also derive significant value from intangible or "hidden" assets: customer lists, patents, research projects, reputation, goodwill, and so forth. These assets are much less prone to direct appraisal, which limits the impact of an asset appraisal approach to business valuation.

As to *relevance,* asset appraisal is less suitable in cases where future earnings, rather than appreciation in asset values, are the main goal. The approach usually has at least some relevancy in the sense that, when earnings are depressed, the value of a business may be buoyed by the worth of its assets or conversely, when earnings grow at extraordinarily high rates, asset values may act to retard the overall increase in business value. In the former case, the prospect of liquidating or divesting rather than continuing to operate at sub-par levels may contribute to the buoying effect on value; in the latter case, the potential tax impact of trying to transfer the benefits of higher earnings directly to investors may contribute to the retarding effect on value (e.g., capital gains, depreciation and investment tax credit recapture, and extraordinary good will).

In terms of *documentation,* the asset appraisal approach to business valuation may incorporate studies by outside appraisers, unless the assets are unique or nonquantifiable. The documentation process can be expensive and time-consuming if several experts are required.

WHAT'S TODAY'S MARKET FOR BUSINESSES?

A third generally accepted valuation approach is to analyze purchases of similar businesses. This approach requires a careful survey and screening of publicly available data on recent acquisitions. With this information, perhaps in the form of a sample of five to ten acquisitions, one can identify relationships of the price paid for each business to its underlying characteristics, such as recent earnings, net assets, revenue growth, location, and acquisition structure.

In many industries, rules of thumb exist for estimating value. Newspaper publishers for example may be priced according to a multiple of circulation, gas station chains according to a multiple of gallons pumped, and fast food chains according to a multiple of weekly revenues per outlet. Persons familiar with a given industry or industry segment usually know these rules of thumb. Often, an acquisition analysis will combine rules of thumb and financial relationships.

The strength of this valuation method is that it draws on actual business transactions between willing and knowledgeable purchasers and sellers—closely approximating the definition of fair market value. Drawbacks to this approach, for which adjustments can sometimes be made, include: the distortions in selling prices caused by peculiar negotiating circumstances; unique acquisition structures or synergies; the relatively low frequency with which comparable acquisitions may occur; and the lack of published detail on acquisitions of or by closely held companies.

With these pros and cons in mind, one can measure the objectivity, relevance and documentation inherent in acquisition analysis as a business valuation method. The method is *objective* in that its inputs consist of *de facto* relationships between fair market value and underlying business characteristics. Acquisitions are historical events, not tenuous hypotheses.

The method is *relevant* when there exists a sufficient number of acquisitions of similar businesses, or acquisitions with similar financial and operational features, to permit the identification of important trends and relationships.

A *documented* analysis of acquisitions may be hard to develop. If the seller has been publicly held, or if the acquirer is publicly held and issues stock to pay for the acquisition, the disclosure requirements of the Securities and Exchange Commission provide a ready and comprehensive source of publicly available information. Otherwise, documentation of acquisition ratios, multiples, etc., may be inaccurate, difficult, or impossible. This is usually the case; in 1980, more than 85 percent of all U.S. acquisitions involved privately held sellers, according to W. T. Grimm & Co., a financial consulting firm.

A fourth popular valuation approach is to compare the business being valued to publicly held companies with similar financial, operational, and marketing environments. Why publicly held companies? Because these companies must regularly disclose details of their activities to the investing public, which in turn assigns a fair market value to shares of these companies through trading on an exchange or over-the-counter market.

Who Values Business?

Valuation Source	Basis of Valuation Expertise
Appraisers	Extensive exposure to most business activities.
	Understanding of asset appraisal techniques.
	Long-time reputation as an independent and professional valuation source.
Financial intermediaries	Frequent contact with merger/acquisition situations.
	Corporate financial specialization.
	Expertise in negotiating and pricing details.
Accounting firms	Industry specialization.
	Familiarity with a wide range of interrelated business problems.
	Financial statement analysis.

THE STOCK TICKER TELLS A TALE

As in analyzing acquisitions, the idea is to relate the underlying business characteristics of similar companies to their market price. In this case, however, the market price is determined by numerous small trades in common stock instead of the acquisition of a business as a whole.

The comparable-company approach is pervasive in business valuation literature. At the broadest level, it underlies even the vaunted price-to-earnings multiples, often the keystone of investment advice. The approach is popular and adaptable because the U.S.

equity capital market is so active, financing new publicly held businesses decade after decade. These businesses, whose shares trade regularly despite their relatively small initial sizes, provide a benchmark against which to measure the fair market value of closely held shares, usually through an analysis of current and historical earnings, net worth, and cash-flow or dividend capacity.

A strength of this approach is that it can be adapted to situations in which DCF analysis, asset appraisals, or acquisition analysis are inconvenient or impossible. For example, if one wishes to value a closely held engineering firm with revenues of $30 million, one can compare it with several dozen such companies whose shares trade actively. What about intangibles such as engineering reputation and skilled-employee satisfaction? A thorough investigation of the company being valued, along with the careful selection of publicly held engineering firms with similar intangible traits, will take them into consideration and will adjust for major differences, such as the marketability of shares, degree of control, differing accounting methods, nonoperating assets.

Does the comparable-company approach have drawbacks? Yes, occasionally. In rare cases, it will be impossible to identify a group of publicly traded companies which, taken together, are broadly representative of the business being valued. Also, the business to be valued may be financially or operationally incomparable: it may be experiencing survival problems such as a negative cash flow; it may be a start-up situation with no operating history; or its activities may be totally without precedent. In such circumstances a comparable-company business valuation will be useless. (Unfortunately, the other valuation approaches may be equally impractical for similar reasons.)

The comparable-company approach is *objective* in that it draws on thousands of anonymous, arm's-length trades in common stock. Investors thus evaluate the financial and operational history and prospects of businesses like the one being valued. The approach is *relevant* when it is based on a careful analysis of companies similar to the one being valued. And it is documentable in that comparable-company information is generated through publicly available filings with the Securities and Exchange Commission.

THE BEST APPROACH DEPENDS ON THE GOAL

Each valuation method has been shown to have peculiar advantages and drawbacks. Situations arise in which one or several methods may not be meaningful. Nevertheless, the four methods are closely interrelated. Each reflects one of the investment alternatives theoretically available to the owners of a business entity at some point in its life cycle. These are

> Continuance of the business in its current financial, operational, and ownership posture.
>
> Orderly termination and liquidation of the activities and assets of the company.
>
> Sale of the business to an individual or corporate owner.
>
> Creation of a public market for the company's shares.

Exhibit I depicts the link between each investment alternative and one of the four common business valuation methods. If owners choose the first alternative, they are looking to the future cash returns on their shares. This is the DCF concept. If owners choose the second alternative, they are looking to the asset values of the business, less liquidation costs, as the primary source of value to them. This is the asset-appraisal concept.

If owners choose the third alternative, they are looking to the net proceeds from a potential acquirer as a primary source of value. This is the acquisition analysis concept. If the owners choose the fourth alternative, they will be looking to the price at which

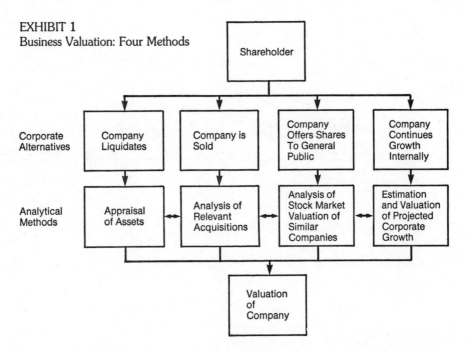

EXHIBIT 1
Business Valuation: Four Methods

an investment banker would underwrite a like public offering of common stock. This is the comparable-company concept.

In short, to evaluate equity in a closely held business, one should consider a number of valuation approaches which reflect one's alternatives. It *is* feasible to value a closely held business. Technically sound methods exist. The valuation process consists not of establishing facts, but rather of influencing perceptions. Business valuation techniques should be closely tailored to the situation: business valuation, carefully thought through, is an indispensable step in corporate planning.

APPENDIX

I

TRENDS AFFECTING BOARDS OF DIRECTORS

Although this article, reporting on a study by Korn/Ferry International, clearly relates to much larger companies (probably all publicly traded) than those which are under discussion in this book, the material may be of interest to private company investors considering the structure and compensation of a board of directors. The material is reprinted with the permission of Deloitte Haskins & Sells and originally appeared in the DH&S The Week in Review, June 24, 1983. [A. L. III]

The 10th annual survey of policies, practices, and compensation of boards of directors has been published by Korn/Ferry International. Over 600 companies participated in the study, including major industrial companies, banks and other financial institutions, insurance companies, and retailers. Some of the findings:

Board Composition. The changing pattern of board representation continues to illuminate the most striking trend in corporate governance over the past 10 years—the trend toward seeking independent outside directors. The top three sources of outside directors continue to be senior executives of other companies (88 percent), retired executives of other companies (66 percent) and academicians (50 percent). When asked to name the primary consideration in asking a prospective director to sit on the board, 76 percent of the companies cited corporate experience.

Compensation. Over 85 percent of the companies compensate their directors on the basis of an annual plus a per-meeting fee. The following table shows the range of average annual compensation paid:

Annual Compensation of Outside Directors Attending All Board Meetings

	Companies Reporting		
Compensation	*1982*	*1981*	*1973*
Under $11,000	21%	27%	70%
$11,000–$16,999	33	35	
$17,000–$19,999	15	13	
$20,000–$24,999	20	18	16
$25,000 and over	11	7	
Unspecified	—	—	14
	100%	100%	100%
Average compensation	$16,990	$15,660	$7,110

Compensation for committee service is not included.

The data this year suggests that the era of structural change is over. Trends in the next decade will show a swing to increased board power and influence. Several emerging trends will unfold during the remainder of this decade. Some seem to indicate management's understanding that the board will participate more fully in the determination of and accountability for corporate strategy, policies, and practices. A few of these trends:

The responsibility of the board in determining corporate strategy will grow. The day of the "rubber stamp" board is over.

Senior executives from outside companies, with strong operating experience, will be the most sought-after directors in the 80s.

The addition of women and ethnic minority directors has peaked. While the 10-year trend was up dramatically, the trend now is flattening.

Former high-ranking government officials, particularly those with sound business experience, will be prime targets for board vacancies.

In order to most effectively carry out their expanded powers, boards will form their own management and administrative groups to support the directors.

Board Issues. Participants were asked to identify and rank the most important issues they deal with as board members. The top 5 issues are:

Relative Importance of Major Issues Facing Boards of Directors

Issue	*Ranking #1*	*Ranking #1 or #2*	*Ranking #1, #2, or #3*
Financial results	55%	82%	94%
Strategic planning	21	51	75
Day-to-day operations	17	34	47
Managerial succession	10	20	37
Mergers/acquisitions	2	11	28

When asked to project the rank of these same issues 5 years from now, the only significant differences reported by companies were the decreasing importance of day-to-day operations and the increasing importance of managerial succession.

The companies were asked to estimate the percentage of time spent at board meetings on these same issues and financial results again was listed first. They estimate that 32 percent of their board meetings are devoted to financial results, 23 percent to day-to-day operations, and 11 percent to mergers and acquisitions. The time estimate for all other individual issues is under 10 percent.

Board Practices and Policies. This year, outside directors reported they spent an average of 123 hours per year on board-related business, the same as last year. There is a direct correlation between company size and time devoted to board matters. Directors of companies with sales of $5 billion and over devote an average of 176 hours, while directors of companies under $200 million spend an average of 85 hours. This year, directors averaged 48 hours on board and committee meetings, 34 hours on review and preparation time, and 41 hours traveling.

APPENDIX

J

BUYING STOCK . . . OR ASSETS

*There's more than one way to buy a company, but a buyer should protect his invest-
ment with certain contractual safeguards. The author is a partner in the New York law
firm of Golieb & Golieb. His article was published in **Venture** in May 1982. [A. L.
III]*

You've decided to buy XYZ Corp. Your army of experts has meticulously examined
the company's financial structure, operations, labor, plant and equipment, markets, rights,
and obligations. After arduous negotiations you've agreed on a purchase price. The only
remaining question is whether to buy XYZ's stock or its assets. What's the difference?
Plenty!

Your tax specialists will highlight the differing tax treatment of a stock purchase
and an asset purchase. For example, the buyer of assets of a manufacturing facility,
including its physical plant and equipment, can increase the value reflected on the sellers
books to a figure taking into account the purchase price. He can then depreciate these
assets without regard to any depreciation previously taken by the seller. If, on the other
hand, stock of XYZ is bought, no new depreciation is allowed.

Which Way Is Best?

The question of whether to buy a company's stock or its assets depends upon circumstances. While there is no clear-cut answer, each type of purchase offers different benefits.

Advantages of Buying:

Assets	Stock
1. Certain assets can be depreciated regardless of prior depreciation claimed by the previous owner.	1. In most cases, contracts and leases come with the purchase.
2. The company is not burdened with unwanted minority shareholders.	2. If minority shareholders exist, control can be gained by acquiring less than 100 percent of the stock, thus reducing the amount of investment.
3. Unwanted obligations, such as union contracts, are not acquired.	3. Sales tax is avoided.

However, there are legal implications as well when acquiring a business. For example, although XYZ may be willing to turn over a lease or contract it holds to a purchaser of its assets, not all leases or contracts may be assigned. If the buyer acquires the shares, there is generally no need for approval by the other party to the lease or contract.

Of course, the seller may be burdened with unfavorable contractual obligations, such as expensive employee benefits. If this is the case, the buyer might benefit by purchasing assets instead of stock.

Minority shareholders may present problems in either case. If you buy a majority block of stock, you'll be marrying partners who have voting rights that may thwart your plans. On the other hand, by acquiring only a portion of a company, your capital investment may be less.

To avoid partners, you may choose to purchase assets. By law, a sale of assets may require the affirmative vote of a stated proportion of the company's shareholders. Even if the required number of shareholders agree, dissenters may be entitled to have their shares appraised and purchased by the selling corporation.

A purchase of assets could also involve sales tax, while stock sales are immune.

Generally, the buyer of assets is not responsible for a seller's liabilities. However, "Bulk Sales" acts provide for prior notice of the impending sale to the seller's creditors. If sufficient notice is not given, the seller's creditors may have a right to the acquired assets. Since the obligations of the business generally are unaffected by a sale of the corporation's stock, the purchaser of shares may be buying potential litigation as well.

Whether the acquisition is a purchase of shares or assets, the contract should contain seller representations in order to disclose any condition that might affect the acquired firm or its assets, and to provide the buyer a remedy (by way of litigation against the seller, if necessary) for any false statements. Typically, such representations provide that the selling corporation was validly organized and exists under the laws of the state where it is located; that the agent who will sign the purchase agreement is authorized to do so by the bylaws; that any required consent to the transaction by shareholders will be obtained; and, that no legal impediments to the sale are known to the seller.

Other representations should state that the seller has good "marketable" title to the assets (whether sold outright or acquired through a stock purchase) and that there are no liens or encumbrances against them; that no legal actions are pending against the seller and that it is not a party in any bankruptcy proceeding. Additional representations that the buyer may ask the seller to make may relate to financial statements, tax liabilities, and employment contracts.

One of the more important safeguards in the purchase contract is the indemnity, a kind of insurance policy that protects the buyer against liability or loss. For example, an indemnity may cover claims of patent infringement. If a court later holds that a piece of acquired equipment violates patent rights of a third party, the seller is responsible for any damages the buyer sustains in litigation. Indemnities should also protect the buyer against the seller's misrepresentations, product liability claims or suits, and tax arrears.

To better ensure that the seller's representations are true, the contract should require an opinion of the seller's counsel confirming that the seller validly exists, that the person signing the agreement is authorized by the bylaws, that there are no legal impediments to the transaction, and that no claims or litigation are pending against the seller. These are some basics to consider, but every acquisition is different. So, have your attorney look at any contract before you sign it.

APPENDIX

K

THE DANGERS OF OVERCAPITALIZATION IN THE
STARTUP STAGE

Richard H. Buskirk

*This article is from **Frontiers of Entrepreneurship Research,** Proceedings of the 1982 Conference on Entrepreneurship, Karl H. Vesper (ed.), at Babson College Center for Entrepreneurial Studies, Wellesley, Mass. The thirteen footnotes and the commentary at the end are mine and did not appear in the original publication of this article. [A. L. III]*

ABSTRACT

A startup venture is faced with a crisis four years after its inception when its technical product is not quite ready for production, no customer exists, and its 1.5 million dollar equity investment is dissipated.[1] Investors hire consultants to evaluate the situation to determine if the enterprise should be folded or new capital be infused. Serious questions

---

[1] Why was the investment made as equity? It would have been better as debt or in some form giving the investors control in the event of nonachievement of objectives.

arise as to the wisdom of management's use of the original 1.5 million dollars.[2] There is evidence that several parties billed the new firm more on the basis of how much money was in the till than on the basis of the market value of their services.[3]

Video Learning Systems, Inc.

On February 1, 1982, the six person board of directors of Video Learning Systems, Inc. of Newport Beach, California assembled in the offices of one of its large, non-director investors, Dr. Brady, an anaesthesiologist, to hear the report of two consultants who had been retained a month previously by Dr. O'Mallery, director and largest investor ($600,000), to evaluate the company's situation and prospects for the future.[4] The consultants had proposed to conduct their study in three stages. The first stage, which was to be completed within the first month, was to answer three questions:

1. Does the company have a workable, marketable product? Does it do what it is supposed to do?
2. Is there a market for the product? If so, what is it?
3. What competitive threats are on the horizon?

The second stage, if approved by the board, was to answer the questions:

4. What organizational structure is needed?
5. How much more money will be needed and from where will the funds come?
6. What marketing plan should be adopted?

The final stage of the project was to be a detailed business plan for the enterprise.

The company had been founded in 1978 by Dr. O'Malley, a family physician of national note, who had been distressed by the poor quality of continuing educational material used by physicians in their efforts to keep abreast of their practices. As national president of his professional association, Dr. O'Malley undertook a comprehensive investigation of alternatives to the existing educational media. He was impressed by some of the work done in video educational media and was told by some of the industry's leaders that the future was to be found in what was called "video interactive systems." In such systems, the student could interact with the program at any point; questions could be asked to determine if the student comprehended the material being presented. For each answer, the program could branch into other material if it were so desired. For example, should a wrong answer be given, the program could present additional material to clarify the point and then test on that new material. Thus, remedial material could be provided where needed. It was this branching capability, in contrast to the existing looping techniques, that gave promise of great things for video interactive learning systems. Such systems consisted of microprocessors that drove either video tape or video disc machines. Thus, the programs were on either tape or discs. The front end costs of discs combined with their inflexibility for program modification led the consultants to conclude that for the time being the Video Learning System unit should incorporate a video tape unit in it. A Panasonic tape drive was used in the prototypes. Several inputs could be used:

---

[2] Was the disposition as promised in the business plan and was it authorized by the board of directors? If not, is there redress possible from those committing certain acts which may be contrary to the plan which was used to induce investment by the investors.

[3] Are any of these billings recapturable by negotiation? Did they overcharge to the extent of a possible legal recovery action being pursued?

[4] Unless "observation" rights had been contracted for by Dr. Brady, I see no reason why he should receive special information not available to other investors. The directors have a responsibility which is special, but all investors have the same inherent rights.

1. A small hand held console was most popular for most programs.

2. A standard computer keyboard could be used.

3. A light wand to respond to screen stimuli was used in several medical programs, i.e., to point to the gallbladder.

4. A wide variety of special sensors could be used for special applications, i.e., a manikin used for a CPR program was wired with 100 sensors that informed the computer if the student were doing the CPR properly.

Dr. O'Malley then retained some local experts in video-computer systems and financed initial research for the project. The initial results were encouraging, so he formed Video Learning Systems and sold some stock to fellow physicians who had become interested in his project.[5] Dr. O'Malley had a good reputation among the local medical fraternity for some of his previous ventures which had proven profitable. Obtaining the needed funds was easy: the profit sharing pension funds of the physicians were overflowing with venture capital ready for work.[6] Over the next four years, $1.5 million dollars was invested by 26 different investors.[7] It was the opinion of the company's legal counsel that the firm was in complete compliance with all laws pertaining to security sales.[8]

In December 1981 the company's capital had been depleted. The firm could not pay its bills except by raising new money. Each point (1 percent) of the company was being sold for $60,000.[9] The company's overhead in the late months of 1981 was running about $40,000 per month. (See Exhibit 1.)

EXHIBIT 1
Monthly Overhead Costs

President's salary[10]	$12,000
Technician's salary	2,000
Occupancy	1,000
Office expenses	1,000
Travel and entertainment	4,000
Legal and accounting	5,000
Consulting fees	15,000
Total	$40,000

[10] Both the president's salary and consulting fees seem way out of line for a startup situation.

In 1979, Mr. McDonald, the former president of a large pharmaceutical supplier, was given a three-year contract to be president of the new concern at a salary of $60,000 a year plus expenses. Much distress among investors developed a year later over Mr. McDonald's performance. One investor said, "We are dead in the water. Nothing is happening. We keep pouring money into that company but nothing comes out." The two consultants had been hired by Dr. O'Malley without the knowledge of Mr. McDonald. One of their assignments was to be an evaluation of Mr. McDonald and the other people involved with the enterprise. The other full-time employee was David McDavid, an electronic technician in charge of developing the prototype. Dr. Connor, the consultant in

---

[5] What representations did he make? Is he liable for the investments of the others?

[6] Is there liability to others in the plans?

[7] What representations were made to the investors at different times and did all the investors and shareholders have the same information available to them?

[7] It would be good for the investors if that legal opinion was in writing and could be looked to in the event the counsel was found to be incorrect.

[9] Was this another round of equity? To what extent did it dilute the holdings of the existing shareholders?

charge of the project, after talking at length with both employees had concluded that McDonald was out of his element; he was a corporate type, not an entrepreneur. He just did not know what to do to make things happen. On the other hand, Connor was pleasantly surprised with McDavid and planned to continue his employment.

One of the consultant's first tasks was to find out what happened to the money. A source and application of funds statement (Exhibit 2) was developed. The consultants were dismayed at how little of the funds actually went into research and productive activities.

EXHIBIT 2
Source and Applications of Funds—1978 to 1982

Source of funds:	
Sale of 25 percent of authorized stock	$1,500,000
Application of funds:	
Management salaries	$ 210,000
Consultant fees	415,000
Legal fees	230,000
Accounting fees	160,000
Occupancy costs	65,000
Research expenses	285,000
Prototype costs	55,000
Office operations	45,000
Marketing costs	15,000
Working capital	20,000
	$1,500,000

The board of directors was composed of:

Dr. Goldberg, M.D., plastic surgeon	(2 percent of stock)
Dr. O'Malley, M.D., family practice	(10 percent of stock)
Dr. Mahan, M.D., retired pathologist	(2 percent of stock)
Mr. Harris, investor	(2 percent of stock)
Mr. Coman, stock broker	(2 percent of stock)
Dr. O'Brien, M.D., family practice	(2 percent of stock)[11]

The board meeting convened at 10 A.M. After 10 minutes of routine business, Mr. Harris asked in brusque tones by what right Dr. O'Malley had hired the two consultants. The two consultants were then asked to leave the room while the board loudly argued for the next 90 minutes. The consultants were then asked to rejoin the group to give their report. The consultant's retention was approved by a vote of 5 to 1.

The consultants gave a three hour report of their findings and recommendations. The essence of the report was:

1. The company had a good product that was a definite improvement on the state of the art. But, it was not quite ready for production. The competition did not have similar capability, particularly the grading and recording cartridge by which each student's performance could be permanently recorded.

---

[11] The whole situation is "amateur night." The way it was set up ensured it would be a loser. No businessperson with entrepreneurial experience was involved. The money went in as equity. No controls seem to have been imposed by the investors. Salaries and fees are silly. The directors hold too little stock and are inexperienced at building businesses.

2. There was a huge market for such a training system, particularly in corporate training programs. It was strongly recommended that the company focus on intercepting existing corporate training dollars as its initial marketing target. The consultants recommended discontinuing existing thrusts into the medical training markets because of marketing difficulties.

After the report, the directors spoke on various matters and asked questions. One pertaining to money caused Dr. Connor to recommend that the firm should terminate not only the contract of the existing president but the consulting contracts of two of its board members. To this, Dr. Mahan took strong exception by saying, "I am owed $55,000 a year by the company for consulting and I expect to be paid in full soon."

The consultant who was running the meeting asked him, "Exactly what did you do for the $55,000?"

"I made myself available. It's not my fault that no one asked me to work," was his reply. Dr. Mahan had some experience in making video training films and had been hired as a consultant for that expertise. Dr. O'Malley also stated he expected to be paid but only after the firm was profitable. He had done considerable work for the firm and was acting as *de facto* president. He had raised all of the money. Mr. Harris then erupted into a tirade against Dr. O'Malley at which point Mr. Coman, who had been silent until then, stood up and threatened to punch Mr. Harris in the face. Dr. Mahan broke in to demand his money, at which point Mr. Connor tried to say something. Dr. Mahan pointed a finger at him and said, "Shut up, you. I am talking to my partners, and it's none of your business." Dr. O'Brien asked the two consultants to leave the room once again. The ensuing verbal fight lasted 45 minutes. When Dr. Palmer, the other consultant, suggested to Dr. Connor that perhaps they should keep walking right out of town, he was told, "No, there's too much at stake here. This can be big, very big."

After the consultants had been asked to rejoin the board, they were told that Mr. Harris had offered his stock for sale for his cost, ($120,000).[12] Mr. Harris was not happy and was most subdued for the rest of the meeting. The consultants then outlined what work was to be done for the next meeting, March 13, 1982.

That night, the board of directors, without Harris, joined several other investors at the home of Dr. Brady for an evening of Irish cuisine. Several potential investors were at the party and were eager to know more about the firm's future. Great care was taken not to "hype" the stock. "Cautious confidence" was the adopted slogan after Dr. Palmer had cautioned several board members about some of their statements.

The next day the consultants delivered their message to a special meeting of the company's stockholders held at the Marriott hotel. All went well. Mr. Harris did not attend.

In planning their activities for the next month, the consultants reviewed where the firm now stood. It had a product, but one that was not quite ready to go into production. About $50,000 was needed to make some needed modifications. Previous management had neglected three simple, but critical, technical factors. Dr. Palmer, who had 10 years experience in electronic production, had quickly detected that the units needed:

1. Ventilation. The heat buildup inside the unit would eventually damage the video tapes. No provision had been made for ventilation. It was a simple matter but had been overlooked.

---

[12] The position of Mr. Harris is typical of the disgruntled investor. He feels that he should be able to get his money back, just because he is disenchanted and wants out. I would guess there is not much chance of this happening.

2. No shielding had been provided to keep radiation from affecting the operations of some of the computer circuitry—again, a simple matter.

3. No provision had been made for quality-control check points in the unit so that the production units could be quickly checked by instruments to detect deviations from specifications. The firm had spent $55,000 for ten prototypes to be made by a large electronics company, but the work had been farmed out to some uninterested unit that was only able to make three units, none of which worked consistently well.

Pursuit of the first customer was at the top of the list. To date, despite all efforts of previous management and the promises of great things, no customer has been developed. The consultants had targeted five potential customers who had indicated great interest in the system.

In his final statement to the stockholders, Dr. Palmer had urged them to give serious thought about what they would want to do in May when the final report was submitted. It was suggested that about $3,000,000 would be needed to take the company to its breakeven point. The stockholders would have to decide if they wanted to provide the additional money or whether they wanted to go outside for it, thus, diluting their position.[13]

COMMENTS BY ARTHUR LIPPER III

The author of this article, Richard H. Buskirk of the University of Southern California, provides a service by bringing this situation to the attention of investors and entrepreneurs, since it contains so many of the usual mistakes made in private company investing. The basic problem in this case was that apparently no sufficient challenge of the business plan was made, if in fact a real business plan was ever developed. The investors simply relied on the reputation (as a doctor, not as a businessman) of Dr. O'Malley and on their general acceptance of the idea for the business. (As it happens, I know something of the business the company originally intended to enter, as well as the reorientation suggested by the consultants. I agree with the consultants, yet I understand Dr. O'Malley's premise concerning medical education. Here, we have a very appealing idea being developed by amateur business people, with the result that time and money were wasted.)

There is no mention of patent protection, and there seems to be no awareness of the fact that the real business investment will be in the software and not in the hardware. The software is the key to the success of the business. All too often investors fail to understand where their company is situated in the development-production-distribution-servicing-utilization cycle. In this case, in a field dominated by giant equipment manufacturers, to try to be simply a manufacturer of equipment is unrealistic. Even if the company was successful in developing a product, a bigger company with greater resources would benefit from their experience and market a rival product. Products have to be sold and serviced, and small companies are at a great disadvantage in the product manufacture and distribution areas.

In any case, if the company's directors do decide to seek an additional $3 million, in all probability the new investors will be senior to the investors of the original $1.5 million, and it will be a long time before the original investors see a profit on their investment, as derived from the buildup of retained earnings. This undoubtedly is another case of investors being less concerned with the growth of retained earnings, as they are with the likelihood of selling their interest to new investors willing to pay highly for projected future earnings.

---

[13] One of the key points the investor should note is that the original money went in all at once and without any achievement requirements for subsequent investment. If there had been a staged investment, not nearly so much money would have been wasted before calling in the consultants.

APPENDIX

L

TERM SHEET USED BY WHITEHEAD ASSOCIATES

Jack Whitehead of Whitehead Associates, one of the most sophisticated and successful venture capital firms, was also the founder of Technicon (the very successful medical technology company, now a part of Revlon). Thus, he has had the experience of both running an important company and managing successfully his own very substantial portfolio. This term sheet is being used with his permission. The addition of my comments is not intended to be critical in any way of the Whitehead form. [A. L. III]

NAME OF COMPANY

Summary of Principal Terms
of Whitehead Associates, Inc.
Investment

A. *Equity Interest*

_____percent (_____%) of fully diluted common stock outstanding calculated based on common shares outstanding, options outstanding, and shares issuable upon exercise of warrants or convertible securities represented by (convertible preferred stock), (convertible debentures), (common stock), (Debt and _____)

B. *Type and Terms of Security*

C. *Price to be Paid by WAI*

D. *Registration Rights*

_____ after closing, one mandatory at the expense of _____, two additional mandatory registrations, the cost of which shall be shared by WAI and _____. Unlimited S-16 registration at company expense. Piggyback subject to underwriters approval.

E. *Voting Rights*

Equal to percentage ownership of fully diluted common stock.

F. *Right of Co-Sale*

If a management stockholder receives a solicitation to sell all or any portion of his equity in _____, such an offer will not be accepted unless a similar offer on the same terms is made pro rata for the same proportion of securities held by WAI. If WAI chooses not to sell on these terms, WAI may, at its option, purchase from the management stockholder group those securities proposed for sale.

G. *Pre-emptive Rights*

WAI will have the right of first refusal for its pro rata share of any sale of securities by _____ prior to the first public offering.

H. *Covenants*

    a. Annual financial statements certified by Certified Public Accountants.
    b. Monthly financial statements, budgets, and business plan, as provided internally.
    c. Noncompete agreements.
    d. Standard contractual covenants and representations.
    e. The Company shall not be merged or sold or sell substantially all of its assets without WAI's approval.

I. *Board Seat*

Same representation as ownership percentage, but in any event at least one board seat for WAI.

J. *Expenses*

Legal expenses to be paid by _____.

COMMENTS BY ARTHUR LIPPER III

A. I would add a provision for Revenue Participation Certificates.

B. I assume that elements of the guarantees which may be required of the entrepreneur, as well as a description of the assets being acquired or used as collateral, would be listed in this section.

C. The staging of the investment(s) would be included in this section, as well as the criterion established for any follow-on investments.

D. Registration rights can be seen as a two-part issue: (1) the requirement of the company's cooperation, since without such cooperation it is almost impossible to effect the filing of a registration statement by the selling shareholders; and, (2) the cost of the filing to the selling shareholder. I have never required more than piggyback rights (allowing my inclusion at such time as others were filing a registration statement to sell stock), believing that my overall controlling features have always been such that it has been unnecessary for me to do otherwise or believing that the controlling shareholders wanted to go public as soon as possible. The registration rights required by WAI are reasonable, and they are but one of the many things I have learned in the preparation of this book. I will insist on similar rights in my own deals in the future.

E. Voting rights at shareholder meetings on which matters? Note that the WAI form refers to a "fully diluted" basis, which I assume means that they vote the shares underlying convertible securities or shares into which warrants are exercisable. Do all shares vote equally on a merger? Do all shares vote equally on a change in capitalization? What about the appointment of auditors? Or the election of directors? Is an acquisition a matter the investor wishes the entrepreneur to control (should he have the major block of voting common stock)? Consideration should be given to embedding, in the bylaws of the company, shareholder percentage voting requirements for certain corporate acts which will permit the investor to veto that which is not in his best interest. The whole problem may also be solved by the issuance of different classes of stock, with the classes having different voting rights on different issues. Investors should not lose sight of the importance of having the company bylaws reflect the desires of the investors. This is one of the advantages the investor has in forming a startup company, and he should not forget the Section 1244 election.

F. This is a highly effective clause that I will use in my own future deals. However, the buy/sell option, described elsewhere in this book, could have the same effect for an investor who wishes to buy the interest of the management group. Yet, the concept of having a right to receive the same offer as management is excellent. A problem exists—one which has arisen in two of my companies—how does the investor value increases in the manager's salary, additional pension benefits, unlimited expense account, country club dues, automobiles, stock options in the acquiring company, and other perks offered "management" by the acquiring company? These perks have a value and can cause the management to urge the acceptance of the offer. The investor has to be aware that managers typically look to their own interests in times of pending enrichment, and their loyalty and prior obligations tend to evaporate with concern for personal gain.

G. This is an interesting requirement, and one which investors would do well to use.

H. I agree with all these covenants, except possibly the requirement for certification, because the added expense is at times not worth the added protection. Also, I would require an attestment by the CEO and entrepreneur as to all financial statements, including monthly reports. If they present them, they should say they are true and complete.

I. The investor should realize that there can be bylaw requirements concerning the number of director votes needed to take or propose shareholder actions, etc. Perhaps division of the board into committees should be part of the shareholders' agreement; for example, the investor or his appointee could be chairman of the finance committee.

J. I am not certain that expense reimbursement should be limited to legal expenses when a technical analysis or survey is required. This is negotiable and should not be thought of as a profit center by the investor. However, the investor must remember that seriously researching deals is an expensive affair and that the better job done the better will be the result. Yet, as Karl Vesper often reminds me, it is possible to have a bad result from a good decision. Such is the case with deals that are passed over by one investor and done by others to their benefit. Looking backward in the private company investment business is profitable only if one learns from mistakes made, and that is not always a function of how much money might have been made or lost in deals passed over. Buyer's remorse and seller's remorse are common afflictions, to which need not be added "passer's" remorse.

APPENDIX

LETTER OF INTENT

This is a fairly typical letter of intent from an investment banker specializing in low-priced new issues. The letter includes some demands which private company investors should seek and some which may be troubling when the company in which they have invested is in the position of going public. [A. L. III]

Gentlemen:

This will confirm our intent to act as the Managing Underwriter in connection with the proposed public offering of units ("Units") of Super New Technology, Inc. (the "Company"). It is contemplated at the present time that New Issue Securities, Inc. ("NIS") shall underwrite for the account of the Company, on a best efforts basis as the exclusive agent of the Company, fifteen million (15,000,000) Units, each consisting of two shares of Common Stock of the Company and one warrant, to acquire one share of Common Stock ("Public Warrants"), at a public offering price of twenty cents ($.20) per Unit or an aggregate of three million ($3,000,000) dollars and that the shares of common stock included in the Units shall result in the public ownership of thirty-seven (37) percent of the issued and outstanding shares of Common Stock. The Public Warrant included in each Unit shall be exercisable for a period of twenty-four (24) months from the effective date of the Registration Statement hereinafter referred to at a price of twenty cents

($.20). It is contemplated that the shares of Common Stock and Public Warrants constituting the Units will be separable ninety (90) days after the commencement of the proposed public offering or such earlier date as we may determine. Our acting as Managing Underwriter shall be subject to the following general terms, conditions, and qualifications:

1. The Company will, as soon as practicable, file with the Securities and Exchange Commission a Registration Statement on Form S-18 or other appropriate form covering the proposed Unit offering which shall include all audited and unaudited financial statements for such periods as may be required. Such Registration Statement, at the time it becomes effective, shall be in form and substance satisfactory to NIS and the Company and to their respective counsel.

2. On or about the effective date of the Registration Statement, it is contemplated that we shall enter into an Underwriting Agreement with the Company in the form and in substance satisfactory to the above-named counsel. The Underwriting Agreement will provide that we shall act as your exclusive agent, on a best efforts basis, for the sale of the Units for a commission equaling ten (10) percent of the initial public offering price thereof and an additional commission equaling five (5) percent of the exercise price of the Public Warrants exercisable at twenty cents ($.20), payable upon exercise. Said Underwriting Agreement will further provide that all funds received from subscriptions for the first thirteen million (13,000,000) Units will be promptly transmitted, pursuant to the terms of an escrow agreement, to an institutional escrow agent acceptable to the Underwriter ("Escrow Agent") and that (i) in the event thirteen million (13,000,000) Units are not subscribed for during the offering period as defined in the Underwriting Agreement ("Offering Period"), all funds will be returned forthwith in full to subscribers without deduction therefrom or interest thereon; (ii) in the event thirteen million (13,000,000) Units are subscribed for during the Offering Period, the funds received therefrom, net of commissions, will be forwarded to the Company against delivery of certificates representing thirteen million (13,000,000) Units; and, (iii) funds received upon the sale of Units in excess of thirteen million (13,000,000) Units during the remainder of the Offering Period will not be subject to any refund provisions and will be forwarded to the Company, net of commissions, against certificates representing such additional Units.

3. On the effective date of the Registration Statement, the Company shall have a capitalization reasonable acceptable to NIS.

4. It shall be the Company's obligation to bear all of its expenses in connection with the proposed Unit offering, including, but not limited to the following: filing fees, printing costs, registrar and transfer agent fees, costs of mailing and transmitting prospectuses, counsel and accounting fees, issue and transfer taxes, if any, and Blue Sky counsel fees and expenses (it is agreed that NIS counsel shall perform the required Blue Sky legal services). NIS will pay its own expenses, including counsel fees and expenses, advertising costs and will have benefit of its expense allowance as provided in paragraph 5 hereof. The Company shall have no obligation to make any payments in the form of underwriting compensation or expenses except as set forth herein to any person who participates in the underwriting described herein.

5. The Company further agrees to pay NIS, on a nonaccountable basis, an amount equal to three (3%) percent of the gross proceeds derived from the sale of the Units underwritten, $20,000 of which is payable upon the execution of this letter.

If NIS does not, or fails to, enter into the proposed Underwriting Agreement, and the reasons therefor are reasonably and directly related to a material adverse change in the business or financial results or condition of the Company or to adverse market conditions, or if the proposed public stock offering is not completed because of the Company's actions or failure to take actions as reasonably required hereunder and NIS is prepared to perform in accordance with the terms herein, then, in either such case, NIS may retain such portion of the twenty thousand dollars ($20,000) payable to NIS upon the execution of this letter as shall equal actual expenses incurred by NIS and, to the extent that NIS' actual expenses exceed $20,000, the Company agrees to promptly pay such additional amount, provided, however, that such expense shall not in any event exceed $50,000 without the prior written approval of the Company. In this connection, Blue Sky applications shall be made in such states and jurisdictions as shall be requested by NIS provided that such states and jurisdictions do not require the Company to qualify as a foreign corporation or to file a general consent to service of process. In addition, the Company shall remain liable for all Blue Sky counsel fees and expenses and Blue Sky filing fees.

6. The Company shall issue and sell, at the closing (or closings, as the case may be) of the proposed underwriting, to NIS and/or its designees, five (5) year warrants to purchase such number of shares of Common Stock as shall equal ten (10) percent of the number of Units underwritten for the account of the Company at a price of 1 mil per warrant (the "Warrants"). The Warrants shall be exercisable at any time during a period of four (4) years commencing at the beginning of the second year after their issuance and sale at a price equaling one hundred and twenty (120) percent of the initial public offering price of the Units. The Company agrees that, for a period of seven (7) years from the date of the closing of the public offering of the Units, if the Company intends to file a Registration Statement for the public sale of shares of Common Stock not covering employee-benefit plans or in connection with a merger and/or acquisition, it will notify all of the holders of the Warrants and/or underlying shares and if so requested it will include therein material to permit a public offering of the shares underlying said Warrants at the expense of the Company (excluding fees and expenses of the holders' counsel) subject to such terms and conditions as shall be agreed to by NIS and the Company. It is understood and agreed that the Company shall not be obligated to register such underlying shares pursuant to the preceding sentence if the offering of such shares would, in the opinion of the Company's then managing underwriter, interfere with a financing for the account of the Company. In addition, for a period of five (5) years from such date, upon written demand of any holder, the Company agrees, on one occasion, to promptly register the underlying shares for purposes of a public offering at the expense of the Company (excluding fees and expenses of the holders' counsel). The Company shall only be obligated to undertake the registration referred to in the preceding sentence at a time when current audited financial statements are available, unless the holders demanding registration agree to bear the costs to the Company of any special audit which may be required. Additionally, for a period of five (5) years from such date, upon written demand of any holder, the Company agrees, on one occasion, to promptly register the underlying shares for purposes of a public offering, at the expense of such holder(s).

7. Except upon the consent of the Company and NIS, the holders of all shares of

Common Stock issued and outstanding on the effective date of the Registration Statement who may be deemed to be "affiliates" of the Company (as such term is defined in the rules and regulations promulgated under the Securities Act of 1933, as amended) shall agree not to sell any such shares publicly (either pursuant to Rule 144 of the General Rules under the Securities Act of 1933, as amended, or otherwise) for a period of not less than thirteen (13) months following such effective date. An appropriate legend shall be marked on the face of stock certificates representing all of such shares of Common stock.

8. The Company represents that consumation of the transactions contemplated herein will not conflict with or result in a breach of any of the terms, provisions or conditions of any written agreement to which it is a party.

9. The Company's financial and operational history, its present condition, financial and otherwise, and its prospects, shall be substantially as represented to us. The Company shall supply us with such financial statements, contracts, and other corporate records and documents as we shall deem necessary, and it shall supply our counsel with all financial statements, contracts, documents, and other corporate papers as may be requested by them. In addition, we shall be fully informed of any events which might have a material affect on the condition of the Company. If, in our opinion, the condition of the Company, financial or otherwise, and its prospects do not fulfill our expectations, we shall have the sole discretion to review and determine our continued interest in the proposed underwriting.

10. It is understood that NIS may enter into other agreements with broker/dealers who shall act as co-underwriters and/or dealers in connection with the proposed public offering contemplated herein, but you shall have no liability to such persons for fees and expenses incurred with their participation in such offering.

11. We shall not be responsible for any expense of the Company or others for any charges or claims related to the proposed financing or otherwise if the sale of Units contemplated by this letter is not consummated.

12. The Company represents that there are no claims for services in the nature of a finder's fee with respect to the proposed public offering. We shall compensate any of our personnel who may have acted in such capacities as we shall determine.

13. The Underwriting Agreement shall provide that the Company will grant to us a right of first refusal for a period of five (5) years after the effective date of the Registration Statement for any public or private sale of securities to be made by the Company or its subsidaries.

14. Prior to the initial filing of the Registration Statement, the Company shall have (i) entered into a three year employment agreement with the entrepreneur acceptable to us and (ii) purchase key-man insurance on the life of the entrepreneur, naming the Company as the sole beneficiary thereof, from a company and in amounts satisfactory to us.

Please affix your signature in the place designated and by doing so you will confirm our general understanding in connection with the proposed public Unit offering referred to herein, subject to the execution of any Underwriting Agreement. This letter shall serve as an indication of our mutual intention as regards to the proposed public Unit offering stated herein and shall not bind either party except to the responsibilities for expenses referred to in Paragraphs 4 and 5 herein. No binding commitment to proceed with the offering of Units will arise until the execution of the Underwriting Agreement which shall obligate us to use our best efforts to sell the Units as your agent during the Offering Period.

Very truly yours,

NEW ISSUE SECURITIES, INC.

By _____,
_____ , President

The arrangements in the foregoing letter are satisfactory to us:

SUPER NEW TECHNOLOGY, INC.

By _____,
_____ , President

APPENDIX N

LETTER OF INTENT

This letter of intent from an old-line investment banker is as underreaching as the letters of intent in Appendixes M and O are overreaching. Note the absence of warrants, unaccountable expense allowance, selection of printers, future fee payments, lengthy stand-off period, sale of principal shareholders' shares, upfront fees, and so forth. [A. L. III]

Dear Board Members:

This letter sets forth the understanding between Company (the "Company") and _____ (the "Managing Underwriter") with respect to the underwriting on a firm commitment basis of a public offering of common stock of the Company.

The Managing Underwriter is interested in underwriting a public offering of an issue of approximately $29,000,000 (exclusive of any over allotment option); $25,000,000 for the Company and approximately $4,000,000 for not more than three selling stockholders subject to (1) satisfactory completion of our due diligence review, including confirmation of the written and verbal information already given us and the receipt and confirmation of such additional information as we may reasonably request in the future, (2) formal approval of this understanding by the Commitment Committee of the managing underwriter, and (3) market conditions which, in our sole judgment, are satisfactory.

The proposed underwriting will be made in accordance with the following general terms:

1. *Security*

    The proposed offering is to consist of approximately 1,750,000 shares of common stock (exclusive of the over-allotment option) of which 1,500,000 shares will be offered by the Company with 250,000 shares offered by selling shareholders.

2. *Price*

The public offering price is to be negotiated, but if the offering were made today, the price would be approximately $16 to $18 per share based on 35 times earnings per share for the fiscal year ended December 31, 1982 and approximately 18 times the estimated earnings per share for the twelve months ended December 31, 1983. The final price will be determined based upon (i) the prices of common stocks of similar companies exhibiting comparable risks, (ii) general market conditions, and (iii) the market's acceptance of such a common stock offering.

3. *Reorganization*

The Company will split its shares so that there are 4,500,000 shares of common stock outstanding prior to the 1,750,000 share offering.

4. *Discount*

The underwriters' discount is not to exceed 7.5 percent of the public offering price.

5. *Overallotment Option*

The Company will grant to the underwriters an option to purchase all, or any part of, an additional number of shares equal to 10 percent of the total number of shares to be underwritten. Such option will be on the same terms as described in Section 2 and 4 above and will extend for a period of 30 days from the date the public offering commences. Any shares purchased under this option will be used solely to cover overallotments, if any.

6. *Board of Directors*

A person designated by the Managing Underwriter will be named to the Board of Directors following the offering described herein. This designation will continue for as long as the provisions of Paragraph 11 are in effect.

7. *Registration Statement*

With the assistance of the Managing Underwriter and its counsel, the Company will prepare and file a Registration Statement in accordance with the provisions of the Securities Act of 1933, as amended, and the rules and regulations of the Securities and Exchange Commission, containing appropriate audited financial statements.

8. *Due Diligence*

The Company will make reasonably available to the Managing Underwriter and its counsel access to the Company's facilities and management personnel. In addition, management of the Company will use its best efforts to cause its independent accountants to be responsive to any inquiries made with regard to the audits of the Company's financial statements, as well as providing to the Managing Underwriter the customary "cold comfort" letters, including acceptable references therein to statistical information contained in the Registration Statement which is based on, or derived from, accounting records. The Company agrees to deliver to the Managing Underwriter a comfort letter which will specifically detail, as of the dates of effectiveness of the Registration Statement and of the closing, the Company's current financial position, and express, in management's best view, the current outlook for its business prospects. The comfort letters described herein shall conform to current accounting practices.

9. *Standoff Agreement*

The Company will agree not to sell any shares of common stock other than those to be registered for sale in the public offering, and the officers and directors of the Company and their affiliates will similarly agree not to sell any shares of common stock owned or controlled by them for a period of 120 days following the date of the public offering without the permission of the Managing Underwriter.

10. *Expenses*

The Company and the selling shareholders will bear all costs and expenses incident to the registration of the securities with the Securities and Exchange Commission, filing with the NASD, transfer taxes and fees and disbursements of experts for the Company, including such Blue Sky qualification expenses and legal fees as are reasonably required by the underwriters. In addition, the Company and the selling stockholders will bear all costs of preparing and printing the Registration Statement and related exhibits, amendments and supplements thereto, underwriting documents (including the purchase agreement, agreement among underwriters, selling group agreement, underwriters' questionnaire, power of attorney and Blue Sky memoranda) and such number of preliminary and final prospectuses as the underwriters may reasonably request. The underwriters will bear the expenses of their own experts and the costs incurred in the formation of the underwriting syndicate.

11. *Future Financing*

The Company will formally agree that the Managing Underwriters will serve as the Company's investment banker for a period of five years from the date of the offering contemplated in this letter of understanding and that during that period the Managing Underwriters will have the right of first refusal to arrange all public or long-term private financing done by the Company.

12. *No Finder*

We have not employed the services of, and will not be paying any fee to, any finder or broker in connection with this transaction and the Company has informed us that it has not employed the services of, and will not be paying any fee to, any such finder.

This letter is not intended to constitute an agreement between us relative to underwriting or purchasing the common stock referred to above, such an agreement being made only by execution of a definitive underwriting agreement. However, it is our intention, and your acceptance and return to us of the enclosed copy of this letter will evidence your intention, to proceed with this proposed public offering on the basis outlined above.

We are pleased with the prospect of working with you and look forward to a successful offering.

Very truly yours,

By _____
Vice President

Accepted:

Board of Directors

By _____
Date _____

APPENDIX

O

LETTER OF INTENT

Clauses 4 and 7–13 of this letter of intent may be found of interest by readers.
[*A. L. III*]

Gentlemen:

Reference is made to our recent discussions relevant to a proposed initial public offering by you of 3,700,000 shares of common stock of NEWCO (The "Company") and based upon our discussions, financial materials which you have submitted to us, and representations which you have made to us with regard to the Company's operations and financial condition, we hereby confirm in principle our interest in underwriting on a firm commitment basis, a public offering of your shares upon the following basic terms and conditions:

1. The underwriters will underwrite on a firm basis for the account of the Company and the Company will register and sell 3,700,000 shares of common stock at a price per share, the "Initial Offering Price," which will be not less than $5.00.

    a. Part of the use of proceeds will be used to purchase 50 percent of the outstanding common stock of OLDCO which operates EXCO, the remaining funds from the offering will be available for new investments.

    In the event that the cumulative earnings of OLDCO do not exceed

$3,000,000 by 12/31/85 or $6,000,000 by 12/31/86, then OLDCO will give back to NEWCO if the earnings are not obtained on 12/31/85 10 percent of the outstanding stock to the Company, and if the earnings are not obtained by 12/31/86 an additional 15 percent of the outstanding common stock to the Company.

2. You have advised us that other than the stock of the Company, there are no classes of stock issued and outstanding nor are there any securities convertible into common stock of the Company. The Company will cause authorized shares to be 5,000,000 shares of which 3,700,000 (4,070,000 in the event the overallotment option referred to in Paragraph 5 is fully exercised) will be issued and outstanding immediately following the public offering contemplated herein.

3. The Company will expeditiously take all the steps necessary to effectuate this offering including the expeditious preparation and filing with the Securities and Exchange Commission of a registration statement as required by the Securities Act of 1933.

4. The gross discount to which we shall be entitled shall be a sum equal to ten percent (10%) of the total proceeds resulting from the sale of the shares. The Company will use a transfer agent approved by underwriters. For a period of two (2) years from the effective date of the Registration Statement covering the public offering contemplated herein, the Company at its expense, if so requested, shall provide us with copies of the Company's daily transfer sheets. In addition, we shall have the right to approve the financial printer to be used by the Company for the preliminary and final prospectus and all related documents.

5. For the purpose of covering overallotments and to be exercisable only for a period of 30 days after the offering is commenced, the Company shall grant to the underwriter an option to purchase up to 370,000 shares at the Initial Offering Price less the underwriting discount.

6. The underwriter will act as principal in purchasing the shares from the Company and be under a "firm commitment" (subject to the terms and conditions set forth in the Underwriting Agreement). The underwriter may, at its discretion, negotiate with other underwriters who shall be members in good standing of the National Association of Securities Dealers, Inc. who acting severally would contract to purchase as principals portions of such shares directly from the Company. Pending completion of the financing contemplated herein, the Company agrees that it will not negotiate with any other underwriter or other person relating to a possible public or private offering of its securities.

7. Provided that proper corporate action by the Company authorizing the issuance and sale of the shares (the "Securities") shall have been taken and an appropriate form of registration statement under the Securities Act of 1933 covering the Securities shall have been filed and declared effective, and subject to the approval of our counsel, we will pay for the Securities not later than ten (10) days after the effective date of said Registration Statement. This tentative commitment is made subject to release of the underwriters: (1) in the event of war; (2) in the event of any material adverse change in the business, properties, or financial condition of the Company (of which conditions we shall be the sole judge); (3) in the event of any action, suit or proceeding at law or in equity against the Company, or by any Federal, State, or other Commission, board or agency wherein any unfavorable decision would materially adversely affect the business, property, financial condition or income of the Company; (4) in the event of materially adverse market conditions

of which event we are to be the sole judge. These usual release provisions are to be duly incorporated in the Underwriting Agreement relative to the sale of the Securities to be entered into between the Company and us.

8. The Company will grant to the managing underwriter individually and not as representative of the underwriters upon closing of the sale of the shares being offered a five year warrant (the "Warrant") to purchase up to 370,000 shares (the "Managing Underwriter's Warrant Shares") at one mill each, such purchase option will be exercisable for a period of four years commencing one year after the effective date of the registration statement and shall be exercisable at 107 percent of the Initial Offering Price for the first exercisable year, 114 percent of the Initial Offering Price for the second exercisable year, 121 percent of the Initial Offering Price for the third exercisable year, and 128 percent of the Initial Offering Price for the fourth or last exercisable year. The Warrant cannot be transferred, sold, assigned, or hypothecated for one year except that it may be assigned in whole or in part to any officer, consultant, or employee of the Managing Underwriter within said one year period. The Company agrees to register expeditiously the Managing Underwriter's Warrant Shares and/or the Warrant at its sole expense at the request of the managing underwriter. This request may be made at any one time during a period of five years beginning one year from the closing of the underwriting transaction contemplated herein. In addition, the underwriter will also have "piggy back" registration rights for the Managing Underwriter's Warrant Shares, and/or the Warrant. In connection with these "piggyback" rights, the Company shall give the holders of the Warrant and the Managing Underwriter's Warrant Shares at least thirty (30) days written notice by registered mail prior to the filing of any Registration Statement with the Securities and Exchange Commission.

9. The Company shall be responsible for and shall bear all expenses directly and necessarily incurred in connection with the proposed financing, including but not limited to the costs of preparing, printing, and filing with the Commission, the Registration Statement and amendments, posteffective amendments and supplements thereto; preparing, printing, and delivering exhibits thereto and copies of the preliminary, final and supplemental prospectus; preparing, printing, and delivering all underwriting and selling documents, including but not limited to the Underwriting Agreement, agreement among underwriters, selling agreement, blue sky fees, filing fees and disbursements of our counsel, legal fees of our counsel relating solely to blue sky matters, and disbursements of transfer agent. You shall pay to us nonaccountable expense allowance equal to three percent (3%) of the total proceeds resulting from the sale of the Shares (including any shares sold pursuant to the overallotment option described in paragraph 5), to cover the cost of our advertising, mailing, telephone, telegraph, travel, due diligence meetings, and other similar expenses including our legal fees. If the proposed financing is not completed because we prevent its completion for any reason (except if such prevention is based upon a breach by the Company of any covenant, representation or warranty contained herein or in the Underwriting Agreement), the Company shall not be liable for our expense allowance set forth in this paragraph.

   a. Upon execution of this letter of intent, you shall pay to the Managing Underwriter $100,000 as a nonrefundable advance against the nonaccountable expense allowance.

10. In addition, we shall have the right for a period of five years from the closing of the public offering contemplated herein, or until the warrants described in paragraph

8 have been fully exercised, whichever is shorter, to designate an individual subject to the approval of the Company, which approval shall not be unreasonably withheld, to serve as a Director on the Company's Board of Directors.

11. The Company agrees that if all the committed Securities are sold in accordance with the terms of the Underwriting Agreement, we shall have a preferential right for a period of five (5) years from the date hereof, to purchase for our account or to sell for the account of the Company or any of its principal stockholders, any Securities with respect to which the Company or any of its principal stockholders may seek a public or private offering pursuant to a registration under the Securities Act of 1933 or otherwise. The Company and its principal stockholders will consult with us with regard to any such offering and will offer us the opportunity to purchase or sell any such Securities on terms not more favorable to the Company or its principal stockholders than they can secure elsewhere. If we fail to accept in writing such proposal for financing made by the Company or its principal stockholders, within thirty days after the mailing of a notice containing such proposal by Registered or Certified Mail, addressed to us, then we shall have no further claim or right with respect to the financing proposal contained in such notice. If, thereafter, such proposal is modified, the Company or its principal stockholders shall adopt the same procedure as with respect to the original proposal. Should we not avail ourselves of such opportunity to act as an underwriter, this will not affect any preferential rights for future financing.

12. At or prior to the closing of the underwriting transaction contemplated herein the Company will enter into an agreement with us providing:

   a. That we will be paid a finder's fee, of from 5 percent of the first $1,000,000 ranging in $1,000,000 increments down to 2 percent of the excess, if any, over $3,000,000 of the consideration involved in any transaction (including mergers, acquisition, consummated by the Company, an "Introduced, Consummated Transaction," in which we introduced the other party to the Company during a period ending five years from the closing of the underwriting transaction contemplated herein; and

   b. That any such finder's fee due to us will be paid in cash at the closing of the particular Introduced, Consummated Transaction for which the finder's fee is due.

13. The foregoing is only a brief outline of the proposed financing and each of the foregoing terms must be interpreted in the form in which it finally appears in the proposed Underwriting Agreement and related documents. While it is the intention of the parties hereto that a public offering of Securities of the Company's shares be made, this letter cannot in any way be construed as a commitment by us to purchase the shares and we may, in our sole judgement and discretion, determine at any time not to proceed with the public offering; nor, except as to the Company's obligation relating to expenses as a commitment by it to sell the shares and shall be conditioned in its entirety upon the execution and delivery of a satisfactory Underwriting Agreement between the Company and us (and this letter is not to be construed as such a contract nor as an agreement to enter into such a contract) to be entered into immediately prior to the time of the public offering, and shall be conditioned further upon compliance by the Company with the terms, contained in this letter and in such Underwriting Agreement. The provisions of paragraph 9 hereof shall, however, be effective and binding upon the execution hereof.

If the foregoing conforms to your understanding, please sign date and return to us the enclosed copy of this letter.

Very truly yours,

By _____
Manager Corporate Finance Dept.

By _____
President

By _____
Executive Vice President

The foregoing is in conformity with our outstanding.

By _____   Date _____

APPENDIX

P

S CORPORATIONS—THE NEW LOOK FOR CLOSELY HELD BUSINESSES[1]

Main Hurdman
Certified Public Accountants

As indicated elsewhere, I believe it better for the private company investor to use a corporation, or possibly a trust, as the vehicle for investment. Not only are there the advantages of reduced liability and a generally more professional format, but the investor has the advantage of representing an entity rather than dealing on his own behalf. Also, in the case of S corporations, there are additional tax advantages of single instead of double taxation of investment income and gains.

This material is being reprinted with the permission of Main Hurdman, the international certified public accountants. [A. L. III]

INTRODUCTION

On October 19, 1982, the President signed into law on Subchapter S Revision Act of 1982 (the Act) dramatically changing the rules for corporations electing to be

---

taxed under Subchapter S of the Internal Revenue Code. The Act is generally effective for taxable years starting after 1982.

Congress originally enacted the subchapter S provisions in 1958 to minimize the effect of income taxes as a factor in making a choice between operating a small business as a corporation or a partnership. By making an election, a corporation's income was taxed to its shareholders. Thus, the double taxation of income at both the corporate and shareholder levels was avoided.

As a practical matter, however, most small businesses found the subchapter S provisions complex and the eligibility requirements restrictive. Unsophisticated taxpayers often fell prey to its many technical traps. Conversely, knowledgeable taxpayers were sometimes able to use subchapter S corporations to obtain unintended tax benefits.

The Act changes this. The old rules have been repealed and replaced with a new simplified framework for taxing the income of subchapter S corporations (now referred to as *S corporations*). Eligibility restrictions were modified and rules relating to income and distributions that created traps for the unwary were revised.

This booklet is intended to serve as an overview of the new provisions for electing and operating an S corporation.

S CORPORATION CONSIDERATIONS

The new S corporation rules, with their simplified framework, provide the shareholders of closely held corporations with a viable choice between regular corporation taxation and taxation at their personal level. Corporations in the following categories that could qualify as S corporations should investigate whether an election would generate an overall tax saving.

New corporations (shareholders benefit from the pass through of losses during the start-up period).

Corporations with adequate cash flow for distributions (taxation of profits at shareholders' level avoids tax at the corporate level; shareholders' tax liabilities can be covered by cash distribution).

New personal holding companies (the new passive income rules make the investment corporation practical in many situations).

However, an S corporation election is not a panacea. In many situations, the election would probably not be advisable, notwithstanding the 4 percent differential between the maximum regular corporation and individual income tax rates. Corporations in the following categories that could qualify as S corporations probably would find it to be more advantageous not to make the election.

Capital intensive corporations (an electing corporation might not have sufficient cash flow available to provide funds for distribution to cover its shareholders' tax liabilities).

Corporations undergoing expansion (again there could be a lack of sufficient cash flow to cover the shareholders' tax liabilities).

Corporations planning to acquire other corporations (The acquisition of other corporations to form a related group of corporations could cause a termination of an S corporation election).

Corporations with net operating loss carryovers that anticipate future profits (the NOL carryovers will not be available to offset future profits).

These situations are generalizations. Since each group of shareholders is unique, the decision to elect S corporation status can only be made after a thorough review of the enterprise's particular circumstances and goals.

ELIGIBILITY

As under prior law, only *small business corporations* can elect S corporation treatment. A corporation must now satisfy all of the following conditions to qualify as a small business corporation:

It must be a domestic corporation.

It must have 35 or fewer shareholders.

Its shareholders must be individual citizens or residents of the United States, estates, or certain qualified trusts.

It can have only one class of stock.

Ineligible Corporations

The following types of corporations are ineligible to elect S corporation status:

Members of an affiliated group of corporations, e.g., parent-subsidiary.

Banks, insurance companies, or other financial institutions.

Corporations electing to claim the Puerto Rican and possession tax credit.

Domestic International Sales Corporations (DISCs) or former DISCs.

Under prior law, subchapter S corporations were allowed to hold foreign corporations, DISCs, or inactive corporations as subsidiaries. However, under the Act, only inactive corporations will be allowed as subsidiaries.

A corporation that had a valid subchapter S election in effect on September 28, 1982, and that held a foreign corporation or a DISC as a subsidiary on that date will be allowed to continue to hold those subsidiaries until more than one half of the S corporation's stock has been transferred (ignoring certain excepted transfers) or the election is terminated for other reasons.

Number and Types of Shareholders

To correspond with the private placement exemption allowed under federal securities law, the permitted number of shareholders in an S corporation has been raised to 35 from 25. For this purpose, a husband and wife (or their respective estates) are treated as one shareholder.

Certain domestic trusts will also qualify as permitted shareholders. These include grantor trusts; voting trusts; a trust created under the terms of a will, but only for 60 days beginning with the date of the stock transfer; and a trust that owns stock in one or more S corporations and distributes all of its income currently to a sole income beneficiary. This latter type of trust, known as a *qualified subchapter S trust,* must also meet certain other requirements with respect to elections, beneficiaries, and corpus distributions.

One Class of Stock

The Act makes two important changes to prior law under which the one class of stock requirement was strictly applied.

First, voting rights are now disregarded in determining whether or not more than one class of stock exists. S corporations can now issue and have outstanding both voting and nonvoting common stock, provided all other rights of the stockholders in the assets and profits of the corporation are identical.

Second, the Act now provides that a *straight debt instrument* will not be treated as a second class of stock in determining whether the one class of stock requirement has been met. This straight debt safe harbor applies to any debt of the corporation that meets all of the following conditions:

The debt is evidenced by a written unconditional promise to pay on demand or at a specified date a sum certain in money.

The interest rate and interest payment dates are not contingent on profits or borrower discretion.

The instrument is not convertible into stock.

The lender is an individual, an estate, or a trust that is eligible to hold S corporation stock.

ELECTION

A small business corporation desiring to be treated as an S corporation must file an *election* with the Internal Revenue Service (IRS). This election may be filed at any time during the preceding tax year or on or before the fifteenth day of the third month of the election year. To be effective, all those who are shareholders on the day the election is made must file a *consent* to the election.

Example A corporation that files its tax returns on a calendar year basis may file an election for the year 1984 at any time during the period that starts on January 1, *1983*, and ends on March 15, *1984*. If the election is filed after March 15, 1984, it will be effective for the year *1985*.

If the election is made after the first day of the election year but before the fifteenth day of the third month of the election year, the consent of anyone who was a shareholder during such preelection period is required. If this consent is not obtained or if the corporation was not eligible to make the election during this pre-election period, the election will not be effective until the following taxable year.

Example A calendar year corporation has 36 shareholders on February 1, 1983, but when it files its election on March 14, 1983, it has only 35 shareholders. Because the corporation failed to meet the eligibility requirements at all times during the pre-election period, the election filed March 14, 1983, will not be effective until 1984.

Comment This new provision is a significant change. Under prior law, qualification deficiencies could be corrected between the beginning of the taxable year and date on which the election was filed. Because of the potential negative impact of this provision, it should be considered when drafting shareholder agreements.

REVOCATION AND TERMINATION

As under prior law, an S corporation election can be terminated by either revocation or disqualification. However, it will no longer be possible to *retroactively* disqualify an election. In addition to terminations by revocation and disqualification, an election may terminate when certain passive income limitations are exceeded.

New Shareholders

Under prior law, if a new shareholder filed an affirmative refusal to consent to the election within 60 days after acquiring the stock, the existing subchapter S election terminated as of the first day of the taxable year. Under the Act, the new shareholder will be bound by the previous election unless the new shareholder acquires more than 50 percent of the corporation's stock and consents to revoke the election.

Revocation

Terminating an S corporation election by revocation will now require the affirmative consent of shareholders owning more than 50 percent of the corporation's stock. An S corporation can file a revocation and choose any future date on which it wishes to have the termination effective. If a future date is not specified, a revocation filed on or before the fifteenth day of the third month of the taxable year will be effective for the current year. A revocation filed after that date will be effective for the next taxable year.

Disqualification

An S corporation's election will terminate if it fails to continue to meet the initial eligibility requirements. Termination under these circumstances will be effective as of the date the disqualifying event occurs.

Example On May 15, 1983, a calendar year S corporation acquired all of the stock of another operating corporation. Under the Act, May 14, 1983, is the last day of S corporation status. Under prior law, the termination would have been retroactive to the beginning of 1983.

Realizing that terminations by disqualification can be unintended, the Act gives the IRS the power to waive the effect of an inadvertent terminating event for any period provided the corporation timely corrects the event and provided the corporation and its shareholders agree to be treated as if the election has been in effect for the period. In such cases, the IRS has the discretionary power to determine what conforming adjustments will be required to waive the effect of the termination.

Excess Passive Income

Under prior law, if more than 20 percent of a subchapter S corporation's gross receipts were from certain forms of passive investment income, its election was terminated by disqualification. The Act repeals this qualification requirement and replaces it with a less restrictive requirement aimed specifically at those corporations that had accumulated earnings and profits prior to their election as an S corporation.

The election will terminate if more than 25 percent of the corporation's gross receipts for each of three successive taxable years is from certain forms of passive income *and* it has accumulated earnings and profits from periods prior to its election as an S corporation. The termination will be effective as of the beginning of the fourth taxable year.

Effect of Termination

When an S corporation's election is terminated by disqualification, the termination will result in two short taxable years. The first or S corporation year will end on the day before the day on which the terminating event occurs. The second or regular corporation year will begin on the day the terminating event occurs and will continue through the end of the corporation's normal taxable year. The two short taxable years will also be required when a revocation specifies a mid-year effective date.

Example A calendar year S corporation sells stock to a nonresident alien on September 10, 1984. For 1984 the corporation has two taxable years. It will be treated as an S corporation for the year beginning January 1, 1984, and ending September 9, 1984, and as a regular corporation for the period beginning September 10, 1984, and ending December 31, 1984.

Income must be annualized when computing tax for the short regular corporation year. However, the two short periods count as one elapsed year in determining the number of years to which net operating losses or other items may be carried. Additionally, although a tax return is required for each taxable year, the due dates for both will be the date the return for the regular corporation year is due.

Under the Act, a corporation with a mid-year termination can compute its income for each short period under one of two methods. It may allocate total income based on the number of days in each period or it may elect (with the consent of all shareholders) to compute income for both short taxable years on the basis of income or loss as recorded on the corporation's permanent records under normal tax accounting rules. Under this method, items will be attributed to the short S corporation and regular corporation years according to the time they were incurred or realized, as reflected in such records.

Planning Points S corporations with mid-year terminations should compute taxable income for the short taxable years under both methods to determine which produces the lowest overall tax.

If an S corporation election is terminated, a new election may not be made without IRS consent until the fifth taxable year following the year of termination. The same rule applies to any successor corporation.

Planning Point Under the Act, corporations that had their elections terminated under prior law can now reelect S corporation status for the first tax year beginning after 1982, notwithstanding a similar five year rule under prior law.

TAX TREATMENT OF S CORPORATIONS

The Act has greatly simplified the tax treatment of S corporations. As under prior law, an S corporation is virtually exempt from all federal income taxes; there are, however, at least four exceptions:

1. In special limited circumstances, an S corporation will be subject to tax on its capital gains.

2. If an S corporation is liable for tax on its capital gains, it may also be liable for the minimum tax.

3. If an S corporation has accumulated earnings and profits and passive income in excess of 25 percent of its gross receipts, it will be assessed a corporate level tax on its excess net passive income.

4. An S corporation must pay any tax that results from the recapture of investment tax credits on an early disposition of property if those credits were claimed while it was a regular corporation.

Computing Taxable Income

Under the Act, an S corporation's taxable income is computed in a manner virtually identical to that of a partnership. Certain items of an S corporation's income, losses, deductions, or credits that could affect different shareholders in different ways are required to be *separately stated* and do not enter into the overall computation of the S corporation's taxable income. Separately stated, however, does not mean nondeductible or nontaxable. That test is passed onto the shareholders who will determine the item's ultimate treatment based on their particular facts and circumstances.

Example An S corporation with two 50 percent shareholders makes a $20,000 charitable contribution to a qualifying organization. The contribution is passed through in equal amounts to high income shareholder A and low income shareholder B. Although the contribution may be fully deductible by A, it might not be fully deductible in the current year by B because of the charitable contribution limitation based on adjusted gross income.

As in the case of partnerships, deductions generally allowable to individuals will be allowed to S corporations. Those Code provisions that are applicable only to corporations, e.g., the dividends received deduction, will not apply. Nondeductible items include, among other things, the net operating loss deduction and the deduction for personal exemptions.

With certain exceptions, elections that affect the computation of items derived from an S corporation are required to be made by the S corporation rather than by each shareholder.

Capital Gains Tax

As under prior law, the Act imposes a tax on certain net capital gains of S corporations to discourage their temporary use as a device to pass through capital gains to the shareholders. The tax imposed is the lower of the corporate alternative tax on capital gains or the regular corporate tax.

The tax will apply if the S corporation's net capital gain exceeds both $25,000 and 50 percent of its taxable income, provided its taxable income exceeds $25,000 for the taxable year. However, the tax will not apply if the corporation has been an S corporation for the three preceding taxable years or if the S corporation has been in existence for less than four years and has had an election to be treated as an S corporation in effect for each of those years.

Tax on Passive Income

As previously explained, the Act repeals the passive income limitation for S corporations that have no accumulated earnings and profit and substantially modifies the limitation for those corporations that do. This modification of the limitation carries with it a price in the form of a corporate tax on certain passive income. However, if an S corporation is newly formed or has no accumulated earnings from years prior to its election under Subchapter S, the passive income limitation and the tax on excess passive income will not apply.

If applicable, the tax is imposed at the highest corporate tax rate, currently 46 percent, on the *excess net passive income* of the corporation. *Passive income* is defined as gross receipts from rents, royalties, dividends, annuities, interest, and gains from the sale or exchange of stock or securities. *Net passive income* is the corporation's passive income reduced by deductions directly connected with it. *Excess net passive income* is that portion of the corporation's net passive income that bears the same ratio to the total net passive income for the taxable year as the excess over 25 percent of gross passive income bears to the total gross passive income for the year. However, excess net passive income for a taxable year cannot exceed the S corporation's taxable income.

The amount of tax imposed will reduce the amount of passive income passed through to the shareholders. Furthermore, gains taken into account for purposes of the S corporation's capital gains tax will not include the portion included in excess net passive income.

Planning Point Corporations that anticipate large amounts of passive income, but have only small amounts of earnings and profits carried over from pre-election years, should consider distributing the accumulated earnings and profits as taxable dividends to their shareholders prior to becoming an S corporation to avoid application of this tax.

PASS THROUGH TO SHAREHOLDERS

Under prior law, income was determined at the corporate level and passed through to the shareholders in the form of actual and constructive dividends in proportion to their stock ownership as of the *last* day of the corporation's taxable year. Losses were passed through to the shareholders in proportion to their stock ownership *during* the taxable year. Certain items, such as capital losses, did not pass through to the shareholders.

Character and Amount

The Act adopts a *conduit* rule, similar to that applying to partnerships, for passing through to shareholders their pro-rata shares of the income, losses, deductions, or credits of the S corporation. A shareholder's pro-rata share will be determined in the same manner as the prior law rule for passing through net operating losses, i.e., per-share, per-day allocation.

In the case of transfers of S corporation stock during the taxable year, income, losses, deductions, and credits may be apportioned to the period of ownership under either the general per-day or elective actual income method in the same manner as when an S corporation election terminates during the year.

Comment To apportion income to the departing shareholder under the elective actual income method, it is necessary to obtain the consent of all shareholders. Departing shareholders may be reluctant to consent unless the elective method is clearly advantageous to them.

Year of Inclusion

Each shareholder's pro rata share will be taken into account in the *shareholder's* taxable year in which the corporation's year ends. If a shareholder dies, the deceased shareholder's portion of S corporation items will be taken into account on the deceased shareholder's final income tax return. Items from the portion of the S corporation's taxable year after the shareholder's death must be taken into account by the estate or other person acquiring the stock.

Losses

A shareholder's deduction for his or her pro rata share of an S corporation's loss is limited to the sum of the adjusted basis at the beginning of the year in the stock of the S corporation plus the adjusted basis in any indebtedness of the corporation. However, unlike prior law, disallowed losses can now be carried forward and deducted by the shareholders in any subsequent S corporation year in which the shareholders have adequate basis in their stock or debt. Special rules apply for recovering disallowed losses upon termination of an S corporation election.

Under prior law, capital losses of a subchapter S corporation were not passed through to its shareholders but were instead carried over at the corporate level to be offset against future capital gains. Under the Act, any preexisting capital loss carryovers will pass through to the shareholders in the S corporation's first taxable year beginning after 1982.

Planning Point Shareholders of an S corporation with a capital loss carryover may wish to generate capital gains to fully use their pro-rata share of this capital loss.

Basis Adjustments

Under the Act, income, including tax-exempt income, and deductible and nondeductible expenses will serve, respectively, to increase or decrease a shareholder's basis in the S corporation stock. When the items that reduce basis (other than distributions) exceed the shareholder's basis in the S corporation stock, the excess is applied to reduce the basis of any indebtedness of the S corporation to the shareholder. If the basis of debt is reduced by application of this rule, the net increases in basis occurring in subsequent years must be applied in the following order:

First, to increase the basis of any indebtedness of the S corporation to the shareholder, but not in excess of the original amount of the indebtedness, and

Second, to increase the shareholder's basis in the S corporation stock.

DISTRIBUTIONS

Under the Act, corporate distributions during the current year will have no impact on how much of the *S corporation's* current income is taxable to the shareholder. As previously described, income will be determined at the corporate level and will be passed through to the shareholders on a pro-rata basis regardless of the amount of distributions received by any shareholder.

The taxability of the distributions themselves will now depend upon the shareholders' basis in their S corporation stock and whether or not the S corporation has any accumulated earnings and profits. The amount of any distribution to a shareholder will equal the amount of cash distributed plus the fair market value of any property distributed.

Earnings and Profits

A major issue in drafting the Act dealt with the proper treatment of an S corporation's accumulated earnings and profits. The Committee Reports indicate that a decision was made that regular corporations with accumulated earnings and profits should not be able to use an S corporation election to distribute those earnings and profits without a shareholder level tax. Therefore, special rules are provided for taxing distributions which are deemed to be paid out of those accumulated earnings and profits.

For this purpose, it is important to distinguish between accumulated *previously taxed income* (a concept of the prior law which the Act repeals) and *accumulated earnings and profits.* Previously taxed income is that amount that was taxed to a subchapter S corporation's shareholders in prior years but that has not yet been distributed to the shareholders.

Comment Under a transitional rule, existing subchapter S corporations that have undistributed previously taxed income will be allowed to apply the prior law rules for distributions of those amounts. Although the Act does not specify how this transitional rule is to be applied, it is anticipated that regulations will be issued to clarify its operation.

Accumulated earnings and profits can be generally defined as the amount of a corporation's cumulative earnings reduced by any taxes paid by the corporation and further reduced by any taxable dividends paid by the corporation.

Example XYZ Company, a regular corporation, has 1982 taxable income of $100,000. XYZ pays federal income taxes of $26,250 on that income and makes no dividend distributions to its shareholders. Assuming no prior accumulated earnings and profits, XYZ has $73,750 of accumulated earnings and profits at the end of its 1982 taxable year.

For years beginning after 1982, an S corporation will no longer generate any earnings and profits. An S corporation may, however, have accumulated earnings and profits attributable to any of the following:

Taxable years for which an election was not in effect.

Taxable years beginning prior to 1983 for which an election was in effect.

Certain corporate acquisitions which resulted in a carryover of the acquired corporation's earnings and profits.

Corporations without Accumulated Earnings and Profits

The amount of a distribution by a corporation without accumulated earnings and profits will be tax free to the extent of the shareholders' basis in their S corporation stock. The distribution is first applied to reduce a shareholder's stock basis. To the extent the amount of the distribution exceeds this basis, the excess will be taxed as a capital gain.

Example Individual A forms an S corporation on January 1, 1983, by contributing $1,000 in exchange for all of the S corporation stock. During 1983, the S corporation has income of $5,000 and makes a $7,500 cash distribution to individual A. Individual A will report $5,000 of pass through income in 1983, increasing his basis in his S corporation stock to $6,000. The $7,500 cash distribution will result in a capital gain in the amount of $1,500, the amount by which the distribution exceeds his stock basis.

Corporations with Accumulated Earnings and Profits

The rules for taxing distributions become more complicated when the S corporation has accumulated earnings and profits. Distributions by these S corporations are treated in the same manner as distributions by S corporations without accumulated earnings and profits up to the amount of the S corporation's *accumulated adjustment account*.

A corporation's *accumulated adjustment account* is equal to its post-1982 *taxable income* (which will not include tax-exempt income or reflect nondeductible expenses) less its post-1982 distributions. Under this formula, shareholders of an S corporation with accumulated earnings and profits will be assured of tax free distributions to the extent of the corporation's accumulated adjustment account, but not in excess of basis. Distributions in excess of the accumulated adjustments account will be taxable to the shareholder as dividends to the extent of accumulated earnings and profits.

Comment Because tax exempt income does not increase an S corporation's accumulated adjustments account, but does increase a shareholder's basis in his or her stock, it may not be possible to distribute that income tax free to an S corporation's shareholders. By distributing these amounts, an S corporation with accumulated earnings and profits could inadvertently convert otherwise tax-free income into taxable dividends.

Distributions of Appreciated Property

When an S corporation distributes appreciated property to its shareholders, gain will be recognized to the S corporation in the same manner as if the property had been sold to the shareholders at its fair market value. This gain, like all other gains of the S corporation, will pass through to the shareholders. The only exception to this rule is for distributions in complete liquidation of the S corporation.

OTHER PROVISIONS

Taxable Years

Under the Act, S corporations will be required to conform to a new *permitted year* rule. Under this rule, S corporations must choose either a taxable year that ends December 31 or a fiscal year for which it establishes a business purpose to the satisfaction of the IRS.

Comment The IRS has an administrative policy of granting requests for the adoption or change of a *partnership* fiscal year in those cases where the fiscal year results in a deferral of three months or less and where the partnership agrees to certain transition adjustments. It is anticipated that a policy similar to this may be adopted for S corporations. However, because of the tax saving opportunities available to an S corporation with a fiscal year, it is unlikely that the IRS will grant a request for a fiscal year that results in a deferral of more than three months.

Existing S corporations will be allowed to maintain their present fiscal year only if at least 50 percent of the S corporation stock is not *newly owned stock*. For this purpose, newly owned stock is the amount of stock of the S corporation owned by any shareholder to the extent such ownership exceeds that shareholder's ownership on December 31, 1982. As soon as more than 50 percent of the stock changes ownership after December 31, 1982, the S corporation must conform to the new permitted year rule. In applying this ownerhip test, the following three transfers will not be counted:

1. A transfer due to a qualified transferor's death.

2. A transfer due to a gift from a qualified transferor to a member of his or her family.

3. A transfer due to the operation of a qualified buy-sell agreement in effect on September 28, 1982, between a qualified transferor and a member of the transferor's family.

A *qualified transferor* is any person who held the S corporation stock on December 31, 1982, or who acquired the stock in one of the above three transfers.

Comment This special grandfather rule allows the continued use of a fiscal year only by a corporation having a valid subchapter S election in effect for its taxable year that includes December 31, 1982. Other fiscal-year corporations that wish to make an S corporation election for taxable years beginning after 1982 will be required to change to a permitted year.

Fringe Benefits

Under prior law, shareholder-employees of a subchapter S corporation enjoyed certain tax favored fringe benefits that were unavailable to partners in a partnership, e.g., group-term life insurance. Under the Act, the treatment of fringe benefits of any person owning more than 2 percent of the stock of an S corporation will be treated in the same manner as a partner in a partnership.

Under a transitional rule, if the qualifying fringe benefits existed on September 28, 1982, and the corporation was a qualifed subchapter S corporation on that date, the new rules will generally not apply until tax years beginning after 1987.

Expenses Owed to Shareholders

Accrual basis corporations have special rules for deducting payments for expenses or interest owed to *cash basis* shareholders who own more than 50 percent of the corporation's stock. For those payments to be deductible, the corporation must make the payments to the shareholder within two and one-half months of the close of the corporation's taxable year.

The Act creates a special rule for S corporations by effectively requiring the matching of an S corporation's deductions and a *2 percent or more* shareholder's income. Accordingly, an accrual basis S corporation will be placed on the cash basis of accounting for the purposes of deducting business expenses and interest paid to cash basis shareholders who own at least 2 percent of the S corporation's stock.

Comment This new rule may pose problems in the normal operations of an accrual basis S corporation. For example, year-end payroll accruals to owner-employees may not constitute deductible expenses until the following year when they are actually paid.

The Act also expands the list of related party transactions to which the rule will apply. When more than 50 percent common ownership exists, the transactions subject to the rule will now include transactions between an S corporation and a partnership, an S corporation and another S corporation, and an S corporation and a regular corporation.

Oil and Gas Production

The Act significantly alters the rules governing cost and percentage depletion on an S corporation's oil and gas production. Unlike prior law, each shareholder is now treated as having produced his or her pro-rata share of the oil and gas production of the S corporation. This will require separate shareholder-level computations of cost and percentage depletion.

Additionally, the percentage depletion rules regarding the transfer of proven properties to and from an S corporation have been revised. This revision of the transfer rules may cause otherwise eligible production to lose its exemption under the independent producers and royalty owners exception for percentage depletion when a regular corporation elects S corporation treatment. The loss of percentage depletion may also occur when an S corporation election terminates unless the limited exception for transfers by individuals to corporations applies.

To mitigate the effect of these changes, *qualified oil corporations* will be allowed to continue to use the prior subchapter S rules. A qualified oil corporation is any corporation that satisfies the following conditions:

As of September 28, 1982, it was a subchapter S corporation or had elected such status after December 31, 1981, and before September 28, 1982.

For the calendar year 1982, the combined average daily production of domestic crude oil or natural gas of the corporation and any shareholder owning more than 40 percent of its stock exceeds 1,000 barrels.

An election is made by the corporation to have the prior subchapter S rules apply.

Comment At this time, it is uncertain what the full impact of these modified transfer rules will be. Pending further clarification by the IRS, it is advisable to proceed with caution when considering an S Corporation election for a corporation holding oil and gas interests benefiting from or that expect to benefit from the percentage depletion allowance.

Effective Dates

In general, the Act's provisions apply to taxable years *beginning* after December 31, 1982. Subchapter S corporations in existence on that date are treated as having elected under the new rules for their first taxable year beginning after 1982.

However, certain provisions of the Act have different effective dates, including:

The passive income limitation and tax are effective for taxable years beginning in 1982 and thereafter.

The provisions relating to S corporation pension plans in effect before October 19, 1982, will continue to remain in effect for all taxable years beginning before 1984 at which time the changes made by the Tax Equity and Fiscal Responsibility Act of 1982 are scheduled to take effect.

The prior law's distribution rules will continue to apply to an existing subchapter S corporation's previously taxed income.

The provisions of the new Subchapter S Revision Act of 1982 have a direct impact on existing subchapter S corporations and on corporations or other businesses that could qualify for the new S corporation status. The professionals of Main Hurdman are available to explain the new Act and to consult with you on the impact of its provisions as they relate to you and your business.

APPENDIX

Q

ANGELS AND INFORMAL RISK CAPITAL[1]

William E. Wetzel, Jr.
University of New Hampshire

Raising risk capital is always a challenging and difficult task. "Business angels" play a key role in the risk capital market by providing seed capital for inventors, and startup and growth capital for small, technology-based firms. This article discusses the investment characteristics of a sample of angels active in New England, offers suggestions for entrepreneurs looking for angels, and recommends steps to improve the efficiency of the informal risk capital market.

William E. Wetzel, Jr., is Professor of Business Administration at the Whittemore School of Business and Economics, the University of New Hampshire. Mr. Wetzel holds the B.A. degree from Wesleyan University and the M.B.A. degrees from Temple University and the University of Chicago. His research interests include the functioning of the risk capital markets, the relationships between entrepreneurship and economic development, and financial strategies for closely held firms. Mr. Wetzel has written for such journals as Business Horizons *and* New England Journal of Business and Economics. *[Sloan Ed.]*

---

[1] *Sloan Management Review,* Summer 1983.

The 1980s have been touted as an age of technological entrepreneurship in the United States. Success stories like DEC and Apple have stimulated expectations for an economy energized by technology and entrepreneurs. A growing body of research data documents the contribution of small, technology-based firms (STBFs) to job creation, technological innovation, and other economic benefits, such as productivity gains, price stability, and favorable trade balances. The Small Business Innovation Development Act of 1982 is testimony to the economic and technological virtues attributed to STBFs (and to the increasing political influence of small business). The act provides for a federal investment of about $1 billion in research by STBFs over the next five years.

Risk capital investors play an essential role in the growth of the high-tech sector. However, despite tremendous growth in risk capital investments in STBFs, there is a continuing perception that gaps exist in the capital markets for smaller firms, and this raises questions about the vigor of any "age of entrepreneurship." Though such gaps have not been convincingly documented, the capital gap folklore maintains that there are shortages of product development financing for technology-based inventors, of startup financing for STBFs that fail to meet the criteria of professional venture capital investors, and of equity financing for closely held STBFs that are growing at a faster rate than internal cash flows can support. Created by Congress in 1958, the Small Business Investment Company (SBIC) program was an early institutional attempt to fill such gaps. Following the 1980 White House Conference on Small Business, more recent efforts to deal with the gap include the Small Business Investment Incentive Act of 1980 and the SEC's new Regulation D streamlining securities law for small business.

The capital gap folklore is based upon the observable behavior of financial institutions, including SBICs and professional venture capital firms. However, the data we have collected suggest that capital gaps may be more apparent than real. The folklore overlooks the investment record of informal risk capital investors—the "business angels." (Angels do not include founders, friends, or relatives.) Not only do these angels exist, they may represent the largest pool of risk capital in the country. According to our data, they tend to invest in precisely the areas that are cited as gaps in the capital markets for STBFs.

The effect of capital gaps can be created when markets fail to function efficiently. Modern financial theory rests upon assumptions of efficient capital markets where all relevant information about sources of funds and about investment opportunities is freely available to buyers and sellers of capital. Efficient risk capital markets require fully informed entrepreneurs and investors. Our data indicate that this necessary condition is not fulfilled in the angel segment of the risk capital markets. In the absence of efficient markets, the flow of capital from less productive to more productive uses will be impeded. The efficiency issue is a cause for concern, because angels play an essential role in the financing of many STBFs. Angels fill what would otherwise be a void in the risk capital markets by providing development funds for technology-based inventors, seed capital for STBFs that do not meet the size and growth criteria of professional venture investors, and equity financing for established STBFs. In 1980–81 Jeffry Timmons and David Gumpert conducted a survey of 51 of the largest and most active professional venture capital firms. The survey showed that the range of an individual investment was from $300,000 to $4 million and that the size of a typical individual investment was $813,000. The figures were similar for SBICs, but substantially higher for corporate venture affiliates.[2] However, it is clear that risk capital financing of between $50,000 and $500,000 is primarily the domain of the angels and is a vital resource for many inventors and STBFs.

---

[2] See D. E. Gumpert and J. A. Timmons, "Disregard Many Old Myths about Getting Venture Capital," *Harvard Business Review,* January–February 1982.

Many entrepreneurs will confirm that, once personal funds and "friendly money" have been exhausted, raising the first piece of external risk capital can be an enormous obstacle to creating or expanding a small, technology-based firm. STBFs tend to be founded by technically skilled individuals; although some of these founders may have management experience and marketing savvy, they seldom have had experience in the capital markets, particularly in the risk capital markets. The problem is compounded by the fact that the most likely sources of risk capital for many STBFs are the least visible—those mythical business angels. They are a diverse, dispersed population of individuals of means; many have created their own successful ventures and will invest their experience as well as their capital in ventures they support.

Informal Risk Capital

Any useful discussion of risk capital must recognize the diverse nature of the commodity and its sources of supply. The market for risk capital consists of at least three segments, each having a unique set of distinguishing characteristics:

The public equity market.

The professional venture capital market.

The market for informal risk capital (business angels).

Although the boundaries separating these segments are indistinct and often overlap, nonetheless an appreciation of the distinctions is essential for entrepreneurs seeking funds. A founder can waste much time talking to sources about deals that are unlikely to occur.

The public equity market and the professional venture capital market are relatively efficient and well understood. At the risk of serious oversimplification, it can be said that if an entrepreneur is trying to raise from $2 million to $5 million (or more) for a venture with sex appeal, the speculative new issues market represents a potential source of funds. The professional venture capital is generally interested in ventures that require $500,000 (or more) of postrevenue financing, that yield projected revenues of more than $20 million within 5 to 10 years, and that can go public or sell out by that time.

The informal risk capital market, on the other hand, is virtually invisible, inefficient, and often misunderstood. Yet searching for an angel is appropriate for a technology-based inventor looking for development funds or an entrepreneur looking for less than $500,000 to start or expand an STBF. Inefficiency and the invisible nature of the angel segment of the capital markets contribute to perceptions that funds for such purposes are unavailable.

There is evidence to suggest that individual investors (despite their low profile) represent the largest pool of risk capital in the country. In 1978 the organized venture capital industry invested approximately $500 million; in 1981 the industry invested an estimated $1.2 billion. Although there are no data documenting the total volume of risk capital provided by individuals, clues can be found. For example, in 1981 private placements reported by corporations to the SEC under Rule 146 totaled over $1 billion. In a 1980 SEC survey of a sample of issuers who filed Form 146, it was found that corporate issuers were engaged primarily in high technology or in other manufacturing or nonfinancial services, and that they were generally young companies employing few workers. The survey indicated that 87 percent of those buying corporate issues were individual investors or personal trusts. The average amount invested by an individual in a corporate issue was $74,000. The $1 billion corporate financing reported under Rule 146 represents only a fraction of the total transactions that occurred in the informal risk capital market. Rule 146 private placements by noncorporate issuers engaged largely in oil- and gas-related activities or in the real-estate business totaled over $3 billion in

1981. Individuals and personal trusts represented 93 percent of the purchasers of noncorporate issues. Note also that Rule 146 private offering data exclude financings exempt from registration because of their intrastate nature (Rule 147) or financing by closely held firms under small-offering exemptions (Rules 240 and 242). Effective June 1982, Regulation D replaced the exemptive provisions that existed under Rules 146, 240, and 242.[3]

Other empirical data confirm the importance of angels in the financing of STBFs. In an examination of capital market imperfections, Charles River Associates, Inc. (CRA) excluded "individuals who act informally as providers of venture funds." Yet CRA commented that "they may represent the largest source of venture capital in the country." The CRA study looked at the composition of external funds received by STBFs prior to making initial public offerings. The study showed that between 1970 and 1974 "unaffiliated individuals" accounted for 15 percent of external funds, while "venture capitalists" accounted for 12 percent. When the data were classified by stage (age of venture), unaffiliated individuals provided 17 percent of external capital during the start-up year, while venture capitalists provided 11 percent.[4]

A similar pattern can be found in David Brophy's study of financial support for new, technology-based firms that were incorporated and operating from 1965 to 1970. In a sample of Boston-area firms, private individuals (excluding founders, friends, and relatives) provided 14 percent of total financing and SBICs, and private venture capital firms provided 15 percent. The figures for a sample of Ann Arbor and Detroit firms were 16 percent from individuals and 2 percent from venture capitalists.[5]

Clearly, angels play a key role in the early financing of many STBFs: one or more wealthy believers will provide seed capital, help solve problems, and exploit the opportunities associated with commercializing an invention or innovation or with starting up a new enterprise. Most entrepreneurs have heard of business angels and some entrepreneurs have found them. However, no one has ever really found out where angels come from, how many there are, how to find them, or what angels look for in a venture proposal.

THE STUDY OF ANGELS

With the SBA's seed capital we undertook a hunt for business angels in New England in an attempt to learn more about this invisible segment of the risk capital markets.[6] Our search turned up 133 investors who fit the description of a business angel, a sample large enough to at least draw tentative conclusions about the characteristics of angels. However, much more study is required before definitive statements can be made about the functioning of the informal risk capital market. Our work focused on the role of informal investors as a source of funds for three types of investment situations:

Financing for technology-based inventors.

Startup and early-stage financing for emerging firms.

Equity financing for small established firms growing faster than retained earnings can support.

---

[3] See *Report of the Use of the Rule 146 Exemption in Capital Formation* (Washington, D.C.: Directorate of Economic and Policy Analysis, U.S. Securities and Exchange Commission, January 1983).

[4] See Charles River Associates, Inc., *An Analysis of Capital Market Imperfections* (Prepared for the Experimental Technology Incentives Program, National Bureau of Standards, Washington, D.C., February 1976).

[5] See D.T. Brophy, "Venture Capital Research," *Encyclopedia of Entrepreneurship* (Englewood Cliffs, N.J.: Prentice-Hall, 1982), ch. IX.

[6] The SBA's Office of Advocacy and Milton Stewart (then Chief Counsel for Advocacy and now president of the Small Business High Technology Institute) were our believers. See W. E. Wetzel and C. R. Seymour, *Informal Risk Capital in New England* (Prepared for Office of Advocacy, U.S. Small Business Administration, Durham, N.H.: University of New Hampshire, 1981).

This article presents the results of our research and our perceptions of the lessons they offer for entrepreneurs.

It took nine months and the assistance of several professional organizations to identify and collect data from our sample of angels. We discovered that angles tend to be found in clusters that are linked by an informal network of friends and business associates. Finding one investor typically led to contacts with three or four more, a tedious but productive "snowball" search technique.

The total population of informal investors is unknown and probably unknowable. Our sample represents approximately 10 investors per million population, or about 1 percent of the 1,000 per million incidence of "millionaires" based upon 1972 IRS data. Given 10 years of inflation and the drop in capital gains tax rates, it is likely that the total population of angels in New England is substantially larger than our sample, perhaps by a factor of 20 or more.

Investment History

Our sample of angels reported risk capital investments totaling over $16 million in 320 ventures between 1976 and 1980, an average of one deal every two years for each investor. The average size of their investments was approximately $50,000, while the median size was about $20,000. Thirty-six percent of past investments involved less than $10,000, while 24 percent involved over $50,000.

In 60 percent of past financings, respondents participated with other individuals in larger transactions. It is clear that informal investors are accustomed to sharing investment opportunities with friends and business associates. Participation with other financially sophisticated individuals permits venture financing that approaches the $250,000 to $500,000 interest threshold of venture capital firms and equity-oriented SBICs.

Venture Life-Cycle Preferences

The data developed by Gumpert and Timmons show that professional venture capital firms currently place from 25 percent to 35 percent of their funds in startup situations; this is an increase from the mid-70s figure of approximately 15 percent.[7] While these professional investors appear to be increasingly willing to look at startups, their interest is generally limited to proposals from entrepreneurs with successful startup track records or to investor-initiated startups in emerging technologies (e.g., genetic engineering and robotics). Even then their interest is only for ventures with enough growth potential to justify liquidation expectations through a public offering or acquisition by a larger firm within 5 to 10 years of initial financing.

Historically, informal investors have been the principal source of external seed capital. The age distribution of ventures receiving financing from our sample of angels is consistent with this record. Forty-four percent of past financings were startups, and 80 percent involved ventures less than five years old. If the definition of startup is tied to the achievement of break-even operations rather than age, 63 percent of past investments were in situations that had not achieved break-even performance. With respect to future investments, 78 percent of our sample expressed a "strong interest" in startup and early-stage financing for emerging firms. The lesson for entrepreneurs is clear: if you need less than $500,000 to launch a new venture, look for one or more angels.

For technology-based inventors the lesson is even more compelling to find an angel. One third of our sample of informal investors expressed a "strong interest" in financing technology-based inventors. An angel with technical and managerial experience in the

---

[7] See Gumpert and Timmons (January–February 1982).

commercialization of related technology can bring a "sense of the market" to the work of an inventor. When asked whether their interests were limited to specific fields of technology, the areas investors cited most frequently were electronics, computers, energy, and health care. However, the principal criterion cited by these investors was that the technology be in a field that they understood and could evaluate:

> "A field in which I have some technical competence."
> "Fields in which I am sufficiently experienced to permit evaluation."
> "Related to my background in organic chemistry and pharmaceuticals."
> "Those I know: electronics, physics, mechanics."
> "It is limited to what I know and understand myself, especially about the marketplace, or can get trustworthy opinions on."

Approximately one respondent in five expressed a "strong interest" in equity financing for established firms. Investors interested in established firms anticipated larger investments (approximately $75,000 per firm). In our sample of angels, the incidence of advanced technical training and startup management experience was lower among investors interested in established firms than among investors interested either in technology-based inventors or in early-stage financing for emerging firms.

Venture Relationships

Both informal investors and professional venture investors typically contribute more than capital to the situations in which they invest. They are active investors, generally playing a consulting role or serving on a working board of directors. The investors in our sample are no exception. They are a well-educated group and experienced in the management of startup situations. Ninety-five percent hold four-year college degrees and 51 percent have graduate degrees. Of the graduate degrees, 44 percent are in a technical field and 35 percent are in business or economics (generally an M.B.A.). Three quarters of the sample had been involved in the startup of a new venture.

The relationship between angels and their portfolio firms was tested by asking respondents about the nature of their contact with portfolio firms. Passive investors were defined as those whose contact consisted of receiving periodic reports and attending stockholder meetings. Active investors were defined as those whose relationship included one or more of the following roles: membership on the board of directors, a consulting role, part-time employment, or full-time employment. Eighty-four percent reported that they expect to play an active role, typically having an informal consulting relationship or serving on a board of directors. In addition to raising capital, the entrepreneur's task is to find investors with a combination of training and experience that will contribute to the venture's success. For first-time entrepreneurs this resource can be more valuable than capital.

Geographic Patterns

The tendency of informal investors to maintain close working contact with ventures they finance is reflected in the geographic distribution of their portfolios. Three quarters of the firms financed by our sample of angels were located within 300 miles of the investor (roughly one day's drive). Fifty-eight percent were within 50 miles. The geographic distribution of portfolio ventures may also reflect the absence of systematic channels of communication between investors and entrepreneurs. The likelihood of an investment opportunity coming to an individual investor's attention increases—probably exponentially—the shorter the distance between the two parties. The lesson for entrepreneurs looking for angels is: Look close to home.

Industry Preferences

Both professional and informal risk capital investors display a broad range of industry preferences. The fields that interest professional venture firms are described in Stanley Pratt's *Guide to Venture Capital Sources*, but information about the tastes of angels is very difficult to find.[8]

Our sample of angels reported a clear preference for manufacturing enterprises in general and for "high technology" manufacturing in particular. Fifty-seven percent of past investments were in manufacturing firms: 28 percent in high technology products, 20 percent in industrial products, and 9 percent in consumer products. Service firms were a distant second, attracting 12 percent of past investments. Reported investment objectives were more broadly distributed. At the top of the list, 64 percent of the respondents expressed "strong interest" in high technology manufacturing, 33 percent in industrial product manufacturing, and 30 percent in service firms. At the bottom of the list, only 5 percent expressed a "strong interest" in wholesale trade, 3 percent in retail trade, and 1 percent in transportation firms. Even in the least attractive categories (retail trade, wholesale trade, and transportation), one investor in three reported either a "moderate" or a "strong" investment interest. These patterns indicate two things to entrepreneurs: first, some types of ventures attract much more interest than others; and second, somewhere there is an angel interested in backing a viable opportunity in virtually any business or industry category.

Exit Expectations

Risk capital is "patient money." Returns take the form of long-term capital gains realized after an extended period during which an investment possesses little or no liquidity or marketability. Liquidation expectations with respect to timing and method are variables that influence risk capital investment decisions. Forty-seven percent of our respondents reported that provisions for liquidating their investment were "definitely" or "generally" included in the initial investment agreements.

The "patience level" of informal investors was tested in terms of expected holding periods. The median expected holding period of respondents was five to seven years. Entrepreneurs will be particularly interested that 24 percent of the respondents either consider the holding period unimportant or expect to hold their risk capital investments longer than 10 years, a "patience level" well in excess of the typical expectations of venture capital firms and SBICs.

Patience and shared exit expectations are particularly critical for ventures with a 5- to 10-year sales potential below $20 million (i.e., ventures with limited prospects for a public offering or acquisition by a larger firm within the typical exit horizon of risk capital investors). Patience is a virtue, and angels tend to be virtuous.

Rejected Proposals

Most entrepreneurial lessons come the hard way—by making mistakes—and the same can be said of venture investing. "Schools" for entrepreneurs and venture investors are out on the street, not on university campuses. However, some entrepreneurial lessons can be learned from the mistakes of others. In order to help guide future entrepreneurs, we wanted to discover the reasons our sample of investors had rejected past investment proposals.

The "typical" angel seriously considers and rejects two or three investment opportunities each year. The most common reasons cited for rejection were lack of confidence

---

[8] See S. E. Pratt, ed., *Guide to Venture Capital Sources*, 6th ed. (Wellesley Hills, Mass.: Capital Publishing, 1982).

in management; unsatisfactory risk/reward ratios; absence of a well-defined business plan; the investor's unfamiliarity with products, processes, or markets; or the venture was a business the investor "did not want to be in." The following comments reflect the range of reasons for rejecting investment proposals:

"Risk/return ratio was not adequate."

"In most cases management did not seem adequate for the task at hand."

"Simply not interested in the proposed businesses. Saw no socioeconomic value in them."

"Unable to agree on price."

"Too much wishful thinking."

"One of two key principals not sufficiently committed—too involved with another activity."

"Unfamiliar with business."

"Wife refused."

Entrepreneurs can learn several important lessons from this:

Be realistic about the prospects for your venture and about the risks and costs of venture investing.

Be sure all essential management functions are staffed with experienced, committed individuals.

If you cannot put your proposal in writing, you cannot finance it.

Risk Perceptions

The world is populated with risk-averse individuals, including venture investors. Risks and, consequently, required rewards vary substantially over the spectrum of risk capital investment opportunities. However, with the exception of a number of highly visible success stories, little is known about the past performance or future expectations of risk capital investors, particularly informal investors. The problem of dealing with risk/return considerations is compounded by the absence of generally accepted risk measurement criteria.

We addressed the question of risk by hypothesizing portfolios of 10 investments of a given type, all of which met the investor's criteria regarding investment size, industry, location, and management qualifications at the time of the investment. Investors were asked to specify how many of the 10 would probably turn out to be "losers." Losers were defined as investments in which eventual losses exceeded 50 percent of the original investment. This definition of risk was selected because it is representative of the way investors think about "downside risk."

We also asked risk-and-return questions for five types of investment portfolios:

Technology-based inventors.

Startup firms.

Infant firms about one year old and approaching break-even operations.

Young firms less than five years old and entering a rapid-growth stage.

Established firms growing too fast to finance from retained earnings.

By measuring risk and return for the five types of investments, it was possible to identify investors' risk/return tradeoffs—not only how expensive risk capital is in general, but also how much more expensive it is for inventors than for startups, established firms, and so forth.

As expected, venture investors perceive noticeable risk differences among the five types of portfolios. The median number of expected losers in a 10-security portfolio covered the following range: 7 for inventors, 6 for startups, 5 for infant firms, 4 for young firms, and 2 in a portfolio of 10 established firms. The dispersion of expectations within each portfolio was also substantial. Informal investors do not have homogeneous perceptions of risk.

The range of loser expectations indicates that perceptions of risk drop dramatically over the developmental stages in the life of a new venture. Since risk and cost are directly related, entrepreneurs can conclude that the longer a venture can survive on personal funds, "sweat equity," and internal cash flow, the lower will be the cost of external risk capital—i.e., the lower the share of equity required to purchase any given amount of venture capital. A startup venture that is at the frontier of some new technology can be an exception to this generalization. Having no track record may then be an advantage. In such a case the dreams (and sometimes avarice) of investors can lead to startling share prices. Recent examples of this include many genetic engineering firms and the Denver penny energy stocks. Selling romance instead of reality is a treacherous game and is not recommended as a strategy for raising funds or for building lasting relationships with sophisticated investors.

Reward Expectations

Entrepreneurs who pursue venture capital are always concerned about the questions, What will it cost? and How much of my venture will I have to give up to raise the capital I need? The answers will depend upon a number of variables, including the amount of capital required and the rewards expected by investors. The other variables, however, are unique to the firm, its history, and its prospects, and this makes the answer also unique to the firm. The methodology for arriving at mutually agreeable terms, however, is not unique, and every entrepreneur should become familiar with it before entering negotiations.[9]

Entrepreneurs are advised to think of fund raising as a process of buying capital rather than of selling stock. The difference is subtle but important. Risk capital is a commodity that is available from a variety of sources on a variety of terms. For every venture some combination of sources and terms will be more appropriate than others and will exert a powerful influence on the future performance of the venture. Besides the price, such factors as exit expectations, the availability of future growth funds, and the quality of management assistance available from an investor will all influence the choice of sources. The final deal should be a partnership of professionals with complementary resources and shared goals.

In our research we undertook an assessment of the reward expectations of informal investors. Within each risk category, we posed two questions dealing with rate-of-return expectations. The first dealt with the "upside potential" of the most successful venture in a 10 investment portfolio. It was an attempt to identify the expectations of returns on individual investments. Presumably, all investments of a given type possess the upside potential of a "winner" at the time an investment is made. Expected returns on winners represent the cost of risk capital to successful inventors and entrepreneurs. This cost is substantially higher than the average cost of risk capital for a given type of investment. As the risk questions reveal, investors recognize that many expected winners turn into

---

[9] For a brief illustration of the technique, see Gumpert and Timmons (January–February 1982). For a more detailed discussion, see: "Structuring and Pricing the Financing," in *Guide to Venture Capital Sources*, 6th ed., ed. S. E. Pratt (Wellesley Hills, Mass.: Capital Publishing, 1982); W. E. Wetzel, "Technovation and the Informal Investor," *Technovation*, Winter 1981.

losers. Substantial returns on the real winners must offset the losers and provide an adequate return on a portfolio of risk capital investments. The second question dealt with portfolio rate-of-return expectations—the average cost of risk capital.

With respect to "winners," investor expectations ranged from median five-year returns of 50 percent per year and capital gains multiples of 10 times for inventors and startup firms, to 38 percent per year and six times for infant firms, to 30 percent per year and five times for young firms, to 23 percent per year and three times for established firms. Rate-of-return expectations were widely dispersed around these medians, again reflecting the diversity of the informal investor population. With respect to minimum acceptable portfolio returns, median expectations were a consistent 20 percent compound annual rate and a five-year capital gains multiple of three times for all portfolios except established firms, where minimum portfolio returns were 15 percent and capital gains multiples only two times in five years.

The data suggest several observations of interest to entrepreneurs. First, seed capital is expensive. Despite every entrepreneur's confidence in his or her "sure thing," investing in entrepreneurs is extremely risky, and investors must be paid to take risks. Remember that risk capital investors win only when a venture succeeds, that is, only when the entrepreneur is an even bigger winner. Entrepreneurs and risk capital investors earn their financial rewards from creating ventures whose economic muscle (cash earning power) supports equity values many times the amount invested. Second, given the extraordinary risks inherent in risk capital investing, the overall level of both winner and portfolio expectations seems low when compared to the range of expectations usually attributed to professional venture capital firms. The relatively low cost of informal risk capital may be due in part to the nonfinancial rewards that often motivate informal investors.

Nonfinancial Rewards

The influence of nonfinancial factors is a characteristic that distinguishes angels from professional venture capitalists. Professional venture investors consider the financial risk/reward relationship to be paramount. Individual investors, on the other hand, often look for nonfinancial returns from their risk capital portfolios. These nonfinancial returns fall into several categories; some of them reflect a sense of social responsibility of many informal investors and some seem to reflect forms of "psychic income" (or so-called hot buttons) that motivate individuals. The influence of these motivators was explored through questions that posed a form of nonfinancial reward and asked investors which ones, if any, represented substitutes for financial returns. Investors responding affirmatively were then asked how large a reduction in the rate of return would be accepted in exchange for the nonfinancial reward. We recognized that tradeoffs may involve undertaking higher risks in situations exhibiting nonfinancial benefits, rather than accepting lower returns. Difficulties in quantifying risk precluded asking the question in this form.

The list of nonfinancial considerations included ventures creating jobs in areas of high unemployment, ventures developing socially useful technology (e.g., medical or energy-saving technology), ventures contributing to urban revitalization, ventures created by minority or female entrepreneurs, and the personal satisfaction derived from assisting entrepreneurs to build successful ventures in a free enterprise economy.

Nonfinancial considerations affect the decisions of a significant fraction of our sample of angels—45 percent in the case of "assisting entrepreneurs." Between 35 percent and 40 percent of the respondents reported that they would accept lower returns (or perhaps assume higher risks) when risk capital investments create employment in their communities or contribute to the development of socially useful technology. Median rate-of-return reductions of 20 percent were associated with investments that create employment and that assist minority entrepreneurs. Entrepreneurs sensitive to the match between the characteristics of their ventures and the personal tastes of investors should be able to raise funds on terms that are attractive to both parties.

Referral Sources

In view of the difficulty entrepreneurs encounter in locating potential investors, we were particularly interested in discovering the channels through which angels most often learn of investment opportunities and their level of satisfaction with these channels. Respondents were provided with an illustrative list of sources of investment opportunities and asked to classify each as a "frequent source," an "occasional source," or "not a source" of proposals they had seriously considered during the previous five years.

The pattern of "frequent source" responses reveals that informal investors typically learn of investment opportunities through a network of friends and business associates. Fifty-two percent cited "business associates" as a frequent source, 50 percent cited "friends," and 41 percent cited "active personal search." The next most common source, "investment bankers," was cited as a frequent source by 15 percent of the respondents. All other sources, including business brokers, commercial bankers, attorneys, and accountants, were insignificant.

Tapping this informal network is not easy. Entrepreneurs can expect little guidance in finding their way through the maze of channels leading to informal risk capital. By the same token, angels continue to rely largely on random events to bring investment opportunities to their attention. There are no systematic techniques for identifying clusters of individual investors or for assessing their distinguishing investment objectives. The best advice for entrepreneurs seems to be: Put your plan in writing and then look close to home for an angel familiar with the technologies and markets you plan to exploit.

The angels in our sample were asked if they were satisfied with the effectiveness of existing channels of communication between bona fide entrepreneurs seeking risk capital and investors like themselves. "Totally dissatisfied" respondents (34 percent) outnumbered "definitely satisfied" respondents (8 percent) by more than four to one. The opinions expressed by our sample of angels support a conclusion reached by Bean, Schiffel, and Mogee with respect to venture capital markets in general: "The issue of little knowledge of the venture capital/new technological enterprise is multifaceted. Entrepreneurs and potential entrepreneurs seem to need better information on financial sources while capital suppliers seem to need better information on new venture/technological investment opportunities."[10]

Respondents were then asked to indicate their interest in an experimental referral service that would direct investment opportunities to their attention. Fifty percent reported a "strong interest" in such a service and 38 percent reported a "moderate interest." Timeliness, objectivity, and confidentiality appear to be essential ingredients of such an activity.

CONCLUSION

Business angels are often the most likely sources of funds for technology-based inventors looking for development funds and for small, technology-based firms looking for startup and growth capital. Collectively, angels appear to represent the largest pool of risk capital in the country, and they finance perhaps five times as many ventures as the public equity markets and professional venture capitalists combined. Based upon our experience, entrepreneurs can expedite the search for informal risk capital by following some basic guidelines:

---

[10] See A. S. Bean; D. Schiffel; and M. E. Mogee, "The Venture Capital Market and Technological Innovation," *Research Policy* 4:1975.

1. First, prepare a comprehensive, documented business plan, including a two- to three-page synopsis of the venture and its management.

2. Be realistic about the risks of and prospects for the venture.

3. Recognize that risk capital is and deserves to be expensive, and understand the process investors follow in structuring and pricing a deal.

4. Look for an angel with relevant experience as well as capital—i.e., look close to home for an investor who understands the venture and will work with it.

5. Be prepared to discuss when and how an investor can cash in his or her chips. Shared liquidation expectations are especially critical for ventures with limited prospects for an eventual public offering or acquisition by a larger firm.

6. If the venture is likely to appeal to an individual investor's "hot buttons," exploit them, for both sides will benefit.

7. Anticipate the need for substantial follow-on financing if the venture succeeds, and be sure that either the initial investors can provide it or they are themselves realistic about the cost of additional outside equity.

PUBLIC POLICY PROPOSAL

Since the end of World War II, the question of institutional gaps in the capital markets serving small firms has periodically been a topic for economic and political debate. The first serious study of capital gaps was conducted by the Federal Reserve Board and led to the Small Business Investment Act of 1958, which created the SBIC program. With the current interest in entrepreneurship and small business, capital formation is again a hot topic in and out of Washington. As examples of "capital gaps," the debate invariably cites problems in raising both seed capital for inventors and new ventures, and equity financing for expanding firms. While institutional gaps may well exist, our data suggest that effectively filling the gaps will depend more on improving the efficiency of the private risk capital markets, and the angel segment in particular, than on creating new institutions or changing the behavior of old ones. With little or no recognition, successful entrepreneurs and other financially sophisticated individuals are filling the void in the institutional capital market. Eight out of 10 investors in our sample would like to examine a broader range of investment opportunities than they currently see.

Recent reductions in capital gains tax rates have enhanced the rewards for all risk capital investors. The impact of the reduction on the size of the professional venture capital pool is well known (increasing from roughly $2 billion in 1978 to over $7 billion today). There is no reason to believe that the impact on the pool of informal risk capital has been any less dramatic. The SEC's new Regulation D will also expedite the risk capital financing of small firms. Mobilization of the pool of "angel money" appears to be impeded by the absence of systematic, efficient channels of communication between entrepreneurs and investors.

The absence of private attempts to improve the efficiency of this market is due in part to the fragmented nature of the informal risk capital market and the existence of "external benefits" that cannot be captured by private investors. Public support for programs that improve the efficiency of private capital markets serving STBFs is justified by the benefits the public receives from STBFs: an enhanced flow of jobs, innovative technology, and tax revenues. Many STBFs will find access to informal risk capital essential to their ability to commercialize the federal investment in their research mandated by the Small Business Innovation Development Act: "To the extent that investment in small, technology-based firms produces external economies, too few resources will be allocated to all phases of investment in them, including generating information about investment opportunities."[11]

Our experience suggests that an experimental effort at expediting the private risk capital financing of emerging, technology-based ventures requires the efficient, systematic performance of four basic functions:

1. Identifying opportunities for risk capital investment in emerging, technology-based ventures and profiling their investment characteristics.

2. Identifying active informal investors and profiling their distinguishing investment objectives.

3. Providing a timely, confidential, and objective referral mechanism that will serve both investors and entrepreneurs.

4. Enhancing the networks of friends and business associates that link risk capital investors with each other, and expanding the flow of information through those networks.

The experimental venture outlined above would act as a clearinghouse of information for investors and entrepreneurs and should be managed, in our judgment, by a respected but disinterested third party. No attempt would be made to evaluate the merits of investment proposals or the qualifications of investors. Given the characteristics of the informal risk capital market, it seems that such an activity should occur at the regional (rather than state or national) level (e.g., the six-state New England region). Professionally managed, such an activity should be at least partially self-supporting once the experimental stage is concluded and data collection and referral techniques are refined.

At the request of committees of both houses of Congress, the Office of Technology Assessment is currently engaged in an eighteen-month study to "determine where high-technology firms are appearing and what factors influence their distribution and growth; [to] identify and evaluate the effectiveness of State and local initiatives to encourage innovation and high-technology development; [to] explore the changing opportunities presented by new and emerging technologies such as robotics and bioengineering; and [to] address the appropriate Federal role in affecting the conditions for such growth in the future."[12] Generating information about opportunities for private investment in STBFs is one federal role worth testing.

---

[11] See Charles River Associates, Inc. (February 1976).

[12] See *Technology, Innovation, and Regional Economic Development* (Washington, D.C.: Office of Technology Assessment, U.S. Congress, September 9, 1982).

APPENDIX

R

THE SUBCHAPTER S CORPORATION[1]

There are about two million corporations in the United States. Of these, 44 percent have sales of less than $100,000 per year and 13 percent have sales in excess of $1 million per year. Less than 1 percent are big enough to be recognized among the big, publicly held corporations whose stock is traded in the stock markets.

Many of the new technologies and their resulting new industries emerge from small corporations. But it takes capital to grow. In order to induce some people in high tax brackets to invest in these promising small businesses, Congress agreed to give them the favorable tax treatment available to a partnership.

With the approval of Congress, the IRS inserted a new paragraph into the tax code at a point in the code identified as Subchapter S. This paragraph says that for small corporations which meet certain criteria, the shareholders may elect to be taxed at the shareholder level on the corporation's income. The corporation does not pay taxes, but its owners pay for their share of the corporation's profits or losses on their own individual income tax return. This is similar to the way partners are taxed.

As long as all of the shareholders agree, Subchapter S tax treatment may be elected or dropped at the beginning of any fiscal year of the corporation. Typically, the owners elect Subchapter S treatment while there are losses so they can include them as deductions on their individual tax returns. When the corporation becomes profitable, they may choose to be taxed as a corporation and avoid adding the profits of the business to their individual tax returns.

---

[1] From the book, *The Entrepreneur's Master Planning Guide* by John A. Welsh and Jerry F. White. © 1983 by Prentice-Hall, Inc. Published by Prentice-Hall, Inc., Englewood Cliffs, N.J. 07632.

CORPORATIONS WITH 1244 STOCK

Congress has a history of approving changes in the tax laws which will help small corporations to solicit high-tax-bracket investors. One is found in section 1244 of the tax code. Under this section, the board of directors of small corporations is given the right to issue stock under section 1244. There are certain requirements, including a limitation of passive income and the need to be largely an operating company.

A shareholder's losses on stock issued under section 1244 is treated as an ordinary loss for tax purposes, while gains on the exchange, sale, or transfer of the stock may qualify for capital gains tax treatment. This may sound similar to the Subchapter S tax treatment. But the difference is that under 1244, the gains or losses are those the shareholder sustains on the subsequent sale of the shares. Under Subchapter S, the gains or losses are the operating profits or losses of the corporation. When a corporation is small and also has a small number of shareholders, it may issue 1244 stock *and* elect Subchapter S tax treatment.

There is sufficient confusion in the minds of the general public that it seems desirable to mention once again that Subchapter S and 1244 stock come from the IRS tax code. They do not change the legal characteristics of the corporation or the steps required to form and maintain a corporation. A Subchapter S corporation is a corporation whose shareholders have elected to be treated in a particular way for tax purposes. A 1244 corporation, a terminology which is a misnomer, is a corporation whose directors have chosen to issue certain shares of stock which have a right to a particular tax treatment when they are sold.

INDEX

TYPICAL BUSINESS PLAN CONTENTS

I. Summary—to convince the venture capitalist to read the whole plan

II. Company background—stage of development, unique features of products or services, any proprietary position (patents, experience)

III. Market Plan

    a. Market segmentation and product viability
    b. Distribution channels
    c. Competition
    d. Sales strategy and projected market share
    e. Pricing

IV. Management

    a. A listing of key managers including detailed resumes
    b. Organizational structure
    c. Compensation and employee ownership
    d. Plans for future staff by job level

V. Operations Plan

    a. Space and equipment requirements
    b. Working capital requirements
    c. Labor force
    d. Geographic location advantages

VI. Financial Statements and Projections

    a. 3-to-5-year pro forma projections, with income statements, cash flow statements, and balance sheets
    b. Projected financing and capital structure
    c. Best- and worst-case outcomes

VII. Amount of Money Sought Now and Use of Proceeds

VIII. Summary of Risks Involved

    a. The industry, the company, and its personnel
    b. Timing
    c. Product market acceptance

Source: *An Overview of Venture Capital*, prepared by Bigler Investment Management Company, Inc.